DÜSSELDORF

INSIGHT *City* GUIDES

Created and Directed by Hans Höfer
Edited by Kristiane Müller

APA
PUBLICATIONS

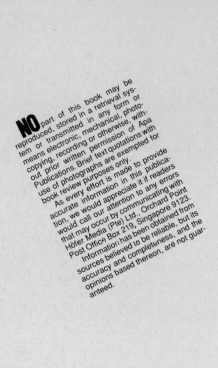
DÜSSELDORF

First Edition
© 1991 APA PUBLICATIONS (HK) LTD
All Rights Reserved
Printed in Singapore by Höfer Press Pte. Ltd

ABOUT THIS BOOK

Düsseldorf, a city of 600,000 inhabitants, is the capital city of North Rhine Westphalia, Germany's most populated state. Just over 700 years old, the city is quite young in comparison to many settlements on the Rhine.

Though always an important provincial centre, its key role in Europe has only developed since the industrial revolution arrived in Germany. Its location and its proximity to the Ruhr with all its coal and steel, are what boosted Düsseldorf into becoming the major administrative, financial and commercial centre it is today.

History has also endowed the city with its fine buildings and monuments and its rich artistic and cultural traditions. Düsseldorf is a city of the Carnival, of old brewery pubs with their *Altbier*. But it is also a city of the Königsallee, of fast cars, trendy jet-setters and high fashion.

Cityguide: Düsseldorf represents a homecoming of sorts for **Hans Höfer**, the Founder and Publisher of Apa Publications. With family roots lying in Benrad, Höfer left Germany equipped with a diploma in printing and graphic design. After an adventurous journey, he settled in Asia, now the homebase for the publication of the internationally acclaimed *Insight Guide* series.

This year marks the 20th anniversary of Apa Publications and the reunion with lots of outbacks in the old city parts where the concept of this book has been mould over with creative Art Director, Professor Vilibald Poffi, a previous school mate of Höfer.

The task of editing *Cityguide: Düsseldorf* fell to **Kristiane Müller,** who has a wealth of experience as author and translator of a number of books and articles. One of the most recent projects she was involved with was in editing APA's Insight Guide to the Rhine, the great European river that flows right past Düsseldorf's front door. Kristiane's team of experienced authors have created a mosaic of history, culture, places to visit and things to do which should entice all visitors.

Klaus Bungert has been Lord Mayor of the city since 1984, and APA was grateful that he found enough time in his hectic schedule to write the introductory page "To the Rhine and Back".

After completing her studies in sociology, **Nina Köster** turned her hand to freelance journalism, a job that keeps her busy, whether while travelling or working back home in Germany. Here she contributes the articles on Düsseldorf's long and varied history as well as the essay on the city's importance as an economic centre.

Johannes Rau, bookseller, journalist and politician, has been the Minister President of North Rhine Westphalia since 1978. Here, Herr Rau gives us his own personal impressions of the State's capital city.

A onetime bookseller and presently a manufacturer of calendars in Frankfurt, **Eberhard Urban** has written on just about every topic under the sun, including steam locomotives, ships and cars, history and the history of art. Here he writes about the Düsseldorf Art Academy and the highly controversial artist Joseph Beuys.

Wolfgang Schmerfeld starts by reporting on the state of the the the theatre in Düsseldorf. Amongst his many other interests is gastronomy, and for this book he takes a look at Düsseldorf's old city, stands at "the longest bar in the world" and discovers something about Düsseldorf's very special kind of beer. He also takes us to the Hofgarten and the

Müller *Köster* *E. Urban* *S. Urban*

equally noble southern part of the city centre, as well as leading us out to the north-east of the city, to not quite so noble Krefeld and the Ruhr District.

Susanne Urban studies German language and literature, a field which has led her to discovering more about Düsseldorf's "most famous son", the renowned German author and publicist Heinrich Heine, about whom she has written an article for this book.

Another subject with which the city of Düsseldorf is inextricably bound, believe it or not, is the production and consumption of mustard. **Kirstin Röll** works for Appel & Frenzel, the manufactuers of the world famous "Original Düsseldorfer Löwensenf". Her article highlights the importance the condiment has always had for the city.

One of the places to head for in the Old City, to get a taste of that *Altstadt* atmosphere, is the famous inn "Zum Uerige". Much of **Michael Richter's** information on the history and unique culture of this traditional brewery pub was gleaned from the landlord himself, Josef Schnitzler.

Birgit Kölgen-Umbach is deputy editorial manager at the "*Neue Rhein Zeitung*", where she is also responsible for features on fashion. Here she describes Düsseldorf in its role as a major city of fashion.

Alexander Scherer has worked in film and TV in Düsseldorf for the most part of 20 years. He escorts us down to the port area on the river, underneath the new Rhine Tower, to discover that after years of decline this part of town is now being transformed into an area really worth visiting.

Rudolf Kottke was press secretary at the airport for 20 years. Here he gives his own personal views on the city in "Düsseldorf Mon Amour".

Freelance journalist **Rudiger Bisping** lives close to the city. He takes us down to the historical jewel Benrath Château in the south, to the racecourse and beyond to the north, and across the river to the town of Neuss, which is older than Düsseldorf, to the west. In addition, he gets involved with certain very important events in Düsseldorf's cultural calendar - its festivals and its carnival.

Michael Bengel is a feature writer for the *Kölner Stadtanzeiger*, a Cologne newspaper. Here he takes us to the Bergisches Land, a beautiful area of hills and valleys to the south-east of Düsseldorf, whose charms have hardly been discovered by outsiders. He also goes up the Rhine to the city of Cologne and the capital city of Bonn, both of which are within very easy reach of the Düsseldorf.

Dieter Vogel, the director of APA's German editorial, takes a peek inside the magnificent Cologne Cathedral.

Hans-Henning Derpa, editor of the magazine "Japan Aktuell" examines the city though other eyes, namely those of the 7000-strong Japanese community living in Düsseldorf, "Nippon on the Rhine".

Finally, **Michael Grixa** explores Düsseldorf's world of sports to give us an intriguing insight into what goes on in some of the more famous arenas.

Erhard Pansegrau has made a name for himself not only by the numerous shots he has had published in other Insight Guides, but also by those which have appeared in his colour volumes on China, Japan, Hong Kong and Korea. Further high-quality contributions come from **Rainer Kiedrowski** and Cologne-based **Wolfgang Fritz** who has also published many of his photographs in other APA Guides.

—APA Publications

Bisping   *Bengel*   *Fritz*   *Pansegrau*

CONTENTS

PEOPLE AND HISTORY

TRAVEL TIPS

TO THE RHINE AND BACK

"The city of Düsseldorf is very beautiful and if I travel abroad and think of it by chance, a strange longing befalls me. I was born in Düsseldorf and I feel as if I should set off for home again."

These words were written more than 150 years ago by Heinrich Heine, Düsseldorf's most famous son. They appeared in his book "Le Grand", a work which firmly established Düsseldorf's name in world literature. It is still possible to find some of the places of Heine's childhood and youth, which he describes in his poetry. They have changed, but then again, so has the whole city.

It was a long road from the small settlement on the River Düssel, which received its city charter 700 years ago, to today's metropolis. But by Heine's day, the city's development had begun to accelerate to such an extent that all that had been achieved in previous centuries faded into insignificance. After the restrictive city walls were done away with, after the city began to shake off its particularism, and, more significantly, after the Congress of Vienna had achieved the conditions for the internationalisation of the Rhine, the way was free for the real rise of Düsseldorf.

The importance of the State capital of North Rhine Westphalia as administrative centre, as industrial and financial city, as a place of trade and exhibitions and not least as a city of culture is well-known. But we also know that 150 years ago it was foreigners and not the indigenous folk who were largely responsible for heralding in the new era. Belgian and Irish businessmen provided the initiative for industrial development. In those days, the people of Düsseldorf welcomed the outsiders. We still like to think that this "openness" towards strangers has remained the hallmark of the true Düsseldorfer.

Confirmation of the cosmopolitan nature of this city of 600,000 souls may best be provided by a stroll through the *Altstadt*, the very heart of Düsseldorf. Nowhere else in Düsseldorf are art and commerce, international cuisine and history, all the ingredients of a thriving city, so inextricably bound together than in the Old City.

The people of Düsseldorf like celebrating, but they also work hard and creatively. Life here revolves around two old local sayings: *"Von nix kütt nix"* and *"Wat mo nit kann ändere, dat muß mo lotte schlendere"*, meaning "nothing comes out of nothing" and "if you can't change it, then wait a while and see how it develops".

Yes, Düsseldorf is a nice place, not least thanks to its citizens. Some of the charm of past centuries has been preserved and a great deal of new has been created. And every visitor should make himself at home in the city - even if he doesn't happen to have been born here....

Preceding pages, pausing for an ice-cream, Thyssen House is reflected in the Hofgarten pond; going home across the Rheinkniebrücke, relaxing in front of a typical pub in the Altstadt. Left, Pallas Athena (1926 by J. Knubbel) stands sentinel in front of the Tonhalle.

The beginnings of Düsseldorf are obscure. The first settlements within the city area were probably founded in neolithic times around 2,000 B.C. During Roman times, when the River Rhine marked the eastern boundary of the Roman province of Gaul, Roman influence on the settlements to the right of the Rhine was very limited and short-lived. Despite incursions into Germania, which often resulted in heavy losses, they generally left its heathen folk alone. Probably of greater impact for the local populace around Düsseldorf, therefore, were the deeds of the Anglo Saxon Christian missionary St Suidbert who established an abbey at Kaiserswerth in 713. It became the focal point of spiritual life in the region until it was demolished by the Normans in 880.

There is actually no official record of Düsseldorf existing until 1135 when it is mentioned as "Düsseldorp". A short time after that, along with other settlements on the right bank of the Rhine, it came into the possession of Duke Engelbert of Berg, for the sum of 100 Marks and on the condition that the previous ruler would provide free board in his castle for the rest of his life. For the next 600 years, Düsseldorf's destiny was bound with that of the Dukes of Berg.

The city charter: Düsseldorf's aspirations for power lay in its status. For years Duke Adolf of Berg had struggled for supremacy on the Rhine with the Archbishop of Cologne, until he won the decisive victory near Worringen on 5th June 1288, in one of the bloodiest battles of the middle ages. Urged on by this success, on 14 August 1288, he proceeded to elevate Düsseldorf - which at that time consisted of a small street and a few houses - to a city. It was bounded in the west by the Rhine and in the north by the northern Düssel tributary. While none of the city's main landmarks existed then, it is

Preceding pages: "The Battle of Worringen". **Left,** washing day in the Middle Ages. **Right,** a favourite meeting place - the clock on the Königsallee.

from this time that they all started to develop; the first town hall, the market place and, of course, the city walls.

With the granting of the city charter, the inhabitants derived certain privileges. While today the city has a reputation for its polluted air, the situation in those days was very different. There existed a saying "Stadtluft macht frei" (city air liberates) and this literally meant what it said. With this promise of becoming free citizens, serfs from the outly-

ing areas were thus attracted to the city, on condition that for a year and a day they incurred no debts. This only applied to the serfs of a foreign master. Serfs of the Duke of Berg were forbidden to immigrate.

A slow start: Despite such privileges, Düsseldorf for a long time remained what it was before the granting of the city charter; a small settlement in the shadow of much larger neighbours. Neuss, Duisburg and naturally Cologne were much more important. And even Kaiserswerth, which had received its city charter as early as 1181, was larger and possessed greater economic clout in the 13th century. Today, Kaiserswerth is part of Düsseldorf. Gerresheim too, also now part of Düsseldorf, blossomed.

Only at the end of the 14th century did Düsseldorf emerge from its deep sleep. While the first city walls, extending in the north as far as today's Ritterstraße, had been completed around 1350, it was only with the accession of Wilhelm of Berg in 1360 that development really took off. Wilhelm, who is known as the second founder of the town, gave Düsseldorf complete judicial sovereignty. He also made Düsseldorf a customs station and the home of the royal mint.

Under Wilhelm, Düsseldorf developed into

a centre of pilgrimage. The city owes the completion of its trademark, the Church of St Lambert, to Wilhelm of Berg. Aisles and ambulatory were thus added to the basic plan of Düsseldorf's oldest church. In 1384, Wilhelm, from 1380 the Duke of Berg, began the planned expansion of the city. New houses and streets were built, extending as far south as today's Flingerstraße.

Wilhelm set about finding ways of attracting new settlers to the city. The inhabitants of Bilk, Derendorf and Golzheim were only granted city privileges if they moved and settled there themselves. Only later did these places, along with the parish of Ham, become part of Düsseldorf. Volmerswerth wasn't integrated into the city until the 15th century. Meanwhile the population grew to 2,000, a figure which, at the end of the Middle Ages, made Düsseldorf the largest city in the Duchy of Berg.

Soon, another leaf in Düsseldorf's history was to be turned, the result of the people of the city allying themselves with the Duke's son Adolf, against their erstwhile ruler. Wilhelm was so broken by this display of blatant ingratitude that he died shortly afterwards, in 1408. But Adolf had no intention of keeping the promises with which he had wooed the populace to his side. On the contrary; he wasn't the slightest bit interested in the city.

The fact that Düsseldorf was rescued from sinking into oblivion was thanks to Adolf's successor. Duke Gerhard instigated a series of measures which resulted in further development, and the small settlement on the River Düssel began to turn into a real city. During his office, Düsseldorf acquired its first very own town hall. The house "Zum Schwarzen Horn" was completed in 1470 and still stands today, although due to several rebuilds and renovations, its exterior now bears little resemblance to the original.

Under Gerhard's son Duke Wilhelm, the foundations were laid for Düsseldorf to develop into the most important town on the Lower Rhine. In 1510 Wilhelm married his daughter Maria to Johann of Cleves, so uniting the two largest reigning dynasties on the Lower Rhine. To all intents and purposes, albeit at the beginning not officially, Düsseldorf became the capital of the new realm which now included the duchies of Berg, Jülich and Cleves, as well as the earldoms of Mark and Ravensberg. Its boundaries roughly corresponded to those of today's North Rhine Westphalia.

Wealthy patronage: The new rulers, Johann and also his son Wilhelm, governed their territory primarily from Düsseldorf. A grand castle was built on the Rhine, as well as a new town hall. Their construction was only made possible through the huge financial support given by Wilhelm, who bore the nickname "der Reiche" - the "Rich". The castle was largely destroyed by fire in 1872. The only part which survived was the tower which today houses the navigation museum. Only the facade of the town hall remains intact. Having escaped the ravages of the centuries, it still gives a good impression of how the building must have looked upon its completion in 1573.

Wilhelm the Rich had new defences built for the city. And work on a citadel, south of the city on the river, was also begun, according to plans drawn up by the master builder Alessandro Pasqualini.

During Wilhelm's rule, a grammar school was also founded, in 1545. Düsseldorf be-

Caught in the crossfire: Due to his illness the Duke was hardly capable of dealing with ordinary, everyday matters of government, and the problem of avoiding involvement in the holy war between Spain and the Netherlands which had begun in 1577. While the Duke sought neutrality in the conflict between the Netherlands and Philip II, he could not prevent the regions of the Lower Rhine being plundered and pillaged by troops as they passed through. Some troops were based in the region as well, and those that were responsible for protecting the city of Düsseldorf turned out to be a complete menace to the local populace.

came a powerful magnet for young people who came from far and wide to study.

Johannes Weyer, one of the century's most eminent doctors, was summoned to the post of court physician. But Weyer could do nothing to cure the the increasingly severe bouts of madness which had been afflicting poor Wilhelm since 1566. After decades of prosperity, there so began a rapid decline in the city's fortunes.

Left, a treasure from the glass museum in the Tonhalle. **Above**, one of Düsseldorf's early bridges.

One of the most flamboyant celebrations in the history of the city took place a short time later. It was the occasion of the marriage between the heir Johann Wilhelm and Margravine Jakobe von Baden in June 1585. Amidst unbelievable pomp, the 1,500 invited guests continued to celebrate the event for a whole week. However, all the hopes which had been invested in the match were soon dashed. No children were forthcoming. Suspected of adultery, Jakobe was imprisoned in 1595 and died in mysterious circumstances in 1597 while still in confinement. The charges levelled against her were never brought before the court. An old saying goes that the ghost of Jakobe continued to haunt the castle towers for some time.

Johann Wilhelm married again, this time to Antoinette of Lorraine. She did not produce any children either, and when the duke died on 26th March 1609, a dispute arose concerning his successor. Elector's heir Georg Wilhelm of Brandenburg and Wolfgang Wilhelm of the Palatinate state of Neuburg, both offspring of the daughter of Wilhelm the Rich, allied themselves against Kaiser Rudolf II, who also staked his claims in the Lower Rhine. After they had defeated his governor, they then proceeded to turn on

The Jesuits played an important role in education; they were granted control of the grammar school.

However, even under Wolfgang Wilhelm's rule, Düsseldorf found little peace. Both the Thirty Years War, which broke out in 1618, and the freedom struggle in the Netherlands, rekindled in 1621, left their mark on the city. Although he managed to preserve the city from the fighting, the countryside roundabout became a battleground. More and more people sought safety within the confines of the city walls and it soon became quite impossible to maintain any reasonable level of hygiene. Between 1620 and 1649, the town was

each other, until they finally realised that in such a conflict neither of them would emerge victorious. In 1614 in Xanten, under the mediation of England and France, they settled the dispute by dividing the region between them. Wolfgang Wilhelm received Jülich and Berg and Georg Wilhelm took possession of Cleves, Mark and Ravensburg. Under the rule of Neuburg Düsseldorf became staunchly Catholic. Monasteries were founded for the Capuchins, the Franciscans, the Carmelites and other orders. In 1622 work was begun on the Church of St Andrew, which remained a Jesuit church until 1842.

struck by six epidemics of the plague. In the year 1627 alone it is said that 2,000 people fell victim to the Black Death.

The cultural centre of Europe: Upon the death of Wolfgang Wilhelm in 1653, his son Philip Wilhelm continued with the policies of his father, and it was during his reign that Düsseldorf established its reputation as a high-ranking European capital. The city continued to flourish during the reign of his son Johann Wilhelm (1679 to 1716) who is still remembered and esteemed to this day as "Jan Wellem". At the end of his reign he had his own memorial built, the famous equestrian statue in the *Marktplatz* which was created by the court sculptor Grupello in 1711.

Jan Wellem turned the city of his birth into one of the cultural centres of Europe. He created the world famous Art Gallery some of whose original contents now form the core of the Pinakothek in Munich. Goethe was impressed by the museum and commented "There is no other such place in the whole of Germany to compare with the likes of this, not even in Dresden". Equally unique was his collection of moulds of antique sculptures. And he also takes great credit for his services to music. The first opera house in Düsseldorf was built during his reign. All kinds of artists

before the city was to reach the size he had envisaged. His political ambitions also remained unfulfilled; the coveted Elector's crown remained beyond his grasp. The princely splendour that Jan Wellem had brought to Düsseldorf ended with his death. His successor moved the court to Mannheim and Schwetzingen. Düsseldorf once more became a provincial city.

Garden city: A further decline was heralded by the Seven Years War, during which in 1758, the Hannovarians bombarded the city. About a sixth of the buildings was severely damaged. But the city's fortunes changed for the better again with the investiture of Duke

and scientists flocked to Düsseldorf.

Jan Wellem was tolerant in religious matters. Not only did he promote the building of Catholic churches and monasteries, but be also sanctioned the construction of the city's first two Protestant churches as well as its first synagogue. However, his ambition to extend the southern limits of the city as far as today's Fürstenwall did not get beyond the planning stages and it was to be 150 years

Jchloß Jägerhof past and present.

Johann Ludwig Franz of Goldstein, the governor of the Elector of the Palatinate, Carl Theodor. From 1769 to 1771, Goldstein commissioned the architect Nicolas de Pigage from Lorraine to lay out the earliest part of the Hofgarten, between the Jägerhof and Goldsteinstraße, and can thus be regarded as the founder of the garden city of Düsseldorf. He also oversaw the completion of the most important Rococo chateau in the Lower Rhine, Schloss Benrath, again designed by Nicolas de Pigage and constructed between 1755 and 1773. Another well-known architect, Johann Josef Couven, a contemporary of de Pigage, carried out much of the design work for Schloß Jägerhof.

Goldstein's name is linked just as much with the cultural life of Düsseldorf as it is with the city's architecture. He founded the first public library on the Rhine and also established an academy of painting, sculpture and architecture.

The French arrive: After his death in 1776, Düsseldorf continued to develop. But a new shadow fell over the city in 1794 when it was bombarded by French revolutionary forces. On 6th September 1795, the French crossed the Rhine and captured the city. There was hardly any resistance. The French occupa-

ment continued apace and work started on the present day Heinrich-Heine-Allee, which had been planned in 1804. Similarly the Königsallee, built on the erstwhile city defences, began to take shape. Under the supervision of the architect Adolf von Vagedes, the city was extended towards the east.

Cheered by the masses, Napoleon made a glorious entry into the city in the Autumn of 1811. He paraded along today's Kaiserstraße and young Heinrich Heine, 14 years old, was also there amongst the crowd. The most visible result of Napoleon's visit was the extension of the Hofgarten to the Rhine, for the purpose of which he had donated the sum

tion lasted six years and they withdrew only after the Treaty of Luneville in 1801. The fact that they destroyed all the city walls before leaving turned out to be a blessing in disguise for Düsseldorf; the city had been relieved of its tight corset and was now free to expand.

But the effects of this "leaving gift" had hardly been felt when the French made another grab for the city. In March 1806, Napoleon made Düsseldorf the capital of the newly created Grand-duchy of Berg, of which Napoleon's brother-in-law Joachim Murat became Grand Duke. The city's develop-

of 91,000 Francs. Heinrich Heine celebrated Napoleon in his book "Le Grand".

It was soon after his sojourn in Düsseldorf that Napoleon's fortunes changed. In 1812 came the split with Russia and the campaign against his erstwhile ally marked the beginning of his downfall. His defeat in Leipzig in 1813 also signalled the end of French rule in Düsseldorf.

Under Prussian rule: The Prussians wrote the next chapter in Düsseldorf's history. With the establishment of the German Federation in 1815, they now took control of the Rhineland. But Düsseldorf had a very disappointing start to its time as a Prussian city; the old arch-rival Cologne became the capital of the newly founded Rhine Province. Nevertheless, when Prince Friedrich of Prussia moved in to Schloß Jägerhof in 1820, a certain amount of the former glory returned. The Prussians were responsible for the revival of the Art Academy. Under its director Wilhelm von Schadow the academy went through a particularly prosperous era. The city became a mecca for art students from all over the world as the reputation of the "Düsseldorfer School" spread.

The rise of industry: During the 1830s it was industry which began to thrive on the banks

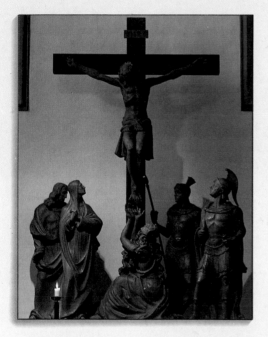

of the Rhine, and which began to alter the whole face of Düsseldorf. A major contributory factor in developments and a turning point in the history of the city was the Rhine Navigation Act of 1831. Previously, a lot of potential business had been diverted away from Düsseldorf to Cologne. The city now won back its freeport status which it had lost in 1818 and from here on, business in Düsseldorf boomed.

Left, the Market Place with the Town Hall and the Jan Wellern Monument. Above, crucifix at St. Lambertus.

Accompanying the developments in river trade was the construction of Germany's first railway. In 1838 the first stretch between Düsseldorf and Ekrath was opened, and nine years later it was possible to travel by train from the Rhine to Berlin. In 1839 the first permanent pontoon bridge on the Rhine was built at Düsseldorf, replacing the "flying bridge" built by Johann Wilhelm in 1699.

Improvements in communications led to rapid developments in industry. Cotton printing, dyeing, weaving and worsted factories sprang up. The steam engine arrived in 1836. With the construction of a puddling furnace in 1839, the Richard brothers from Belgium laid the foundations for Düsseldorf to develop into the centre of Germany's iron and steel industries.

Movements representing the interests of the new proletariat were founded in the wake of these developments. Their best known leaders were Ferdinand Lassalle, the co-founder of social democracy in Germany, and the poet Ferdinand Freiligrath. In 1848/9, in the "Bockhalle", Lassalle held passionate speeches before the populace. It was the year of the revolution and the workers' revolt on 8th May 1849 was brutally crushed.

Lassalle's ideas - he himself had been in prison during the rising - led to the founding of a workers' association in Düsseldorf in 1863. Trades unions were soon formed and the workers of the city were united.

Industrialisation led to a sharp growth in the population. Between 1840 and 1870, the number of inhabitants doubled to 70,000. More and more people from outlying areas arrived in the flourishing and expanding metropolis. The end of the Franco-German war in 1871 gave a further boost to economic development on the Rhine and Ruhr. Well-known companies settled in Düsseldorf. In 1871, the Irish industrialist Thomas William Mulvany founded the "Association of Common Business Interests in Rhineland and Westphalia." Further associations followed, including the "Association of German Iron and Steel industries" in 1874.

Within five years, the population rose by 15 percent and by 1882 the magic figure of 100,000 had been reached. Düsseldorf had become a large city.

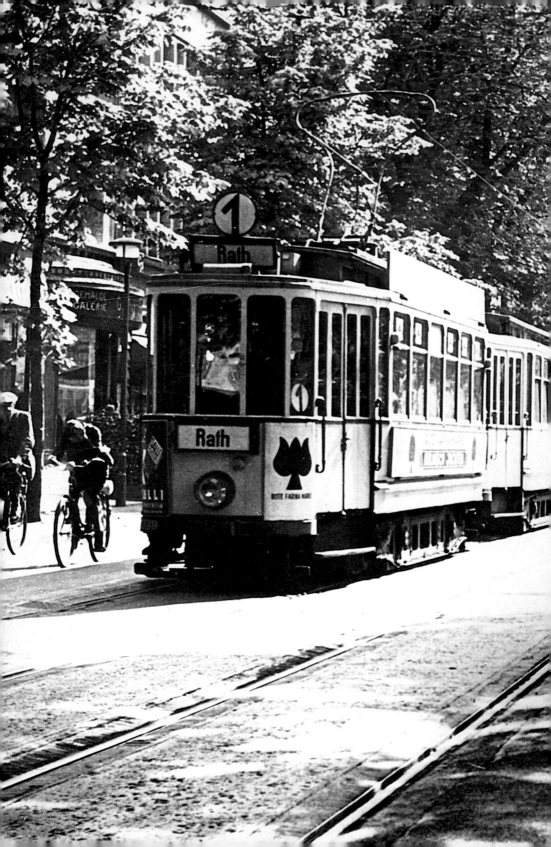

It took virtually six centuries before the "Dorf" by the River Düssel had expanded to something resembling a city. It took only a few decades for that same sleepy rural city to become one of Germany's principal industrial centres. As time went by, the traditional structures changed, preparing the way for present-day Düsseldorf.

One of the prime aspects in this metamorphosis was the re-structuring of the transport system. By 1891 the scattered collection of inadequate railway buildings had been replaced by a central passenger terminal in the east of Düsseldorf and two new goods train stations in the north and south. All lines now converged at the main station. The new port was opened in 1896 and that same year the first electric tram joined the city centre with the suburb Grafenberg.

Surprisingly little changed as far as the old city centre was concerned. Machine-tool companies, steel mills, chemical and glass industries comglomerated in the suburbs. The new workers' settlements rimmed the old city centre. A far-sighted urban development plan was drawn up to ensure that the inner city remained virtually out-of-bounds to industry. It also prohibited too great a density of new housing projects. The development of backyard building space, so frequent in other major cities at that time, was practically taboo in Düsseldorf.

This was all the more remarkable considering the population explosion. Around the turn of the century the population of Düsseldorf already exceeded 200,000 inhabitants and it was considered to be a very much up-and-coming city. A milestone in its development was the trade and art exhibition in 1902. Bigger than the hugely successful first exhibition in 1880, it ran for six months. A new exhibition site was especially prepared for the fair, which stretched for two kilometres along the Rhine embankment. More than five million people visited this exhibition. There were thus not only new impulses for industrial Düsseldorf, but the city also enhanced its reputation as a con-

ference, arts and administration centre.

In 1905 Louise Dumont and Gustav Lindemann founded the Düsseldorf *Schauspielhaus* (theatre), after their attempt to establish a resident theatre company in Weimar had failed. The theatre was built between Kasernenstraße and the Königsallee on what had formerly been the parade ground. After the Second World War, Gustav Gründgens, one of Germany's most famous actors, became the director.

Industry and commerce consolidate: The Theatre was only the first of a number of stately buildings on the erstwhile parade ground. In 1906 the foundation stone was laid for the *Stahlhof*, the headquarters of the Deutsche *Stahlwerksverband* (German Steel Association). This further increased Düsseldorf's reputation as the "administration centre of the Ruhr". The Law Courts are housed in what was formerly the British Military Headquarters. Before that it had been the command centre of the German Arms industry. The Lord Mayor at the time, Wilhelm Marx, encouraged important companies and large associations to set up their offices in Düsseldorf. Two architectural masterpieces built at this time deserve special mention. One was the *Tietz* Department Store, designed by Joseph Maria Olbrich, which was totally renovated by the *Kaufhof* in 1985, the second was the administration centre of the *Mannes-mann Werke* on the Rhine embankment, designed by Peter Behrend.

Düsseldorf developed at a spanking pace, as indeed did some of the adjoining villages and communities, where many commuters now live. In 1908/9 several outlying communities were fused with Düsseldorf, thus doubling the city area and increasing the

number of inhabitants by 63,000 to 300,000. By now Düsseldorf had spilled over to the left bank of the Rhine. The first road bridge over the Rhine had been financed by entrepreneurs as early as 1898.

The armaments industry takes over: Düsseldorf was most certainly an up-and-coming place and the population was soon expected

Preceding pages: today, line 1 is still going to Rath, only it is called Number 701 now. **Left**, Art Nouveau decoration on the Königsallee canal. **Above**, a part of the classicistic Ratinger Tor, one of the entrances to the Hofgarten.

to reach one million. But the First World War put a stop to any such notion and in due course the city seemed only to consist of soldiers and wounded. Industrial production was confined to the armaments industry. In 1914 the arms industry had employed 48,000 people. By 1918 this number had increased to 90,000, of which 33,000 were women and 7,000 foreigners. By 1918 the *Rheinmetall-werken* alone employed 39,000 people.

The events in Russia had not gone unnoticed. Workers' and soldiers' committees were established in Düsseldorf. In January 1919 the radical members of the Workers' Committee, the so-called *Spartakists*, were in the majority and for some months they ruled the city. Government troops eventually crushed the rebellion.

The return of the French: The stipulations of the Armistice stated that German troops had to be withdrawn from the left embankment of the Rhine. In November 1918 Belgian soldiers had already begun to occupy that area. But in March 1921 French troops began to occupy the right embankment of the Rhine, in contravention of the agreement. They occupied Düsseldorf, Duisburg, Mülheim an der Ruhr and Oberhausen.

In 1923 the so-called *Ruhrkampf*, the battle of the Ruhr, broke out and Düsseldorf became the troop base of the French and Belgians. The Government of the Reich and the people offer passive resistance, and the citizens of Düsseldorf did not need much persuading. A far-reaching act of sabotage was perpetrated by Albert Leo Schlageter, a member of the National Liberation Corps when he blew up a railway line near Kalkum. The French captured him and sentenced him to death. For the National Socialists Schlageter was to become a heroic figure, a so-called "Blutzeuge" (blood witness).

After protracted negotiations, the French troops finally withdrew in August 1925. Robert Lehr, the new Lord Mayor since 1924, made a rousing speech on the market square and the Düsseldorf population celebrated the end of the French occupation.

A fresh start: For ten years Düsseldorf's erstwhile booming development had, perforce, come to a standstill. Now the time had come to start again with renewed vigour.

Already in 1924 Wilhelm Kreis had designed a 56-metre high brick building, which was to be the first high-rise office block in Germany. Eventually this became known as the *Wilhelm Marx Haus* - symbolising a renewed period of growth despite the prevailing economic gloom. That same year plans were completed for the first exhibition devoted to National Health Care. For quite some time the project seemed to be unviable for financial reasons. But Robert Lehr, the Lord Mayor, was determined to succeed and, not least due to his unsparing efforts the "Gesolei" (GEsundheitspflege, SOziale Fürsorge, LEIbesübungen - health care, social welfare

ment dispute arose in the Rhine-Westphalian industrial area concerning communal restructuring. The result was a compromise, which, while not exactly mirroring the concepts of the city administration, was one with which Düsseldorf could live well. In 1929 the fusion with Kaiserswerth, Benrath-Reisholz and the small community Garath, parts of Wittlaer and Kalkum, as well as Lohausen increased the Düsseldorf area by a third, the number of inhabitants increased by 36,000 to 473,000. Benrath and Kaiserswerth were two particularly dainty morsels for Düsseldorf. Apart from the castle, Benrath was industrially important as the *Henkel Werke*,

and physical exercise) opened on 8th May 1926. It was an overwhelming success. Seven and a half million visitors came to this gigantic exhibition, not the least of whose effects was to boost the development of the city. The *Ehren-hof* - now the culture centre of Düsseldorf - built according to the plans of Wilhelm Kreis on the Rhine side of the *Hofgarten*, is all that is left of the exhibition. The building complex houses the municipal Art Museum, the Concert Hall, the Art Palace and the State Museum of Society and Economy.

Further expansion: In the late 1920s a vehe-

already then world-famous, had their headquarters here. Kaiserswerth was a favourite excursion area. Robert Lehr, the Lord Mayor, used the short period of the economic boom before the world economic crisis, to strengthen Düsseldorf's position. In 1927 the airport with the four Lufthansa flight-routes was opened. That same year it was also reported that an electrically-operated tram, replete with dining car, would commute between Düsseldorf and Duisburg.

But soon the signs of the times indicated imminent catastrophe. In 1929, 112 enterprises ceased operations, the number of unemployed increased from 15,700 in 1927 to staggering 64,000 in 1932. That same year the city had to spend 35.5 million Marks in unemployment benefit. That was more than the annual revenue from income tax, but still insufficient to afford a tolerable standard of living to the unemployed.

The fascists gain control: The woeful economic conditions and the political instability during the time of the Weimar Republic was a boon for the radicals. Hitler's NSDAP with its blatant slogans found more and more supporters. The Communist Party (KPD) constituted the main opposition to the Nazis. Up until 1932 nine people had been killed

Social Democrats eight, the *Kampffront Schwarzweißrot*, which supported the Nazis, five, the *Wirtschaftsbund* three and the *Deutsche Volkspartei* one. This result, while not constituting a majority for the NSDAP, nevertheless did not stop the Nazis from usurping power. SPD and KPD were prohibited henceforth, while the Centre Party and the right-wing parties voluntarily disbanded.

Parallel to the elimination of the parties, the National Socialists, led by Gauleiter Friedrich Karl Florian, concentrated on bringing the city administration in line. Above all Lord Mayor Lehr was a thorn in their flesh. Despite the fact that Lehr was a mem-

and 28 seriously injured in political strife.

When Hitler came to power in 1933, the number of those sympathetic to his aims was quite considerable in Düsseldorf. After the elections in March 1933, accompanied by massive obstructions of the other parties, the National Socialists held 31 of 79 seats in the city parliament. The strongest faction up to that time, the *Zentrums-Partei* (Centre Party), held 17 seats, the Communists 13, the

Left, the canal divides the shopping half of the Königsallee from the business half. Above, the Königsallee in the thirties.

ber of the *Deutsch-Nationale Volkspartei*, which was not wholly out of sympathy with the Nazis, the NSDAP forced him out of office. He was arrested in April on a pretext and forced to resign from office. After the Second World War, Lehr was able to resume his political career. As chairman of the CDU he was the head of the *Landtag* of North-Rhine Westphalia for some time.

As was the case in other German cities, the National Socialists "cleansed" the authorities, associations, economic institutes and other organisations from adversaries. Trade Unions were prohibited. Even before the official book burning, the works of Heinrich Heine were burnt in Düsseldorf. The National Socialists also stepped up pressure on schools, theatres, libraries, museums and churches.

The net woven by the brown rulers was drawn tighter and tighter. Mass demonstrations by the NSDAP and their organisations were an everyday occurrence. On the tenth anniversary of the death of Schlageter, whose execution the National Socialists shamelessly exploited for their own purposes, 300,000 marched through Düsseldorf to commemorate his death. As the previous two exhibitions had been so successful in Düsseldorf, the

rationing and hoarding of food supplies were indicative of the evil things to come. The persecution of the approximately 5,000 Jewish inhabitants reached its first culmination point with the expulsion of the 361 "*Ostjuden*". On the night of the 9th November the synagogues in Kasernenstraße and Kreuzstraße went up in flames. Like in other German cities, the National Socialists took the murder by a Jew of the Secretary in the German Embassy in Paris, Ernst von Rath, who hailed from Düsseldorf, as a pretext to start a pogrom. They marched through the streets, maltreated and murdered Jewish citizens and destroyed or looted their flats and

new rulers planned the *Reichsausstellung*: "*Schaffendes Volk*" in 1937 (exhibition: "creative population"). No expense was spared. On the Rhine embankment a huge exhibition site was prepared, with 87 exhibition halls, 26 pavilions and a 280,000 square metres garden exhibition. Today it is the *Nordpark*. About 6.9 million people came to see this propaganda fair, which was primarily intended to prepare the population for the coming war.

One year later there could be no further talk of any kind of normal life. The preparations for war were running at full tilt. Food

shops. That was the beginning of the mass extermination. When the Third Reich ended in 1945 only 57 Jews survived in Düsseldorf. Almost 5,000 had been killed in the concentration camps.

On 1st September 1939 the German army attacked Poland and the Second World War began. The first years of war were a relatively tranquil time in Düsseldorf. That changed in the summer of 1942 when Düsseldorf was first bombed. The city centre went up in flames. Constant air raids caused the population to panic. On Whit Monday 1943 more than 1,300 H.E. bombs and more than 250,000 incendiary bombs were dropped on the city. 3,900 buildings were reduced to rubble and 1,200 people were killed.

Reduced to rubble: When the Americans marched into the city on 17th April 1945, the centuries-old city of Düsseldorf no longer existed. 96 per cent of the public buildings, 93 per cent of the business buildings, 94 per cent of the industrial buildings and 93 per cent of housing were destroyed or seriously damaged. Ten million cubic metres of rubble covered the streets and squares. A total of 6,000 civilians had been killed and 250,000 were homeless. The population was now an estimated 235,000 people. After twelve years

the elected City Council and the Municipal Director was the head of the City Administration. In the first free election since the Weimar Republic, on 13th October 1946, the newly established CDU received 47.2 per cent of the vote, the SPD 31 per cent and the KPD 12.3 percent.

The political leadership changed repeatedly in the first post-war years, up until 1964 when the Social Democrats gained the absolute majority. Since then they have only had to relinquish office once, from 1979 to 1984 when the CDU was in office again. In 1984 the Social Democrat Klaus Bungert, who had been the chairman of the city council

of National Socialist rule, Düsseldorf once more had to start from scratch.

The Americans left in June and the British arrived in their stead. They made the *Stahlhof* - not destroyed during the war - their headquarters. Based on the British model, a dual communal self-administration was set up, where the Lord Mayor was the chairman of

Left, destroyed by the bombs of the Second World War: the Oberkassel Bridge. **Above**, the clock tower of the Neander Church in Bolker Straße. It was one of the few buildings in Düsseldorf which did not have to be built anew.

from 1974 to 1979, returned to power, with the support of the Green party. In the communal election in autumn 1989 they lost their majority, however.

A new capital: In 1946 the British did not only set up a new communal order, they also made Düsseldorf the capital city of a new state. The province "North Rhine", the province "Westphalia" and the former state "Lippe" merged to become the new "North Rhine Westphalia", with Düsseldorf as the capital. This was not due to any royal tradition but to the fact that Düsseldorf was some way away from the Ruhr where, because of the uncertain future of heavy industry, social unrest was feared.

The founding of the new state was announced on 17th July 1946. The first Minister President, nominated by the British, was the President of Westphalia, Rudolf Amelunxen. On 6th August 1946 the first cabinet assembled in the *Stahlhof*. On 2nd October 1946 - largely unnoticed by the population - the first North-Rhine Westphalian Parliament held the first session in the Düsseldorf Opera House. The Social Democrat Ernst Gnoß, who had been persecuted by the Nazis, was the first elected *Landtagspräsident*. On Gnoß's insistence, the recon-

homeless, food was scarce. The meagre food rationing was 1550 calories per day and even that was frequently not available. There was virtually no heating as coal was in short supply. Only very slowly did the transport system get going. All bridges had been blown up by the Wehrmacht shortly before the end of the war and thus crossing the Rhine necessitated frequent detours.

The Currency Reform in 1948 brought some improvement. The shelves of the stores gradually filled and the queues began to disappear. But accommodation was still a problem. Despite official warnings, most of those evacuated during the war years re-

struction of the *Ständehaus* (Guild Hall) which had been severely damaged during a bomb attack was undertaken in order to afford "the Landtag a worthy domicile". Until reconstruction was completed, the City Parliament assembled in the cinema of the firm Henkel in Holthausen. On 15th March 1949, the Ständehaus was ceremoniously opened. Gnoß was not present to enjoy his triumph. Three days before he had succumbed to the lung disease that he had caught while imprisoned by the Nazis.

The inauguration was only a brief highlight in a desperate time. Many people were

turned. The flood of refugees continued unabated too. In 1948 the Düsseldorf population was back at 466,000. The housing projects simply could not cope with such a number. Only at year end 1955 was the available housing at the 1939 level, but the population was meanwhile 150,000 higher than in 1939. It reached its peak in 1970 with 705,000 inhabitants. Since then the numbers have steadily declined. Currently the population is approximately 600,000.

A new city emerges: During the time of the reconstruction, the city centre was totally re-planned too. Friedrich Tamm, the head of the city planning authority, drew up plans to make Düsseldorf the centre of the West German service industries. In the past 150 years there had always been plans to build a parallel road to the Königsallee as a new North-South axis and these were now realised. In 23rd April 1960 the *Berliner Allee* was opened by Willy Brandt, at that time the Lord Mayor of Berlin. To cope with the increasing traffic, Kölner Straße and Immermannstraße were also widened and Breiten Straße was extended.

At the south of the Hofgarten the Jan Wellem Platz was built. A serious dispute arose as to whether a 500-metre flyover which was completed in 1960 and became the new symbol of the city.

But the city did not only expand upwards. In Garath, to the south of Düsseldorf, a complete new town was built after the plans of Professor Guther. It is designed to accommodate 30,000 people. It is remarkable that despite the dearth of accommodation not only high-rise blocks of flats were built. There are bungalows as well.

To link this new suburb with the city centre, an urban railway line was opened up in 1967 between Düsseldorf-Garath and Rating-Ost - the first in West Germany.

The link-up with the left Rhine embank-

QUERVERSCHUB OBERKASSELER BRÜCKE

7. - 8. April 1976 · Düsseldorf

SONDERPOSTKARTE

should be built for this square. Ultimately the city planners had their way and the flyover was opened to the traffic in 1962.

Düsseldorf grew upwards too. High rise buildings sprang up everywhere. The first was the 88-metre high Mannesmann House. The highest building is the almost 100-metre high Thyssen House on Jan-Wellem-Platz

Left, the new Navigation Museum in the erstwhile Castle Tower on Burgplatz. **Above**, a miracle: the new Oberkassel Bridge was built next to the old one, and later pushed over into the original position.

ment was constantly improved too. By August 1946 the Hammer railway bridge had been repaired. The first road connection between Oberkassel and the city centre was the Oberkasseler bridge built in 1947. In 1951 this was superseded by the new *Südbrücke*.

Meanwhile six bridges straddle the river: the Südbrücke, the *Theodor Heuss Brücke* (1957, the first cable-stayed bridge in the world) the *Rhein-Knie Brücke* (1969), the new *Oberkasseler Brücke* (1971), the *Schleher Brücke* (1979) and the new *Eisenbahnbrücke Hamm* (1988). The seventh Rhine bridge is planned for Stockum.

Düsseldorf had an airport as far back as 1927. Expansion was prevented by the war but subsequently the city and the state continued to expand the airport at Lohausen. Between 1969 and 1986, at a cost of DM 500 million, a new passenger terminal was built. In 1986 the Rhein-Ruhr airport had 8.8 million passengers. After Frankfurt it is the second biggest airport in the Federal Republic.

Progress was made in other spheres as well. In 1965 the medical academy that was founded in 1907 became the University of Düsseldorf. On 1st January 1966 a mathematical-natural science faculty was opened, later a philosophical faculty. By 1987 approximately DM 1.2 billion had been spent on expanding university facilities.

Exhibitions and art: Düsseldorf's development into a major West German metropolis was enhanced by the decision to build a new exhibition site. In 1969 the foundation stone was laid for the *Neue Messe Düsseldorf*. In the incredible time span of only 900 days, a hyper-modern exhibition area was built in Stockum, near the Rhein-Ruhr airport, with an area of 131,500 square metres. Despite the cost of approximately DM 400 million, it has proved to be a worthwhile investment for the city. In 1982 the Düsseldorf Fair became the No. 1 in West Germany.

Back in the days of the Elector Jan Wellem, Düsseldorf already had the reputation of being an art and culture centre. This reputation was consolidated by the building of an Art Gallery. The initial collection consisted of 88 paintings by Paul Klee, and since 1961 a remarkable number of world-famous 20th century paintings have been assembled. In 1986 the collection was moved from Schloß Jägerhof, which had meanwhile become too small to house the vast number of paintings, to a new domicile in Grabbeplatz. With its curved, black, reflecting facade it is a distinguished landmark on this square. Together with the municipal *Kunsthalle*, this new building is the centrepiece of the Düsseldorf "art area" which stretches from the Karlstadt in the south with its many museums, galleries and studios to the Ehrenhof in the North with the Art Museum, the *Tonhalle* (a concert hall) and the *Kunstpalast*.

Upwards and outwards: The rebuilding necessitated by the war continued well into the 1960s. The last twenty years have been more a time of restructuring. For years the city gave the impression of being one huge

Botanical Gardens of the University.

building site. In readiness for the 700th anniversary of the city, a number of projects were started in the 1970s. The first was in 1973 - the building of the underground railway, which triggered the restructuring of the city centre. Where the old city and the new city fuse the face of the city has changed considerably. Extensive building projects were carried out at the Grabbeplatz, Heinrich-Heine-Platz, Königsalle and in the area of Berliner Allee and Platz der deutschen Einheit. Especially worth mentioning is the 123 metre-high office centre of the *Landesversicherungsanstalt* on the south exit of the Königsallee which was designed by Harald Dallmann.

In 1981 the underground railway tunnel between Kennedy Damm and Heinrich-Heine-Allee was already 1600 metres long. By 1988 it had reached the *Hauptbahnhof* (main station). Three years before the reconstruction of the new Hauptbahnhof had been concluded.

For a long time there had been criticism that the Hauptbahnhof cut off the Altstadt from the east of the city. But development of that area was well-nigh impossible because of the location of the industrial sites. In 1980 the *Oberbilker Stahlwerk* moved its production site to the Reisholzer Bahnstraße and thus the Hauptbahnhof could be integrated into the city centre.

On the old industrial area around the newly created Bertha-von-Suttner-Platz, office blocks, apartment houses and the Municipal Further Education Centre were built. The Hauptbahnhof, modernised at a cost of DM 650 million thus became the centre of the city once more.

This modernisation also introduced a new S-Bahn line, which links Düsseldorf, Hagen und Mönchengladbach. The Deutsche Bundesbahn has invested more than DM one billion in this 82-kilometre route. DM 500 million alone were spent on the stretch between Gerresheim and Neuss. Especially for the S-Bahn a new, four lane bridge was built over the Rhine, to replace the old Hammer railway bridge. Just in time for the 700th anniversary of the City, the East-West axis, where more than two million people live, could be taken into service in 1988.

The Löbbecke-Museum with Aquarium was also completed only recently. Since 1987 ten huge aquariums, 68 small water containers, 31 terrariums, 26 insectariums and a hot house, present an incredible range of fauna.

An important event in recent city history was the Federal Garden Show in 1987. An 87.5 hectare park with man-made lakes was designed. Approximately 450,000 cubic metres of earth had to be moved to create what is now the *Südpark* . The preparations for this also gave much-needed impetus to the hitherto underdeveloped areas of Oberbilk and Flingern. Millions of Marks were invested in the creation of new green areas.

Birthday celebrations: In August 1988 the city of Düsseldorf celebrated its 700th birthday. A 300-metre long buffet counter had been set up between the *Landtag* and the Castle Tower. All the while ships from times of yore and the present day sailed along the Rhine. The parade was headed by a specially built replica of an ancient raft (110 metres long and 20 metres wide). One week before, it had already aroused much curiosity when it was tried out on the Rhine. In the wake of this pre-industrial mode of transport came all kinds of iron sloops, paddle-wheel steamers, sailing boats, cargo ships, ferries etc.

Further highlights of the anniversary year included a medieval city festival, a Kö-festival and a number of cultural events such as the Rhenish music festival, a sculpture exhibition and a Medici exhibition in the city museum. More than five million visitors attended the three main presentations.

Although initially the events had been planned on an even more spectacular scale - a gigantic Rhine project all the way from Basle to Rotterdam had originally been envisaged - nevertheless, in the end everybody was satisfied.

A vital part of a birthday party are birthday presents. The most beautiful was undoubtedly the new *Landtag* on the Rhine, the Parliament building of North Rhine Westphalia which was officially inaugurated in October 1988. The cost was originally estimated at DM 190 million, but, as usual, this sum was exceeded. Now the round building contributes to enhancing the status of Düsseldorf as a capital - in every sense of the word.

Düsseldorf

1600 m/ 1.0 miles

KLEMENSPLATZ

ZEPPEN-HEIM

Schwarzbach

LANGST-KIERST

KITTELBACHSTR.

KAISERSWERTH

LICHTEN-BROICH

ALTE LANDSTR.

Rhine

Düsseldorf
Airport

HOTER - HEIDE

STRÜMP

LOHAUSEN
FLUGHAFENSTR.

Niederrheinstr.

Nordring

Eckener Str.

Hamborner Str.

UNTER-RATH

BOVERT

Meerbusch

HAUS MEER

STOCKUM
D.- MESSE /
RHEINSTATION

FREILIGRATH
PLATZ

Danziger Str.

Kalkumer Str.

Mühlenbach

Morser Str.

BÜDERICH

Rhine
Stadium

Exhibition
Ground

NORDPARK
AQUAZOO

GOLZHEIM

Heinrich-

Ehrhardt-

NECKLEN-BROICH

MB.-BÜDERICH

NIEDERDONK

Düsseldorfer Str.

LÖRICK

TH. KEUSS - BR.

Ulmenstr.

Münsterstr.

LÖRICKER STR.

Krefelder Str.

Brüsseler Str.

KENNEDY-DAMM

Brüsseler Str.

Brüsseler Str.

Landstr.

Heerdter Str.

OBER-KASSEL

KLEVERSTR.

Academy
of Arts

Kaarst

VOGELSANG

Str.

HEERDT

LUEGPL.

TONHALLE

NEUSSER-FURTH

Gladbacher Str.

Heerdter

BELSERPL.

Rheinknie-
brücke

Königsallee

Golf Course

Rhine

H. HEINE
ALLEE

Harbour

DÜSSELDORF STATIO

Post Office

Neusser Ring

Federal State
Parliament

Intimate Theatre

FRIEDRICHSTADT

Bilker Allee

Academy of
Science

Volklinger Str.

UNT. - BILK

BILK

Wizelstr.

HAMM

Südbrücke
Düsseldorf -
Neuss

Südring

Südring

Neuss

St. Quirinius
Cathedral

FLEHE

Universi

Himmelgeis

Landstr.

Str.

Rennbahn

Neusser Ring

POMONA

Kölner Straße

VOLMERS-WERTH

Jülicher

Neusser Ring

GNADENTAL

Bonner Str.

GRIMLING-HAUSEN

Berghener Str.

Erft

DERIKUM

UEDESHEIM

Jülicher Landstr.

SELIKUM

REUSCHEN-BERG

Castle
Reuschenbg.

Norf

Bonner Str.

Rhine

HOLZHEIM

Erft

Gille

WECK-HOVEN

STÜTTGEN

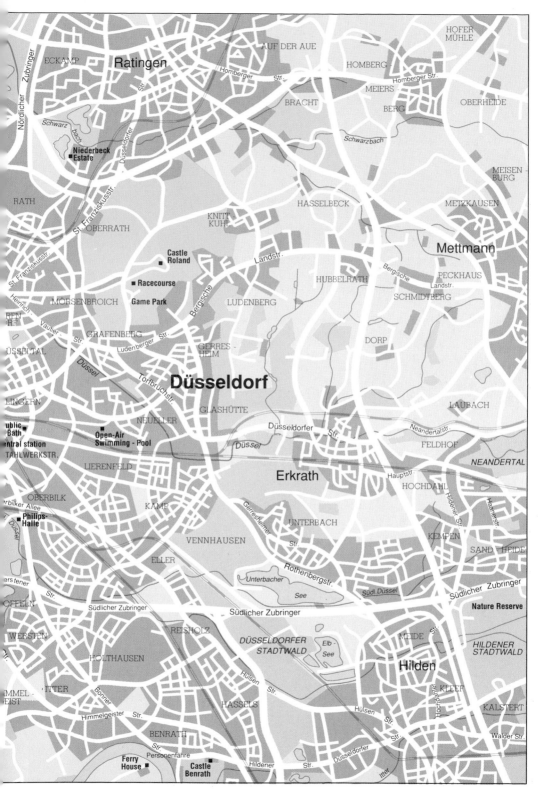

THE CAPITAL OF NORTH RHINE WESTPHALIA

In history the "ruse of reason" occasionally works out. One example of it is the decision of the British Military Governor in 1946 to make Düsseldorf the capital city of the newly established German state of North-Rhine Westphalia. More than 40 years later there is no doubt that this was a fortunate decision not only for the state but the city as well. In retrospect no one can say if Düsseldorf would have become a leading trading centre as well as one of the most important banking centres without having become the capital of the industrial heartland of Germany. Certainly, however, being the *Landeshauptstadt* was not exactly an obstacle for the economic, cultural, scientific and city planning achievements.

The state and its administration is the most important employer. The city has developed together with North-Rhine Westphalia. Both profit reciprocally. Düsseldorf has become a service centre with superb international connections. 320 Japanese companies have established their headquarters on the Düssel and Rhine - only New York provides a comparable magnet for companies from the Far East. More than 350 enterprises from the Netherlands, 300 from USA, 250 firms from Great Britain and 150 from France have subsidiaries in Düsseldorf.

With the development of international trade, Düsseldorf's reputation as a city of flair and chic increased. The Königsallee is quite rightly compared to the famous Champs Elysee and the Via Veneto. Whether or not you will be able to verify the statement that on the "Kö" you can see the most beautiful women in Germany, is up to you.

It seems, in fact, that the creative professions have decreed Düsseldorf as their centre. More than 200 advertising agencies are based here, more than 10,000 architects have offices in and around Düsseldorf. Critics of the city see fit to claim that Düsseldorf is a city of superficiality rather than inner values. Every visitor will be able to prove them wrong. Of course, elegance is the key word for the city centre, but hospitality and warm-heartedness are encountered everywhere.

Especially so in the Düsseldorf Altstadt. What I like about it is the atmosphere, the famous German *Gemütlichkeit*, the immediate possibility of making contact with interesting people. It is easy to strike up a conversation - whether it concerns *Altbier*, politics, culture or fashion. In the old city, ideas hatch quickly - and sometimes they drown in beer. Singing is allowed, making deals as well. *Joie de vivre* is the motto. Who you are is important. Where you come from is as irrelevant as your title, profession or personal wealth.

True to the motto: "Don't always work - just like a beast, enjoy yourself - come out and feast" in spring the tidal waves of joy are especially high. In Düsseldorf, the most northern of the three Carnival cities along the Rhine, the *Rosenmontagszug* (carnival parade) is the high point of the season - just as it has been ever since 1825, in fact. Tradition is valued highly, but not the "stick-in-the-mud" type. The same applies to the world-famous, nine-day "fun fair", celebrated every July. This tradition goes back to the year 1288 when the city was granted its charter. Every summer, from my office overlooking the Rhine, I can see a mottled conglomeration of helter-skelters, Ferris wheels, carousels, beer tents and lottery kiosks. Strains of music waft across the river...and the succulent whiff of fried sausages makes it difficult to resist the temptation for a quick snack.

Düsseldorf is especially proud of being the art metropolis of an area steeped in artistic endeavours. The North Rhine Westphalian Art Collection, the *Kunsthalle*, the Art Museum, the Theatre and the Opera House attract visitors from all over.

With its multiple engagements, the state itself demonstrates that it has accepted Düsseldorf as its capital. The citizens of North-Rhine Westphalia agree: The British knew what they were doing in 1946. Conversely Düsseldorf has managed to become a pars pro toto for North-Rhine Westphalia - a state whose very strength lies in its diversity.

Left, in front of the Thyssen House is the Schauspiel haus, a modern concrete building that has been nick-named the "sinking ocean liner". **Above**, Johannes Rau, in charge of North Rhine Westphalia.

Although Düsseldorf has recently turned 700, it has only been ranked among the major European cities for a mere hundred years or so. It can boast of many things: fashionable shopping city, important financial metropolis, international trading centre, significant industrial location, high-ranking administrative centre, Germany's No. 1 trade fair site, capital of Germany's most populated state. All that is true and yet none of these decorums - by itself - does the city justice.

Düsseldorf owes its rise to fame and glory to industry. When special shipping rights to the Rhine were annulled by the Rhine Shipping Act in 1831 and Western Germany's first train rolled into the region of the Bergisches Land in 1838, the industrial era marched into the small provincial town with all its might.

The industrial base: A booming textile industry was the first manifestation of industrial progress in Düsseldorf. As early as 1836 there were 200 people employed by J. A. Deus' steam-operated calico printing and weaving mill. The textile factories, however, could not hold their ground for long; soon they were surpassed by the iron and steel industry, which began when two Belgian brothers established a steel mill in Oberbilk in the 1850s. They were followed by companies from the Eifel, other German states and England.

The pipe manufacturers Poensgen and Inden from the Eifel set up business in the city in 1860 and thus account for Düsseldorf's leading position in the pipe manufacturing which has lasted to this very day. The triumphant advance of iron pipes "Made in Düsseldorf" is, however, linked with another name. The brothers Max and Reinhard Mannesmann from Remscheid invented the first method of rolling seamless steel pipes in

1886. Soon they both realized that the new product could be marketed most effectively in Düsseldorf, which at the time was already a leading pipe centre. They duly transferred their headquarters to the Rhine.

Today, pipes from Düsseldorf are exported to 120 countries around the world. Pipeline technicians in Siberia and Alaska have absolute confidence in the products manufactured by the Mannesmann Company which has, in the meantime, become a huge techno-

logical combine. The company's nine groups had a turnover of 16.7 billion Marks in 1987. Of the 122,000 employees at Mannesmann only 11,000 work in Düsseldorf where, apart from the pipe works, the machinery division and the business headquarters are located.

Industrial giants: Iron and steel was soon joined by an efficient machine-building industry which is represented by such illustrious names as Schiess, Jagenberg, SMS Schloemann-Siemag and Rheinmetall. The Rheinmetall Group was founded in 1889 as the *"Rheinische Metallwaren- und Maschinenfabrik Aktiengesellschaft"*. Rhein-

Preceding pages, in the foundry at Rheinhausen; Düsseldorf's trade fair and exhibition site. **Left**, children play in front of the Mannesmann building. **Right**, Düsseldorf's women are known for their chic and self-confidence.

metall GmbH, which specializes in defence technology, is part of this concern. By being a majority shareholder at Jagenburg AG (machine-building industry) and Pierburg GmbH (automobile technology) the group also controls these companies. It has an annual turn-over of approximately three billion Marks and employs 15,000 people around the world. All activities in the High-Tech enterprise are controlled from its head office in Düsseldorf.

The SMS Schloemann-Siemag AG has also developed into a large multinational company. The firm started out as a blacksmith's workshop set up by Carl Eberhard

name Henkel. Fritz Henkel, a native of Hessen, had founded a factory manufacturing detergent in 1876 in Aachen, employing an initial staff of only three people. He transferred his business to Düsseldorf only two years later. The town's favourable location, good communications and nearby markets had been decisive factors.

His decision was soon rewarded. It wasn't long before the rented factory on Schützenstraße (formerly a soap factory) grew too small. Henkel moved his business to a newer building on Gerresheimerstraße. But even here there was soon not enough room. The expanding business then moved to the sub-

Weiss in Siegen in 1871 which merged with a trading company for fittings and technological products founded by Eduard Schloemann in Düsseldorf in 1901. By 1987, the company, which now specializes in machine and plant manufacture, had an approximate turnover of 2.3 billion Marks. 1,100 technicians and clerks work at the firm's headquarters on Eduard-Schloemann-Straße in Düsseldorf.

Detergents: Apart from heavy engineering, the chemical industry also became firmly established in Düsseldorf at a relatively early date. Its growth is closely linked with the

urb of Holthausen where the factory is still located today. It was from this suburb that the world's first all-in-one detergent - Persil - set out to conquer the sculleries of the western world.

Today Henkel Enterprises is the largest private company in the city. Over 13,000 people are employed by this giant in the chemical industry and it has over 34,000 employees around the world. In 1989 the Henkel Group had a turnover well in excess of 10 billion Marks.

The chemical industry has now seized the top position that was once held by the iron and steel industry. One in five of the city's 77,000 industrial workers earns his living in the chemical industry, whereas only 7,000 are now employed in the production of iron and steel. The engineering industry takes second place with some 11,000 workers, followed by the automobile industry that employs approximately 9,500 workers.

Cars: Düsseldorf owes its strong position in the automobile industry largely to the exquisite star from Untertürkheim that has firmly expanded its production in the city. Germany's leading car manufacturer has now moved its entire manufacturing of transport vehicles to the Rhine. Since industrial areas

resheimer Glas, Krupp, Siemens, Thyssen and Veba are also represented in North Rhine Westphalia's capital city. Altogether there are 260 companies that account for an annual turnover of 20 billion Marks. With a gross turnover of 85,000 Marks per employee Düsseldorf's industry is in a much better position than most German cities. And yet it is no longer industry alone that determines the economy of the city.

Since the early 1950's Düsseldorf has been undergoing a rapid structural change. While in 1950, 50% of the workforce was employed by manufacturing industry or the building trade, today numbers have sunk to

are hard to come by in Düsseldorf a number of small allotment gardeners were driven out to make room for Daimler-Benz. The fact that the city decided in favour of the giant car manufacturer has paid off. The company has become trade tax payer no. 1 in the metropolis on the Rhine.

There is really no lack of renowned industrial enterprises in Düsseldorf. International companies such as Feldmühle-Nobel, Ger-

100,000, about a quarter of the workforce. Although many of the resulting unemployed have been absorbed by the flourishing service sector, the city still has to cope with a two-digit unemployment rate.

Though it might seem paradoxical, Düsseldorf's favourable location largely accounts for the adverse balance in the job market. Every day 130,000 people, one third of the total workforce, commute to Düsseldorf from nearby cities and communes. Only 20,000 residents earn their living outside the city. This daily influx has presented the city with unprecedented traffic chaos. In the

Left, finding the way around a trade fair. **Above**, in this city of fashion, everything goes.

morning and the evening an avalanche of cars build up for kilometres at the Mörsenbroicher Ei and other traffic junctions. As a survey showed only recently, the citizens of Düsseldorf are more worried about their congested roads than their job situation and their city's finances.

While the industrial sector has suffered drawbacks in recent years, the service sector has boomed. Although Düsseldorf is also traditionally known as an administrative centre, the great breakthrough to a "the city of service industry" did not come until after World War II, though the "Ruhrgebiet's desk" is an expression which even circulated at the

Düsseldorf's growth into a significant trade centre went hand in hand with its expansion as an administrative metropolis, although the city only established its reputation as an international trading centre after 1945.

Foreign investment: Today the metropolis on the Rhine can claim to be Germany's leading centre of foreign business. The offices of about 3,000 foreign companies, manufacturers and other businesses, have settled around Königsallee. Among them are 50 multinational combines that have selected Düsseldorf as their main European seat.

To the Japanese, Düsseldorf is No.1 city in Europe. Japan realized at an early stage

turn of the century when numerous companies and federations of industries in the Ruhr Region first started moving their head offices to Düsseldorf.

Administrative and trading centre: While the royal splendour of the old days is now gone, Düsseldorf's economic and political importance as a capital city remains. The province of North Rhine-Westphalia with its administrative bodies and institutions is today the city's largest single employer. A total of 42,000 people work for the ministries, the State parliament, the district government, the municipal and other authorities.

that the Rhine metropolis could not only be a stepping stone to the German market but also to the entire European market. Around 320 Japanese companies have now settled in this city - more than anywhere else except New York. 7,000 Japanese live in Düsseldorf. There is a Japanese Club with 4,500 members, a Japanese Chamber of Industry and Commerce, a Japanese school and since 1975 a Japanese Garden for whose construction the Japanese community spent 1.8 million Marks. The Far Eastern touch has endowed Düsseldorf with its nickname "Nippon's Capital on the Rhine".

Yet the Land of the Rising Sun only holds third position in the ranking list of foreign companies in Düsseldorf. The Netherlands and the United States lead the field with about 350 representatives each, followed by Japan (320), Great Britain (250) and France (150). In the meantime an ever-increasing number of developing countries have discovered Düsseldorf. 26 Indian companies, for example, have chosen the city as their place of business in the Federal Republic. About 15% of Germany's foreign trade is cleared via Düsseldorf. This is all the more remarkable as less than one percent of Germany's population lives here (the city has 562,000 inhabitants). But 30 million people live within a radius of 150 kilometres, making up the European Community's largest concentrated market.

Following the footsteps of the business community, many federations have also settled in Düsseldorf. Apart from the Central Association of the German Iron and Steel Industry and the German Federation of Trades Unions, the Federation of Chemical Industry, the Retail Trade Federation and the Trade Association of German Advertising Agencies reside here. They are joined by 25 foreign and interstate chambers of commerce and almost 60 different consulates beginning with A for Argentina to Z for Zaire.

Trading centre: Eight of Düsseldorf's business firms are ranked among the top 100 German commercial enterprises: Metro-International, Thyssen Handelsunion, Mannesmann Handel, Salzgitter Stahl, W. und O. Bergmann, Deutscher Supermarkt, Kaufring and Deutsche Kraftverkehr Ernst Grimmke.

It isn't only in iron and steel that Düsseldorf maintains a dominant trading position; the metropolis on the Rhine is also a step ahead when it comes to trading with machinery, vehicles, technical instruments and consumer goods. The wholesale business, with a total of 28,000 employees, has a turnover of 53 billion Marks, almost six percent of the national total.

As far as Düsseldorf's retail trade is concerned, the annual turnover of six billion Marks, some 9,900 Marks per person, accounts for the second highest retail figures of any city in the Federal Republic. And it wallows in the publicity. The city on the Rhine likes to call itself "Little Paris".

All the latest fashion: Königsallee in particular has contributed to this reputation. It is affectionately called "Kö" by friends from far and near. For less than a kilometre along the Kö, 250 different retail shops offer top international goods. To see and to be seen; that is the motto to be lived up to by the rich and the *nouveau riche* as they are drawn towards this frightfully expensive shopping

paradise. A select ambient in marble and brass make up the background to fashion, fashion and more fashion. But electronic equipment, art and junk are also sold along the Kö.

Strollers along the Kö always go for new things. For example chocolates created especially for the 700th birthday of the city found a ready market. Experts estimate that annually 500 million Marks change hands along the Kö. Visitors are particularly generous with their money: they account for 85 percent of the turnover. Besides Kö, Schadowstraße has become a popular shopping street.

Left, there is no shortage of theatrical or musical events in Düsseldorf. **Right**, just for show.

The high society likes to go shopping for shoes here.

Fairs: Fashion isn't only the preserve of the Kö and Schadowstraße; Düsseldorf's trade fair grounds are also seized by the fashion disease several times a year. The international world of fashion meets four times a year in Düsseldorf. Some seven thousand fashion designers from all corners of the globe display their newest creations at the Igedo. Over 200,000 visitors from 70 European and overseas countries come to marvel at their creativity. Nearly ten billion Marks worth of purchasing orders are placed during the show. But it isn't only high fashion that

Nowea (Nordwestdeutsche Ausstellungs-gesell-schaft) established Düsseldorf's reputation as a city of exhibitions, although the city had already built up a reputation at the turn of the century. Now Düsseldorf is Germany's No. 1 exhibition site, with broad international appeal. The new exhibition centre, which is located in the vicinity of the airport and only ten minutes away from downtown, was opened in 1971 and is unrivalled in the Federal Republic.

Advertising: New innovative ideas are a feature of Düsseldorf's advertising community. For Düsseldorf is also the city of advertising agencies. It is said to have over 200

is represented in Düsseldorf. Other fairs and exhibitions enjoy an interntional reputation.These include the GDS (International Shoe Show), the Investment Goods Shows Drupa (International Fair for Print and Paper), Interpack (International Trade Fair for Packing Machinery, Packaging Materials and Sweets Vending Machines) and "K" (Plastics).

The trade fair "Boat" is the most popular with the visitors; 400,000 fans of aquatic sports come together every year in January. Düsseldorf organizes a total of 20 top international fairs. The Trade Fair Organization

advertising agencies, among them 15 of the top agencies in the Federal Republic. Daimler-Benz polishes up its image here. In addition, VW, Citroen, Toyota and other car manufacturers try to boost their turnover with the help of Düsseldorf's advertising specialists. They are joined by customers from other fields: Procter & Gamble, IBM and Dresdner Bank.

People with fantasy can find a wide field of activity in Düsseldorf. Rhenish creativity is much in demand. And yet it was a branch of Doyle Dane Bernbach, an advertising agency from New York, that with its lively maxims established the reputation of the city almost 30 years ago as a "creative melting pot". The advertising business has grown in the meantime. The international character lingers on and endows the agencies with an annual turnover of 3.5 billion marks.

The citizens of Düsseldorf also like to hear their town being talked of as the city of media. But there is still a long way to go for the city to live up to this reputation. The fact that apart from "*Handelsblatt*" there is not a single national daily paper published in the capital city of Germany's most populated state only indicates that the press is still rather backward and provincial here. And

And where else can one do more business than in the banking trade. After Frankfurt, Düsseldorf is the second most important city in Germany as far as the banking and stock exchange businesses are concerned.

Altogether 190 German and 70 foreign joint-stock companies as well as 3,000 national and international bonds are quoted at the Rhenish-Westphalian Stock Exchange which emerged from a fusion of the Düsseldorf, Cologne and Essen Stock Exchanges in 1935. One third of all German share transactions are made in Düsseldorf. The Rhenish-West-phalian Stock Exchange is the second strongest in the Federal Repub-

the city needs to catch up in electronic media as well. Its old regional rival, Cologne, is a clear step ahead in radio and television broadcasting. WDR (West German Radio) has, nevertheless, built a fancy regional studio in Düsseldorf and also *Zweites Deutsches Fernsehen*, Germany's second national television channel, has a studio here.

Financial centre: The citizens of Düsseldorf have always had a knack for doing business.

Left, part of the new State Parliament building. **Above**, a traditional way of transporting goods– a barge on the Rhine.

lic with an impressive annual turnover of over 150 billion Marks.

Over 100 German and 62 foreign banks have an annual turnover of 350 billion Marks. Numerous German banks such as the *Landeszentralbank*, the *Westdeutsche Landesbank* and the *Commerzbank* have their head offices here. The central offices of 51 different credit institutes are located in Düsseldorf. They are joined by six foreign banks that control their business transactions in the Federal Republic from Düsseldorf. How could it be otherwise: all banks are from the Land of the Rising Sun.

HEINRICH HEINE - ROMANTIC AND ICONOCLAST

Heinrich Heine was born in Düsseldorf on 13th December 1797 but decided to glamorize his actual date of birth by declaring that he was "one of the first men of the century", having been born on New Year's Eve 1800.

His parents were Jewish and he was given the name Harry. Little Harry Heine was fortunate enough to grow up in a city that had long since pursued a liberal policy towards Jews and had abolished the ghetto. His contemporary Löb Baruch, better known as the political author and eventual Heine critic Ludwig Börne, was not so lucky, having to spend his childhood and adolescence in the *Judengasse* (Jews alley) in Frankfurt.

At that time Düsseldorf witnessed a decisive epoch of European history. Initially Napoleon's troops were stationed there, from 1806 onwards Düsseldorf joined the *Rheinbund*, a French protectorate, and eventually, after Napoleon's exile in 1815, Düsseldorf joined the newly founded German Federation.

In 1814 Heine left school, without passing his final examination, and in 1815 he started two apprenticeships in Frankfurt, but returned to Düsseldorf shortly afterwards.

One year later he went to Hamburg to work at his uncle's bank. His unsuccessful courtship of his cousin, Amalie, caused him to write his first poems, instead of devoting himself to his business activities, and these poems were published under a *nom de plume*. In 1819 Heine decided to give up any thought of a commercial career and registered at the University of Bonn to study law. Again he found his course of studies unsatisfactory. He continued writing poems, tried his hand at writing drama and succeeded in getting some essays and a volume of poetry published. After registering at Göttingen University and later the University of Berlin he attended lectures on literature.

Preceding pages, the west bank at Oberkassel, with the famous "purple" house; at the *Kirmes* (the fair), old carousels are making a comeback. **Left**, the monument to Heinrich Heine by Bert Geresheim in the Schwanenmarkt. The work is not uncontroversial. **Right**, students in front of the University Mensa.

In Berlin Heine frequented the literary salon of Rahel Varnhagen, a Jewess who had converted to the Christian faith and it was there he met Ludwig Börne, Hegel, Chamisso as well as other contemporary poets and philosophers. In his autobiography Heine was to write: "Of the seven years I attended German universities before graduating, I wasted three beautiful years studying Roman casuistics and law, the most illiberal of all sciences".

In 1825 he, too, converted to Christianity, a step that was generally considered the "entrance ticket to European culture." He also changed his name to Heinrich. Although he was now a baptized Jew, high society looked down its collective nose. His attitude to Judaism was on the one hand characterized by his love for a persecuted people, but, on the other hand, he watched in disbelief how those that clung to their orthodox faith seemed unable to fight for equal rights.

At the time of his conversion, Heine wrote: "I admit that I supported the fight for equal rights for Jews and their rights as citizens, and in those troubled times to come, unavoidable as they are, the German mob will hear my voice resounding in the beer halls and palaces".

The "troubled times" came some 120 years later. In May 1933 Heine's life's work was publicly burnt by the Nazis. And Heine's warning that "There where books are burnt, people will be burnt one day too", went unheeded in the German beer halls.

In 1826 and 1827 the publishers Hoffmann und Campe issued two books of travelogues and a "Book of Songs" - a collection of romantic poems. The main theme of the book, which quickly became a best-seller, was Love, with a capital L, which Heine saw,

time Heine had already been in exile in France for four years.

In 1831 he had left for Paris and, initially, France was not so much the country of exile, but a new home. He began writing increasingly political articles for the *Augsburg Allgemeine Zeitung*. In 1832, not least because of the influence of the Austrian statesman Metternich, the publications ceased; however, the publisher Julius Campe continued to publish his writings. France, in contrast, took to him at once. Today "Henri" has a firm footing in the history of French literature, and is regarded as one of the first mediators between France and Germany.

above all, as synonymous with pain. Heine's ironic and irreverent mockery of the German Federation, oppressive as it was, is already hinted at in his travelogues.

Heine heard about the July 1830 French Revolution while he was staying in Helgoland, and he looked upon the news as "sunbeams, wrapped in paper". These sunbeams were metamorphosed into political activity. Heine became an important member of the literary-political movement *"Junges Deutschland"*, a movement that fought for democracy and liberality. In 1835 the government prohibited his publications and issued warnings to his movement, but by this

66

After 1837 the first symptoms of the illness that was eventually to confine him to permanent invalidism and early death became apparent. In 1841 Heine married his close companion of many years, Crescentia Eugenie Mirat, whom he called "Mathilde". Before she came into his life Heine had only enjoyed a few, discreet, fleeting affairs. Now he began to suffer the pangs of love again.

From January 1843 the ironic verse epos "Atta Troll. A Midsummer Night's Dream" appeared in the *"Zeitung für die elegante Welt"*. In his verses Heine not only attacked the jingoistic *"Schwäbische Dichterschule"* but also the lauders of pan-Germanism, whom he accused of being poetasters, degrading ideals like Liberty and Equality.

In autumn 1843 Heine travelled through Germany where he witnessed oppression and a great deal of anxiety among democratic circles. Around Christmas time he met Karl Marx. While he was undoubtedly influenced by communist ideals, dogmatism remained anathema to him.

In autumn 1844 he again set out for Germany; it was to be his last journey. His health was deteriorating rapidly. The verse epos "*Deutschland. Ein Wintermärchen*" (Germany. A winter's tale) appeared in the volume "New poems" and was prohibited soon

tinued writing, even if he could barely hold his pen. In fact he continued writing poems, novella and even his autobiography right up to his death, which he knew was imminent:

*"In meine dunkle Zelle dringt
Kein Sonnenstrahl, kein
Hoffnungschimmer
Ich weiß nur mit der Kirchhofgruft
Vertausch' ich dies fatale Zimmer"*

(No sign of hope, no sunbeam fell
into this dark and gloomy cell.
When I shall leave this fatal room
They'll take me to the churchyard tomb)

after its publication as Heine unmasked all the hypocrisy and illiberality he had encountered. He spared nothing and no one and castigated the rigidity of the system and its perpetrators.

In 1848, the year of the revolution, Heine's health deteriorated so rapidly that from then on he was confined to his so-called "Matratzengruft" (mattress tomb). He con-

Left, relaxing by the round pond in the Hofgarten. **Above right**, the Heinrich-Heine-Stuben in the old city is located only a few metres away from the poet's birthplace. But that house no longer exists.

His illness racked his body but not his spirit. Heine died in Paris on 17th February 1856, an upright "champion in the struggle for freedom".

As was the case during his lifetime, he continues to have his admirers as well as detractors.

Although Düsseldorf has long since had a Heine archive and a museum, and, since 1981, even a memorial, it was not until 1989 that the authorities deemed it appropriate to name the University of Düsseldorf after one of its most famous citizens. Let's hope that Heine's spirit will leave its mark there, too.

A City of Theatre and Music

Theatre stages: Düsseldorf is an eldorado for the Art connoisseur - that's well-known. But there's more to Düsseldorf than that. It is also one of the most important cities in the Federal Republic as far as the theatre is concerned.

Ingrid Brant's and Alfons Höckmann's boulevard stage *Komödie* in Steinstraße 3 is one of those contributory stones to the scintillating mosaic that makes up the Düsseldorf theatre scene. Not that you should confuse this with the *Kom(m)ödchen,* which evolved from the "*kleine Maler und Literatenbühne*" in the early post-World War II period. Founded and still run by Kay and Lore Lorentz, it has long since been a firm fixture in the German cabaret scene and the sallies and direct hits scored still make those that are their target flinch perceptibly.

Then there is the amazing Puppet Theatre run by the Zangerles. Every evening - ever since the family started their theatre, sixty years ago - their carved wooden puppets seem to come alive, and perform well-known plays at a quality level rarely equalled. Kleist's "*Der zerbrochene Krug*" (The Broken Jug), Nestroy's "*Frühere Verhältnisse*" (Earlier Times), Saint Exupery's "*Der kleine Prinz*" (The Little Prince) are in the repertoire. Operas like Mozart's "Abduction from the Seraglio" and Weber's "*Freischütz*" are performed and there is occasionally even ballet. The director of the wooden ensemble is Winfred Zangerle. His triple category theatre is in Palais Wittgenstein.

A dual category stage is the Music Theatre. In 1951 Gustav Gründgens split up the hitherto customary three genres, so that the straight theatre section moved to a separate house. After this divorce there was an immediate wedding between the opera house in Düsseldorf and that in Duisburg - and the marriage has since continued as a thriving joint venture. The unification of these two stages as *Deutsche Oper am Rhein* would

A circus on Gustav-Gründgens-Platz in front of the Theatre. The legendary Gründgens was director of the Schauspielhaus.

appear to be exemplary, yet, despite its evident cost-saving efficiency, few other cities in Germany are willing to follow suit.

The ballet company also enjoys an international reputation. In the post-war era there have been three directors, Hermann Juch, Grischa Barfuß and Kurt Horres. All three enhanced the quality of the two houses, not least by engaging many young singers and by catapulting talented singers from the provinces to stardom. The same applies to conductors. Karl Böhm - one of the most important Mozart conductors of his time - occasionally made guest appearances in the city. During the rehearsal of a Wagner opera,

conditions performances were staged. Yet one can't say that the days when Germany's theatre elite met on the stage in Düsseldorf are over. The times have changed. Due to the omnipresent media, the voracity for new faces and personalities is greater than ever and hence the requirements of the audiences have changed too. Nevertheless the *Schauspielhaus* in Düsseldorf has lost none of its fascination. It is still in the top rank of straight theatres in Germany, even if the successors of Gründgens - that superlative Mephisto - were not always innundated with praise for their productions.

Since 1970, the Schauspielhaus has been

he once tried to cajole the trombones to modify their brassy splendour by saying: "Gentlemen, don't forget we're in Düsseldorf and not in Jericho." However, it is well known that it wasn't exactly the trombones that caused Düsseldorf's walls to collapse. And when in 1947 Gustaf Gründgens decided to accept the offer to become director of the Theatre, this was a great boon for the city. At the time the city was still little more than a pile of rubble and yet the first tender shoots of a reviving cultural life were already very evident.

The debris has long since been cleared away and few remember in what dilapidated

housed in a futuristically-styled building which the locals call "sinking ocean liner". But there's nothing of the Titanic about it. On the contrary. The schedule of performances ranges from classics to avant-garde, from subtle comedies to heroic drama and the liner can only dock in a port where there are sufficient passengers willing to participate in the exciting voyage. And Thalia is a persuasive goddess - for even if all the world is not a stage - Düsseldorf is trying hard to make up for it.

After all, there is a tradition. The first theatre was at the Rathausplatz. When the elector Carl Theodor announced that he would come for a visit, within six weeks a theatre was built - solely to impress him. But construction work was slapdash and in 1818 the building had to be pulled down. Sixteen years later the company moved to a new house. Justice of the Peace Dr. Karl Leberecht Immermann was appointed director of the theatre and Felix Mendelssohn director of the opera.

Despite such famous people as Graf Spee, Prince Friedrich of Prussia and the Academy director von Schadow the theatre languished for a considerable time. Not until Louise Dumont and Gustav Lindemann took over at the beginning of this century did matters pick up. Soon the theatre quality was regarded as exemplary. It was they, too, who started a theatre archive, which Lindemann later donated to the city. It has now grown so substantially that it has its own museum: the *Theatermuseum* in the Hofgärtnerhaus.

Music: Music in Düsseldorf certainly doesn't play second fiddle either - a rich musical tradition goes back to the 18th century. And musical giants have conducted here: Mendelssohn, Schumann and Brahms were the first music directors and virtually all the great conductors active this century have made music in Düsseldorf. Every year there is the concert cycle given by the "Düsseldorf Symphony Orchestra" conducted by David Shallon. The former planetarium (seating capacity 2,000) has been converted into a concert hall - the *Tonhalle* - and the acoustics are superb. Many people have compared the acoustics to those in the Berlin Philharmonie and some say that, with the sole exception of that hall, the Tonhalle is Germany's best concert hall. And when the *Städtische Musikverein*, one of the most famous amateur choirs in the Federal Republic performs the masterpieces written for choir and orchestra, and the fortissimi thunder forth, the venerable brick building seems to shudder in aural splendour.

Yet this is not the only concert hall. More subdued music is performed in the *Schumann Saal* and chamber music is normally given in

the Palais Wittgenstein - where, as already pointed out - the Puppet theatre is also housed. All these diverse concert halls are also the site for visiting international orchestras, soloists and chamber ensembles.

More raucous music is performed in the *Phillipshalle*, with shows and revues, Jazz, Pop and Rock music. 5,600 fans frequently afford their idols a riotous reception.

Two anecdotes show that Rhenish good cheer has deep-seated roots and that "culture", too, can have a jocular aspect. An actor tried to cajole Gründgens into allowing him to play Hamlet. After some hesitation, Gründgens consented. After the premiere,

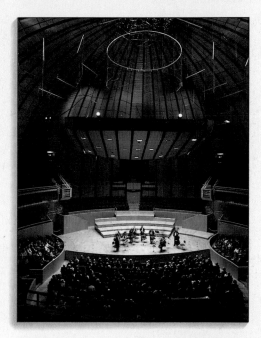

the young man rushed up to the famous director: "How was I?" "Splendid", the latter replied superciliously. "I'm much obliged to you. Only now do I realize why Ophelia drowned herself."

Robert Schumann is said to have been asked to play a piece on the piano at a soiree once. The assembled dignitaries of the city listened in rapt attention. When he had finished, a society lady rushed up to him, raised her glass in a toast and said: "Cher maitre, I'd like to drink in your honour." Schumann smiled whimsically and replied: "Oh, I'm mightily pleased that you're as great a guzzler as I am."

<u>Left</u>, the Düsseldorf Puppet Theatre in Bilk has a long tradition. <u>Right</u>, inside the Tonhalle. The building used to be the planetarium.

SATIRE CANNOT DIE

An interview with LORE LORENTZ of the Düsseldorf Kom(m)ödchen

On one side of the Art Gallery, in Hunsrücken-straße, is the entrance to the "Kom(m)ödchen", Düsseldorf's renowned cabaret stage. From within emanate political and other messages which delight some and are an intense source of irritation to others. Just one year older than the Federal Republic of Germany, the "Köm(m)ödchen" is an institution.

APA: What does it mean to you, to have been in cabaret for so long, Frau Lorentz?

Lorentz: To have sur-vived for so long maybe just means that you're no longer quite as vulnerable as you once were. To have made it through with dignity counts a great deal more than froever spong-ing off others: Our opin-ions, our risks, our caba-ret, mean everything to us.

APA: Could you cast your mind back and tell us how it all began?

Lorentz: The story of this place starts right back in the middle of the Sec-ond World War. One day a male student at the in-stitute of politics decided not to turn up at his Ara-bic seminar, and a female history student decided to miss the lecture on "Ger-man Foreign Policy 1914 -1918". Instead they both

found themselves in the main auditorium listen-ing to a lecture about "Publishing in the USA". After he had returned to the Front and while she was trying to prepare for her exams in the more comfortable location of Vienna, albeit amidst the bombs and mortars raining down on the city, both began to dream of emigrating after the lost war and starting up careers in journalism overseas. Having got married, however, they both came to the realisation that the energies let loose by a lost war would be so great that it might be worth staying around to see how things developed. Indeed, they finally concluded that emigration would be the cowardly alternative.

They swapped an old Leica for 36 cartons of Pall Mall, which in turn were traded for tiles, curtain material and two lamps. Then they met

"Fatty", one of those rare people who could turn his hand to anything, whether it was painting, barkeeping, drawing caricatures, a Jack of all trades, and the journalist Bert Markus who was to write the scripts. They were joined by the up and coming newspaper man Hanswalter Clasen, who also sang soprano when necessary, the opera singer Werner Vielhaber who could play every-thing apart from the villain, and Emil Schuachardt, a composer with a background in church music. And there was Eduard Marwitz to do the stage design and some acting. He knew someone with a relative who could deliver paint on the never never. 120 people they met warned them against it and 240 thought it was a good idea. 50 people actually offered their help as they founded a political-literary cabaret, without ever having seen what one looked like.

APA: And how did you get to be star of the show, Frau Lorentz?

Lorentz: Please let me continue. Because there was nobody who was pre-pared to confront the au-dience, in a rough enough voice, with the plain truths, he simply said to her: "There's nothing for it, you have to do the sing-ing!" - "With pleasure", she said, because nothing really mattered to her anyway, "What shall I sing?" - "I'll buy you a chanson", he said, and jumped on the back of a coal train bound for Mu-nich, arriving there some 48 hours later. He went straight to a famous song-writer to get his chanson. "That'll be three pounds of bacon", demanded the author. "Who's going to sing it?" - "My wife", he said. "Four pounds, then", haggled the famous poet. He left, bought himself a pound of butter on the black market, spread it on a piece of bread and with the strength thus gained, wrote his own chanson for his wife. It was his first, her first, and when they tried it, it fitted like a glove. Just as they began to get cold feet, the curtain went up and that was that.

APA: The story of Kay and Lore Lorentz and their comedy sounds so simple, but surely it wasn't quite as easy as all that.

Lorentz: No, it was really very easy. The story continues like this: The CDU was a month ahead of us with its programme, the Federal Republic had hardly been thought of, Strauß was the chair-man of a rural district council, Kohl was about to take his High School exams and the 74 year old Adenauer was doing his bit... everything, whether accidental, fortunate, or totally imponderable, seemed to happen at once to woo the the public to listen to our act. We were banned after 14 performances; they said there was no need for us in Düsseldorf because there were already enough pubs in town. In those days all that one did, said and experienced, was politics. Today, nothing is politics any more; its just tactics, the voice of the party and pretending as if... Politics doesn't really happen any more. Technocrats have no vision.

APA: The "Kom(m)ödchen" is both loved and feared. You are known throughout the country for your performances, guest performances and appearances on TV. But how long have you had an international reputation?

Lorentz: We performed abroad at a time when no other German cabaret deigned to do so. We had 14 sell-outs in New York, and the New York Times described us as being the embodiment of the "German people's critical sense". In The Hague, we had one of the most difficult performances of all, but Kay, who was first on stage, hit the right note from the very beginning. After the performance, while relaxing in the dim light of the theatre, we heard steps, slow steps, accompanied by the tapping of a wooden crutch. Suddenly, a man appeared, offered Kay a little referee's whistle and introduced himself as the deputy of former concentration camp prisoners. He had actually wanted to demonstrate against the first post-war performance of a German troupe in Holland. But now here was the whistle, as he thanked us for the great evening.

APA: Can cabaret change the world?

Lorentz: When I leaf through old scripts, I am reminded of the moving pathos of the early years, the belief in being able to change everything. I realise today that you can't change anything with political cabaret, for it is nothing more than an articulation of the disenchantment with the times. Perhaps cabaret makes people aware - that would be an achievement. While we have often predicted developments, we have more often been caught up by them. I shall never forget the awkward expression on the face of the American officer-in-charge at Radio Munich who forbade

the broadcasting of an anti-militaristic scene. It was no longer expedient in 1950. One month earlier, in Düsseldorf, the same officer had congratulated us for the same show. I also remember a discussion which lasted the whole night in the half-finished "Breidenbacher Hof" in Düsseldorf, with Herr Bucerius.

APA: You mean the newspaper tycoon?

Lorentz: I was against the re-armament of Germany and he was for it. When I asked in a rage who it was that I had been talking to, they told me he was "Erhard's young man" - Erhard was the Minister of Economics in those days.

APA: You have been a citizen of Düsseldorf for quite some time now. Could you tell us how you feel about the city?

Lorentz: A city influenced so much by its position and history can only welcome new settlers with open arms. It doesn't really matter whether your great great grandfather drank with the legendary comedian Tailor Wibbel, or indeed whether some fictitious ancestor was amongst those who put the fear of God up the Archbishop of Cologne at the Battle of Worringen in 1288, when Düsseldorf fought successfully for its city charter. You'll never get asked about that. Just let everyone see what you can do and show what you are - and get the Düsseldorf seal of approval. The city doesn't make the people, here it is the people that make the city. That doesn't necessarily make things particularly easy. Arms are stretched out so wide that they can't pamper. And no display of tenderness can console that initial feeling of being a stranger. Open cities are by no means cosy havens. They are a challenge.

APA: You accepted this challenge, and since then the city has had the Kom(m)ödchen. How long do you think cabaret will last?

Lorentz: Ever since cabaret has existed, they have said that cabaret is dead. I would naturally disagree with that. I do believe that different ways of expressing criticism, whether protest songs, straight comedy or outright ridicule tend to drop out of fashion from time to time. But satire will always be there as long as there are situations about which it is difficult for someone not to write.

APA: Thank you very much, Frau Lorentz.

THE DÜSSELDORF ACADEMY

Beauty arouses desire, admiration often leads to acquisition - in art as in love. In 1691, Jan Wellem, the elector Johann Wilhelm, a widower, married the archduchess Anna Maria Luisa of Tuscany from the House of Medici. And the love he felt for her kindled his love for art. Among the artisans and artists thereupon summoned to Düsseldorf was Gabriel de Grupelo. The elector commissioned a memorial from this famous sculptor, which was duly erected in 1711, during his life time. The Düsseldorf populace esteemed Jan Wellem so highly that they connived at the fib that it was they, the grateful citizens, that had commissioned this memorial - one of the most beautiful equestrian statues in all Germany.

The elector commissioned and collected works of art, his envoys scoured the European art scene. Soon his collection of paintings and sculptures was so substantial that he had a gallery built in 1710 to house it.

Jan Wellem's successor, his brother Carl III Phillip, decided not to reside in Düsseldorf and part of the collection was transferred to Mannheim, where he had his new residence built in 1720. In 1777 Carl Theodor succeeded Carl III Phillip as elector of the Rhineland Palatinate, but was subsequently invested with the insignia of the Bavarian elector as well, and moved to Munich.

Nevertheless, building work continued in Düsseldorf: Benrath Chateau, for example, was built by Nicolas de Pigage. The custodian of the elector's art collection in Düsseldorf, Lambert Krahe, founded a private school of art which was granted the elector's charter in 1774, and was henceforth known as the "Academy of Fine Arts". During the Napoleonic wars, a part of this collection was brought to Munich for safe-keeping, where it remained even after the victory against Napoleon, when Düsseldorf was integrated into the Prussian state in 1815. The renown of the *Alte Pinakothek* in Munich is partly due to

The building housing the North Rhine Westphalia Art Collection is clad in beautiful marble. A huge variety of international art is on display.

74

this infusion from Düsseldorf.

Preeminent in Germany: In 1819, the Academy became the Royal Prussian Academy of Arts, the centre and sponsor of fine arts in the Rhineland. The director was now Peter Cornelius, born in Düsseldorf in 1783, and a former student of the Academy. In 1811 he had left for Rome, where he joined the group of religious artists known as the *Nazarener* but returned in 1819. Eventually, in 1824, Cornelius went to Munich and subsequently to Berlin, where he died in 1867. His successor in Düsseldorf was again a Nazarene: Wilhelm Schadow. In 1819 he left Rome, where he had founded his own private

poetic inspiration should not take precedence over the skill required to express these: "It is thought that poetic inspiration ceases on completion of the draft; the execution is considered subservient, merely question of technique - what a erroneous idea: I think that inventiveness ceases only when the artists lays down his paint brush." Schadow insisted on the harmonious interaction of emotion, invention and execution. Although he himself concentrated on portraits and human figures, he encouraged all categories of painting.

Allegorical depictions enjoyed great esteem in Düsseldorf and, at that time, they still

academy, and was appointed professor at the Academy in Berlin. He was appointed successor to Cornelius in 1826. Not only were his academic qualifications the reason for his appointment - he had judiciously converted to Roman Catholicism, and was therefore acceptable to the Prussian Rhineland, which was predominantly Roman Catholic. His best students followed him to Düsseldorf, where he set about restructuring the Academy to make it pre-eminent in Germany. "The most commensurate perception of the object, the utmost verisimilitude is the aim and method of the Düsseldorf school." Another of Schadow's principles was that motion and

had artistic merit. One of the masters of this genre was Alfred Rethel. He was only 13 when he was accepted as a student at the Academy. In 1836 he left for Frankfurt where he continued his studies, moving to Dresden in 1848. During a journey to Italy in 1853, he became mentally deranged and died in a Düsseldorf asylum in 1859.

One of Rethel's teachers in Düsseldorf had been Karl Friedrich Lessing. Born in 1808 in Breslau as the grand-nephew of the poet Lessing, he had joined the train of students that followed Schadow from Berlin to Düsseldorf. Another teacher at the Düsseldorf Academy was the bookbinder Johann

Wilhelm Schirmer, born in 1807 in Jülich, who had initially begun to paint only as a leisure time occupation. In 1825 he was appointed professor at the Düsseldorf Academy. Lessing and Schirmer became friends and together started on landscape studies.

Lessing became the founder of the realistic landscape and historical genre painting in Düsseldorf; with his huge canvases depicting the history of the Czech reformer Jan Hus, he fought for freedom of speech and against Prussian reaction and Catholic clericalism. His paintings were considered deeply divisive and, in fact, attracted the attention of a well-situated young man from Wuppertal

school of art. Both Schirmer and Lessing died in Karlsruhe - Lessing in 1880 and Schirmer in 1863.

Progressive ideas: In his autobiography, Schirmer criticized the rigid academic manner of the Düsseldorf school. "The ruins of castles, palaces and monasteries were sought out and drawn and our imagination, transfused with legends and folk songs, did not clearly recognise the unsuitability and the lack of plasticity of these themes. The motto of my current state of development, namely that everything in God's wonderful natural world may be depicted, guided me, yet the romantic dreams of knights, monks and nuns were

who was subsequently to become rather more famous as a revolutionary: Friedrich Engels. In 1858 Lessing was appointed director of the Academy in Karlsruhe. Schirmer, since 1840 head of the newly established landscape class in Düsseldorf, taught a whole generation of young artists, emphasizing that "the sun of reality should conquer the mists of obscure meaning." In 1854 he too left for Karlsruhe to become the director of a new

Far left, Friedrich Wilhelm von Schadow– *Allegory of the Poetry*. **Left**, a piece of modern art stands out against the Renaissance facade of the Art Academy. **Above**, *Westphalian Water Mill* by Andreas Achenbach.

the sickly preparation which later led to the notorious court page and church-goer period in the Düsseldorf Academy that gave rise to the all-too-justified accusation of a costumized poeticism."

An opponent of this very faction was Caspar Johann Nepomuk Scheuren who was fortunate enough to have both Lessing and Schirmer as tutors. Another progressive Düsseldorf painter was Jakob Becker who commenced his studies at the *Städel* before moving on to Düsseldorf in 1833, where he joined the Schadow class. Becker specialized in landscapes, historic genre paintings, illustrations of romantic poems and scenes of rural life - above all peasants, a new subject matter at that time. In 1841 Becker was appointed teacher at the *Städelsche Kunstinstitut* in Frankfurt am Main where he taught many subsequently important painters. Other artists that contributed to the worldwide fame of the Düsseldorf Academy were: Eduard Bendemann, a pupil of Schadow in Berlin, later his son-in-law. He became professor in Dresden and, from 1859 to 1867, was professor in Düsseldorf. There was Johann Peter Hasenclever, a pupil of Schadow who joined the revolutionary movement 1830-1848 and concentrated on social themes and class warfare depictions.

mention must also be made of three of the many pupils who left the Düsseldorf Academy (which had meanwhile become bogged down in academicism) in order to rejuvenate the art world - Arnold Böcklin and Anselm Feuerbach. Both left for Italy; a third, Otto Modersohn, went to Woprswede.

Students from all over the world were introduced to the fine points of painting in Düsseldorf. Indeed even American painting was decisively influenced by the Düsseldorf school. Emanuel Gottlieb Leutze's family (Schwäbisch Gmund 1816-1868 Washington) emigrated to Philadelphia when he himself was still a child. On completion of his

Karl Wilhelm Hübner was a student of Schadow from 1837 onwards. Hübner was mainly interested in rural and social themes. After the failure of the 1848 revolution he turned to more sentimental subjects. Karl Ferdinand Sohn followed Schadow to Düsseldorf in 1826, taught there between 1832-1855 and again from 1859 to 1867. Then there were the Achenbach brothers - Andreas, a leading landscape artist who left the Academy in 1835 and subsequently returned in 1846 and Oswald, a pupil of Schadow and of his brother, who later became head of the landscape class. Special

studies and after a time as a free-lance portrait artist he returned to Germany in 1841 to continue his studies in Düsseldorf. Lessing was Leutze's great exemplar, and it was he who decidedly influenced the latter's revolutionary realism. In Düsseldorf he painted "Washington crossing the Delaware", a painting that has meanwhile become an American icon. In its first version it aroused great enthusiasm among German democrats and revolutionaries. The painting was displayed in the *Kunsthalle* in Bremen, but was destroyed during a bomb attack in 1942. A second version was acquired by a New York art dealer and is now on display at the Metropolitan Museum.

In 1859 Leutze went back to the USA. Shortly before his death he was offered the post of director of the Düsseldorf Academy. Other Americans, some of German descent, who received their decisive impulse for American art from the Düsseldorf Academy were: Albert Bierstadt, George Caleb Bingham, Jonathan Eastman Johnson and Karl Ferdinand Wimar.

The "paint box": The Rhineland and Westphalia Art Association, founded in 1829 by Schadow, had Prince Friedrich of Prussia as a chairman and deemed its main task to be

around Friedrich Engels, Karl Marx and the *Neue Rheinische Zeitung*, and hence the *Malkasten* was suspected of "blood-red, democratic tendencies", although, like in a real paint box, it was intended to have a multi-coloured spectrum. In 1849, in order to regain control of the *Malkasten*, the government ordered Schadow to become a member. That following year the poet Ferdinand von Freiligrath, a friend of Marx and Engels, also joined the Malkasten which now sported a left - and a right wing. The activities of the Malkasten were numerous; apart from looking after the interests of artists and enforcing welfare services, huge

the furtherance of works of art glorifying throne and church. In 1844 independent artists founded the "Association of Düsseldorf Artists", to afford mutual assistance; here Lessing, Leutze and Andreas Achenbach were the prime instigators. Later, in 1848, the year of the revolution, this became the so-called *Malkasten* (Paint Box). Some members were closely associated with the group

Left, encounters in the Art Gallery. <u>Above</u>, the artist Günther Uecker stands in front of his work. He is a member of the famous Group Zero, and professor at the Art Academy.

parties were arranged - complete with tableaux vivants and theatre performances. Welfare institutions were funded through auctions of works of art. But the members of the Malkasten also supported the idea of German unity, first of all insisting on the establishment of a National Gallery. They also propounded the establishment of a General German Art Cooperative Association, which subsequently organised the first pan-German art exhibition.

Schadow, who had meanwhile been raised to the nobility for his services, died in 1862. His demise was not only a loss for the conservative forces. The once flourishing Düsseldorf Art School ossified and not even the move to a new site in 1879 could revive it. After a fire in the palace had destroyed the rooms of the Academy, a new building in renaissance style was built according to the plans of Hermann Riffert.

The social disputes prevalent around the turn of the century eventually also rejuvenated the art scene in Düsseldorf. The *Sonderbund West-deutscher Kunstfreunde und Künstler* (Association of West German Art Lovers and Artists) was founded; the *Sonderbund* exhibition in 1910 in Düsseldorf, in which the painters of the expressionist

ful to her, rhymed: "Ey! hallowed be our patron's name/thy acumen we've always praised/the Rhineland bows before your fame/and buys before the price is raised."

When the National Socialists, who called themselves socialists to deceive the workers, came to power in 1933, not least through the machinations of industry and landed gentry, the battle of the revolutionary artists of the young Rhineland was by no means over. They continued working underground or in exile. Its members were persecuted. Peter Ludwigs was executed in 1943, Franz Monjau was murdered in Buchenwald in 1945.

Mention must also be made of the names

movement *"Die Brücke"* (the bridge) also participated, was of decisive importance.

Germany's endeavour to become the pre-eminent power in Europe had, perforce, to end shamefully in misery and blood. Horrified by the outcome, the young artists intended to work for a better world. *Das Junge Rheinland* (the young Rhineland) was the first association founded shortly after the abortive revolution in 1919. The Düsseldorf innkeeper and gallerist Johanna Ey (1864-1947) was a devoted patroness and enterprising supporter. Max Ernst, the dadaist and surrealist, who had much reason to be grate-

of the other young Rhinelanders who remained faithful to themselves and art: Carl Barth, Mathias Barz, Hanns Kralik, Willi Küpper, Carl Lauterbach, Otto Pankok, Karl Scheswig, Gert Wollheim; in 1922 these Rhinelanders in Düsseldorf had been joined by Otto Dix, who came from Dresden and attended the Academy until 1925. By 1933 the Düsseldorf Academy had acquired the reputation again that it had enjoyed at the time of Schadow.

Paul Klee, coming from the *Bauhaus* school, was appointed professor. Heinrich Campendonk, who had worked together with the artistic group *Blaue Reiter*, had been professor since 1926.

Nazi persecution: In 1932 Ewald Matare became professor for sculpture. In 1933 both were forced to tender their resignation and, like many other artists, were forbidden to continue painting or exhibiting their works. Many artists were forced to leave Germany, many were arrested, some joined the resistance groups and were persecuted and killed. Others arranged themselves with the new regime or allowed themselves to be deceived. Franz Radzwill, vacillated between socialism and National Socialism and succeeded Paul Klee as professor at the Düsseldorf Academy. But after only two years, in 1935,

the market square in Düsseldorf a pyre of priceless painting was set alight.

The thousand year *Reich* lasted twelve years and at its end Düsseldorf, too, was devastated. Time to begin afresh and to link up with the good traditions of yore. Ewald Matare returned as professor. Otto Pankok who had already contributed to the revival after the first World War, was called to the Academy, where he taught until 1958. Later Teo Otto, Georg Meistermann and Bruno Goller were appointed and the Academy was transfused with fresh impulses, again making Düsseldorf an artistic centre.

Some of the post-war art students are now themselves teachers at the academy. But just

he suffered the same fate as his upright colleagues; he was dismissed and forbidden to work. His paintings are now a testimony of the horrors of war.

During the Nazi terror, many artists and their works were defamed as being "degenerate". The Düsseldorf museums were "cleansed" by the Nazis, the paintings were confiscated and destroyed or sold abroad to replenish the foreign exchange reserves. On

Left, Naegli, the Swiss "sprayer", has left his mark all over Düsseldorf. **Right**, Professor Konrad Klapheck giving a lecture at the Academy.

as many Düsseldorf artists leave for new pastures, so artists are attracted to Düsseldorf. Konrad Klapheck - who depicts magical machines, Ulrich Rückriem, sculptor, who allows the stone to retain its strength, both enjoy world-wide fame. Felix Droese, Gotthard Graubner, Jörg Immendorf, Gerhard Richter and Klaus Rinke came to Düsseldorf and subsequently became famous. And the group "Zero"? Günther Uecker, Otto Piene, Heinz Mack. In 1957 they started out on a new artistic venture. And what about Joseph Beuys? That's another story.

Joseph Beuys "Everyone is an Artist"

Düsseldorf in autumn 1984: "This is where it all starts!" - Kasper König, a gallerist, presents contemporary German art. Amongst all the pictures and objects is a small room containing a warehouse shelf, sparsely stacked with parcels and packages, victuals and washing powder from the 1950's - before fancy wrapping was invented - from the time of the German "economic miracle".

Joseph Beuys called this display "economic values". Wishing to document that art is part of the life's staple necessities and demonstrate his kindred spirit with the artists that had aspired improving the world after the First Word War. Beuys, a former World War II fighter pilot, too regarded this his life's aim.

The veneration Beuys enjoyed up to the time of his death on 23rd January 1986 was not unqualified. Some considered him a genius, others a charlatan. Nowadays the general public as well as art commentators approach his oeuvre with respect - for many, indeed, he is the greatest contemporary artist, at least in Germany. Who was Beuys and what were his aims? He was born on 12th May 1921 in Cleves and attended a local Grammar school. In 1941 he was drafted into the Army. He was severely wounded in the war and subsequently covered his head injury with a hat - which was to become a "trade mark" of his. In 1947 he commenced his studies at the Düsseldorf Academy, studying with Joseph Enseling and, from 1949 to 1951, with Ewald Matare. Later he gave master classes. In 1961 he was appointed Professor for monumental sculpture at the State Academy of Art in Düsseldorf. In 1963 he organised the first fluxus concert, a gesture-acoustic action he called the *Festum Fluxorum-Fluxus*. He made his international debut at the Documenta 3 in Kassel in 1964 where he presented 12 year old wax plastics, arousing considerable controversy.

A vital part of Beuys' artistic endeavours were political "actions". In 1970 he organised the "Organisation of Non-voters, Free Referendum", in 1971 the "Organisation for Direct Democracy through Referendum", and in 1973 the "Free International High School for Creativity and Interdisciplinary Research". This last association was a reaction to his immediate dismissal from the Academy in 1972, as he had allowed all the 142 art students who had applied for the academy, but were not accepted, to join him.

At the Documenta in 1976 Beuys installed his "honey pump", and at the Biennale in Venice that same year his "tram stop", the reminiscence of the school child irritated by the adult world. Beuys' aim was to establish a network of associations - associations between man and nature, man and object, man and society, man hovering between thinking and feeling, knowing and sensing. Like his friend Andy Warhol, Beuys cultivated an "extended concept of art", indeed he went even further: social art should solve the formative aspects of society, all else he considered mere decoration and beautification of the ruling system. The helplessness of the viewer when confronted with the enigmatic Beuys oeuvre is intended to evoke emotion and thought - about objects, about reality, indeed a BETTER reality. Beuys' concept of plastic, "social plastic", was always associated with life. "Once one has got away from the ideology of "visual art", one tries to promote stimulation of all the human senses".

Exhibitions all over the world and "actions" - as, for example, his application in 1981 for the post of Director of the Academy in Düsseldorf, in 1982 at the Documenta his "Action 7,000 oak trees" with which Beuys wanted to establish a city forestry programme rather than a city administration; the melting down of a czar crown into a "peace hare"... He worked with copper and felt objects, energy and isolation, fat and honey life, warmth and movement. The irritation that Beuys caused, continues - and if he had read the graffiti on a wall "Better girls than Beuys" he would have smiled.

Left, Beuys meets Warhol. The two great contemporary artists both died in the eighties.

DÜSSELDORF - HUB OF THE CARNIVAL TRADITION

The Carnival undoubtedly provides the climax to Düsseldorf's winter traditions. And by Monday before Lent at the latest, when the big parade in the city is televised nationwide, it becomes clear that Düsseldorf is one of the main centres of the carnival tradition on the Rhine.

The parade on Monday before Lent and the public festival celebrated between the old part of town and Königsallee is one of the main highlights of the year. If the weather is good, hundreds of thousands of people pour onto the streets. Often more than a million spectators line up along the roads to watch the parade pass by.

The carnival season officially begins on 11th of November at 11 minutes past 11. The heralds of the carnival arrive by ship on the banks of the River Rhine. "Hoppeditz" marches off to the town hall and makes a witty speech. The Lord Mayor responds to his speech in the same way. Then people gather at the market-place in front of the town hall, sing and sway rhythmically, arm in arm. But this is a mere prelude to the major carnival events.

The entire city of Düsseldorf gets involved in the carnival. After all, 60 societies have joined to form Düsseldorf's Carnival Committee. The committee is in a way the ultimate authority in matters concerning the carnival and its president can be considered the very embodiment of the carnival spirit. The committee chooses the Prince for the carnival season, coordinates a number of events and organises the parade on the Monday before Lent.

Düsseldorf's carnival reaches its first climax just after the Holiday Season when the official Princely Couple is proclaimed. Up to 2,500 spectators gather in the town hall to watch the "Coronation". At this point people start to get wound up for the events to come. No less than 300 sumptuous meetings, balls, jubilees, receptions and fancy dress parties are on the carnival's agenda.

Prince for a Season: Being the carnival's Princely Couple means a lot of hard work. All 60 associations expect the couple to put in an appearance and each time they are required to make a short but witty welcoming speech. This is expected of them because all members want to admire their "Royal Foolishness" while they summon their subjects to participate in the grand parade on Monday before Lent. On some weekends when they have to show up at about two dozen or more events, the royal duty becomes really hard work. Still, the committee appears to have no difficulty in finding candidates. There are always enough willing individuals who are even prepared to pay money for the pleasure of joining royalty for one season. The princess has as many public obligations as the prince. Apart from her first name, she carries the title "Venetia".

The carnival in Düsseldorf has a long-standing tradition. It all started with medieval jousting and tournaments, balls and fancy dress parties at the court.

Then, at the turn of the last century, people began taking pleasure in making fun of the authorities. The military way of life, which the French and the Prussians had introduced in Rhineland, were ridiculed. The uniform of the Guards, wooden rifles, male and female cheer-leaders dressed up in military attire and the foolishly lax discipline of the Guards, but also medals and decorations, are reminders of a martial period.

In Düsseldorf the first prince was elected in 1825 and the first parade on Monday before Lent was initiated in the same year. That was two years after Cologne but still eleven years before the Mainz Parade. The annual event has taken place ever since and only war and great catastrophes have so far been able to stop it. When in 1949 for the first time after the second World War the parade marched through Düsseldorf's demolished town centre, many regarded this as a clear indication of the Rhinelanders' unabashed will to enjoy life.

After many merry celebrations in the halls of the entire city, people are finally in the right mood for the last phase of the carnival, the "wild days". They begin on the Thursday prior to Monday before Lent. On this Thursday the "*Möhnen*", the women older than fifty, take over the city. Men have no say. The "assaults", however, can be tolerated since a real beauty is often disguised behind the ugly mask!

The carnival's final rehearsal takes place on Königsallee on Sunday. During the entire day people in costumes gather here, and whole families, clubs and groups of friends are out to have fun and make fun of others. Often the tomfoolery is centred around a barrel of beer placed in a perambulator that has been turned into a buggy. Year after year the number of those who enjoy dressing up

forces of the carnival.

The parade is two and a half kilometres long when all floats and groups are lined up. When the parade marches through the old part of town it becomes twice as long and it takes four to five hours for it to pass through. As many as a million gather in the streets; they cheer, dance, sway and otherwise participate in the boisterous merry-making.

Some 800 policemen are on duty along the streets where the procession passes through. They are unarmed for this event. More than 600 first-aid attendants line the streets. Apart from the 150 horses which take part in the parade, there is no less than 7,000 horsepower contained under the bonnets of the tractors

as clowns and participating in the merry-making on the Kö increases.

"D'r Zog Kütt": All rules are broken when "*d'r Zog kütt*", the parade on Monday before Lent, is in progress. The "carnival dragon" lines up along the banks of the river Rhine: 60 floats, most of which are decorated magnificently, dozens of bands and costumed groups on foot - in other words the armed

Preceding pages, "royalty" for one season at carnival time; on the Thursday before the carnival, the *Möhnen* take over the city. Above, in 1990, the carnival was postponed from February to May.

that pull the street-parade floats. The municipal refuse disposal team follows the procession, to clear up all the tons of rubbish that it has left in its wake, including all the confetti thrown from the floats.

Ash Wednesday marks the end of the carnival. People meet to eat fish or to burn Hoppeditz in the company of their friends. When Hoppeditz is officially burned at the stake the carnival season is definitely over, at least until 11th November when everything begins again - provided the weather holds; in 1990 the parade had to be postponed until May because of the hurricanes.

When on a Sunday in July the command *"Mösch raus"* is heard over the town hall's square, then all Düsseldorf knows that on the following Saturday the shooting match and the accompanying public festival will be opened in the State capital. Then the bird is displayed, because in Düsseldorf's dialect *"Mösch"* simply means sparrow. The symbol of this summer ritual is nothing but a wooden bird covered by a layer of gold foil.

Things begin happening a week later: On and another on St. Lambert's Day. A weekly market was also permitted to take place. Almost 200 years later, in 1482, Duke Wilhelm II allowed the city to organize another open fair on St. Albin's Day. Today, the day of Düsseldorf's patron saint, St. Apollinaris (23rd July), occasions marksmen to celebrate their major public festival.

The shooting match is the excuse for what has long become the largest festival on the Rhine. Every year this spectacular event

Saturday gun salutes announce that the Lord Mayor has opened the Festival of Marksmen on the Rheinwiese, the Rhine Meadow, opposite the old part of town, in Oberkassel. A barrel is then tapped in the beer tent and people go for a ride on the super roller coaster. The shooting match and the festival are celebrated at the same time. Ever since the old days the marksmen and the citizens have come together on the fairgrounds.

Steeped in tradition: As early as 1288, the year the city was founded, Düsseldorf obtained permission from Count Adolf V. von Berg to organize two fairs, one at Pentecost attracts two to three million people from all corners of the North Rhine Westphalia, and beyond, for nine consecutive days.

The St. Sebastian Marksmen's Association, with its centuries-old tradition, organises the festival. A whole city of caravans, showmen, lottery ticket kiosks and beer tents descends onto the Rhine meadows of Oberkassel. It is a vibrant scene, with ever more fascinating attractions for young and old.

The Fair's "Mayor", Ludwig Kreutzer, who has been in charge of the fair's organization since 1958, always manages to find the right combination: "Things used to be a little more primitive and simple in the past, although High-Tech hasn't completely taken over. The old merry-go-rounds are still part of the paraphernalia and seem as popular as ever". The event has grown year by year and the Festival's turnover is now estimated at being over 60 million Marks.

The marksmen: There are about 15,000 marksmen grouped in 47 districts and altogether 450 associations affiliated to the Düsseldorf Marksmen's Association, the umbrella organization of all associations participating in this summer ritual. They describe their common motto as follows: "Marksmen are bound to the Christian phi-

actions: support funds for unemployed colleagues are a common thing, as are public functions for senior citizens, etc.. Marksmen have recently begun taking active part in the care and integration of foreign workers, emigrés and refugees.

Today, marksmen stress that shooting is only of secondary importance to them. Although numerous marksmen have joined their associations and fraternities to take active part in shooting events, the majority, however, primarily view their associations as circles where people can meet up and where old traditions are cherished. Tradition is actually held in great esteem by Düsseldorf's

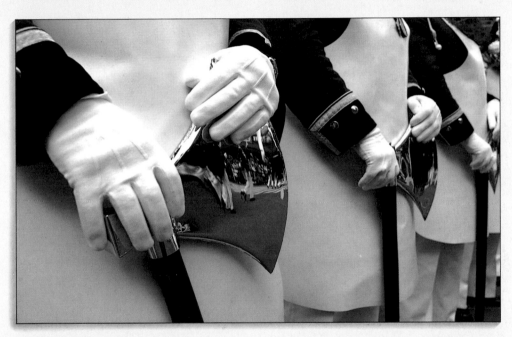

losophy of life." Although they come from all classes they tend to keep to a happy medium in all spheres of life, disapproving of extremes and thus having a stabilizing effect on the life of the community. Membership of a marksmen's association calls for tolerant behaviour and enhances the democratic outlook. The marksmen's associations show their solidarity with the needy and the weak. Their words are made good by their

Far left, a banner waver. **Left**, young marksmen. **Above**, the gun isn't the only weapon the marksmen carry.

marksmen. The associations, without exception, can look back upon a centuries-old history: Derendorf's marksmen established themselves way back in 1410; those of Kalkum in 1428; the Altstadt marksmen in 1435, Angermund's marksmen in 1450, Gerresheim's marksmen in 1455, and the marksmen of Kaiserswerth in 1467.

The most renowned King of Marksmen in the San Sebastian Association was no less than Jan Wellem. The elector, "His Highness Prince and Lord Johann Wilhelm, Count Palatine of the Rhine" managed to shoot the bird from its perch in 1671 and 1683.

St. Martin's Day in Düsseldorf presents the inhabitants of the Lower Rhine with a cheerful festival that is brightened by parades with colourful, elaborately-made Martin's lanterns. For about two weeks a Martin's Procession takes place in at least one of the town's districts. Children and adults sing traditional songs as their lanterns light their way and they march behind the holy man, St. Martin, mounted on horseback. 70 similar parades are organized throughout the city.

dorf date back to the Middle Ages. The reputation of Saint Martin had reached Franconia and Saxony by the 11th century. While it is not clear how St. Martin's customs spread to the Rhineland, a document from the year 1431 shows that Martin's Day was celebrated in one of Düsseldorf's inns. The same celebration continues to this day.

Saint Martin was born in Western Hungary as the son of a heathen Roman officer in 316 and was baptized at the age of eighteen.

The most famous one is the parade on St. Martin's Eve, 10th November. It leads through the old part of the city and ends in front of Düsseldorf's Town Hall. The traditional legend according to which Martin shared his coat with a pauper, who was almost frozen to death, is played at the Town Hall's square. Thousands of children and their parents gather and watch the play with great enthusiasm.

Churches, monasteries and hospitals chose St. Martin, a fervent Christian, as their patron saint as early as the 5th century. The traditions of St. Martin's Festival in Düssel-

Before being baptized, still a pagan, he had shared his soldier's coat out of charity with a pauper. Shortly after converting to Christianity, Martin left the army and was finally elected Bishop of Tours against his own will in 370. He is said to have died in 397.

The customs of St. Martin's Festival, which evolved in the following centuries, are deeply rooted in pagan rituals. The church, however, had no objections to make. On the contrary, just as with other festive occasions it once again tried to reinterpret pre-Christian traditions to suit its own needs. Thus, St Martin's Festival took the place of the Teutonic "Thanksgiving". On this day a goose was immolated for the God Donar - and even today roasted geese are served on St. Martin's Day.

A Christian legend about the Saint gives us a further clue why geese are chosen for this festive occasion. Martin is said to have hidden in a goose coop when the citizens of Tours came looking for him to persuade him to accept the episcopate. Frightened by Martin, the geese cackled and gave him away.

At the turn of the century the groups of children marching through the streets with their lanterns and knocking on doors to collect sweets, had grown in number and size to such an extent that they joined forces to make up one single procession. At the beginning it was only the bishop, St. Martin, who led the parade. Later, from 1905, he was accompanied by a Roman horseman. The St. Martin legend was performed for the first time at the market place in 1930.

Schools, societies engaged in the preservation of local customs, or marksmen's associations, are in charge of the organisation of the parades in the different town districts. The Society of Friends of St Martin's Festival organizes the big parade through the old part of the city. This society was founded in 1925 to prevent Martin's Festival from becoming commercialized and used for propaganda purposes.

Today, it not only organises the parade but also other events that are supposed to reinforce the traditions that have evolved around St Martin's Festival. An exhibition of hundreds of colourful Martin's lanterns made of cardboard, coloured paper and other materials is one of the major events organized by

the society. After the parade, singing children go from house to house and shop to shop to collect sweets in a paper bag. Often children receive paper bags full of sweets and a "*Weckman*", a sort of a biscuit, from their school or the organising society.

In 1979, inspired by Saint Martin, the city of Düsseldorf asked people to make donations in keeping with his example. The paper bags were to be filled with only half the amount of sweets as the year before. The money for the other half was donated to a variety of different aid projects in Third World countries.

Left, St Martin's parade ends in front of Düsseldorf's town hall. **Above**, splendid fireworks accompany the big fairs.

Düsseldorf is considered West Germany's number one city of sports. Almost 100,000 of the city's 600,000 inhabitants are not just content with following sports events on television, radio or in the papers; they engage actively in sports themselves. One in five in Düsseldorf has joined one of the city's 350 sports clubs. 260 sports fields and 130 gyms are booked almost every day of the year. Fitness centres such as the Cosmo Sports Palast with its tennis, squash and badminton

and 1975; in 1989 they were runners-up and in 1990 they won again.

But ice hockey is more than just a classy, tough man's sport, more than just a wild duel on ice. In Düsseldorf the sport is very much an excuse for huge social event. Most fans try and attend every single game and the sport has developed a real cult following in the city. The Ice Hockey "temple" on Brehmstraße attracts a capacity crowd of 10,500 just about every week. At big games,

courts, its body-building equipment and golf simulators are a big thing. Be they young or old, the citizens of Düsseldorf try their best to keep fit.

The ice-hockey "temple": But let us turn to those who earn their living from sport. Professionally speaking, there are two major sports clubs in Düsseldorf; Fortuna Düsseldorf, the local football team, and the *Düsseldorfer Eislaufgemeinschaft*, the ice hockey club, called DEG for short.

The latter has a resounding string of successes to its name; the club became the German national champion in 1969, 1972

such as the major local derby when the DEG plays at home against the arch Rhenish rival Kölner EC from Cologne, otherwise known as *Die Haien* (the sharks), the stadium is bursting at the seams.

At such games there is a flourishing black market. It has been known for tickets in the most expensive category (50 Marks) to have been sold and bought for almost ten times their original price.

A cult or a religion, call it what you will, needs its ceremonies, and in Düsseldorf the fans have developed their own very special rituals. Right before bully-off all the lights are turned off and the stadium is bathed in the light of thousands of sparklers. The supporters hum in the stands and the atmosphere becomes ghastly and solemn. The atmosphere on Brehmstraße is thrilling, and totally unique in Europe.

Even top tennis player Ivan Lendl, who recently came to watch a match in the Ice Hockey Stadium, was beside himself with enthusiasm: "I have never experienced such a fantastic atmosphere," he remarked. The crowd is said to be the best in the world. But God forbid if the DEG ever has a bad day or at least lacks the enthusiasm of the crowd; the fans are sure to draw on a few choice

VIPs (and all those who would like to be one) assemble in the "Small Talk Room" beneath the grandstand, which has been decorated for 80,000 Marks. They take a sip of champagne and indulge in smoked salmon sandwiches. Ordinary mortals have to spend 15,000 Marks every season for the pleasure of gaining access to this particular sanctuary.

Mixed fortunes: The football club Fortuna Düsseldorf, however, has fewer supporters among the upper crust. Based in the district of Flingern, the club has had to struggle hard for survival in recent years. In 1979 the team made it to the finals of the European Cup Winners Cup, losing 3:4 to CF Barcelona.

epithets to register their displeasure, with such choral strains as "You are just ruining the ice!".

"To see and to be seen", that is the motto in the grandstand. In the winter months spectators are seen wearing mink and cashmere. Every self-respecting person in Düsseldorf (who is the lucky owner of a ticket) goes to watch DEG play. In the breaks crowds of

Preceding pages, happy DEG fans at the ice hockey stadium in Brehmstraße. <u>Left</u>, the DEG players are wearing blue jerseys. <u>Above</u>, every time the DEG scores, the stadium is a sea of sparkles.

But in later years severe economic problems and a lack of good players almost caused Fortuna to disappear from the German league. But their luck turned when a new coach was taken on. Aleksander Ristic, a vivacious man from Yugoslavia, managed to rescue Fortuna from the doldrums of the Second Division and lead it to promotion. This was not always an easy task since Ristic, an explosive character, stands firm in everything he does. He shouts, grumbles and complains but nothing will deviate him from his path to success.

Fortuna's fans are very fond of Aleksander Ristic. In fact none of his predecessors was ever as popular. They love the former player of Hajduk Split and Velez Mostar and even the sponsors believe that this lively character from Sarajevo saved the club. Some people worship him as a "Messiah of football".

Soon, "Aleksander the Great" hopes, his team will be able to compete on the international level again and return with renewed glory. Once again the magnificent Rhine Stadium, one of the most beautiful in Germany, will be filled with a capacity crowd of 70,000 people.

Many famous German footballers have emerged from Fortuna over the years. Toni Turek, "the Hero of Berne", in particular,

its only league championship title way back in 1933.

Other sports: Handball is also a popular sport in Düsseldorf. In 1988 TURU, Düsseldorf's handball team, was runner-up in the German national championsips and in 1989 sensationally managed to win the European Cup. Horst Bredemeier, who also coaches the German national handball team, has made handball a popular sport in Düsseldorf. A former postman, Bredemeier has brought fresh ideas into the game. TURU has been playing in the first division only since 1982. With all the recent successes of the club, handball now holds a well-deserved

will never be forgotten. When Germany won the World Cup in 1954 for the first time by beating the Hungarian team, which was said to be invincible, at 3:2 Toni Turek played a major role in the final defensive battle. Herbert Zimmermann's radio coverage and his delighted exclamation: "Toni, you are a football God!" became famous as well. Also Fortuna players such as the Gramminger brothers, Matthes Mauritz, Gerd Zewe or Klaus Allofs will go down in football history. Jupp Derwall, former national coach, who is now successfully coaching clubs in Turkey, also played for Fortuna which won

third place in the popularity stakes in Düsseldorf's sports scene.

Table Tennis for a long time was not very popular in Düsseldorf although BORUSSIA, having been the national champion 13 times, is the German record holder. Two young players, however, helped the club gain unexpected popularity and the stadium is now sold out when they play at home. To the great astonishment of all experts, Stefan Fetzner (21) and Jörg Roßkopf (20) won the gold medal at the World Championships in spring 1989 in Dortmund, so destroying the hopes the Swedish and Chinese favourites. Ever since, the two of them have been among the most popular sportsmen in Düsseldorf.

Even those who are interested in basketball and who like to watch pretty girls at the same time will find what they are looking for in Düsseldorf. AGON has been dominating Düsseldorf's female basketball scene for more than a decade. Having won the championship ten times, the club is the German record holder. And anyone who watches the ladies chase the ball with such commitment will soon become a devotee.

But, apart from regular international athletics events, it is the World Team Cup of tennis professionals that brings sports of

organizing the event for years. The highly paid tournament, which goes on for a week, is normally booked out for spectators months in advance. It always attracts celebrities from show business and the world of sports and politics. While the tournament could never be compared to Wimbledon, it nevertheless generates a considerable atmosphere, in amongst all the lobster and champagne, or sausage and mineral water for the not so well-off. In 1990 the teams played for the total prize money of 1.5 million Dollars.

Those who are looking for a social event should not miss a visit to the picturesque racecourse out in Grafenberg. Even if you do

international quality into town every year. The matches take place in beautiful surroundings, in the Rochus Club on Rolander Weg in the district of Grafenberg. Be it Boris Becker or John McEnroe, Ivan Lendl or Mats Wilander, Jimmy Connors or Pat Cash - many star tennis players are regulars at the club.

Horst Klosterkemper, the manager of Düsseldorf's Fair Company Nowea, has been

Left, **Fortuna Düsseldorf at a home game. Above**, **during the World Team Cup at the Rochus Club Boris Becker comes to the net.**

not intend to bet on any horse you will find a relaxing and yet thrilling atmosphere at the racecourse.

The game of golf is becoming more and more popular on the Rhine. The most beautiful golf course is only a quarter of an hour's drive out of town, at the scenic course of the exclusive Golf Club at Hubbelrath. Any hobby golfers looking for a few hours of fun and do not want to pay through their noses, will be able to pursue their favourite pastime at the municipal golf course in Lausward down by the river, beyond the parliament building and the Rhine Tower.

For visitors to Düsseldorf who arrive by train and walk from the main station along Immermannstraße in the direction of the Königsallee, the first impressions likely to be gained may not quite match the pre-arrival visions one might have had of the city. Indeed, noticing all those shop signs written in Japanese characters, inquisitively peering in through the windows of Japanese restaurants and coming face to face with all those Japanese people walking in the same street, one might well ask whether this really is the capital city of North Rhine Westphalia.

But it is quite true: While in the past Düsseldorf, with its elegant stores, its street cafés and tree-lined avenues was always compared to Paris, today the city is better known as "Tokyo" or "Nippon on the Rhine". For Düsseldorf is now home to some 7,000 Japanese, making up the largest single Japanese "colony" in Europe.

Immermannstraße, indeed, seems to be firmly in Japanese hands. Most Japanese companies have their offices here. There are Japanese food stores, bookshops and many other small businesses. Here too is the Deutsch-Japanische Zentrum (German Japanese Centre) with the Nikko Hotel. It must be the only hotel in Germany where both the teachings of the Buddha and those of the Bible are offered as evening seminars.

Living in Düsseldorf doesn't necessarily mean to say that a Japanese person has to go without the things that he treasures from his homeland. He can satisfy his desire to hear *Karaoke* singing in the "Limelight" on Charlottenstraße as well as the "Katorea" on Immermannstraße. He can feel at home in the sushi bar of the "Nippon Kan" restaurant. In the "Takagi" or "Mitsukoshi" bookshops he can keep up with the news at home by buying yesterday's papers, while next door in the food store he can buy fresh fish, rice

Preceding pages, the Japanese Garden, donated by the Japanese to the city, forms part of the Nordpark. **Left**, Japanese children at carnival time. **Right**, the Japanese Centre, Nikko Hotel.

and dried seaweed. Japanese golf fanatics too can now play on their own Japanese golf course. For years they had to play on other municipal courses.

The Düsseldorf business community is particularly happy that so many Japanese live in the city. And the landlords too! Japanese firms generally pay for the accommodation expenses of their people working in Düsseldorf, and the owners of houses and flats tend to exploit this as far as they can.

They know that the Japanese will pay almost any price, although the boss of a Japanese company also knows that any rent in Düsseldorf will still be lower than the astronomic rents levied in Tokyo.

The Japanese, mainly resident in the more expensive districts of Oberkassel, Mettmann and Zoo, earn well and spend well. And the proprietors of jewellery and fashion shops are naturally over the moon about the spending power of their customers from the far east, particularly as they are so polite!

The Japanese, discrete and pleasant neighbours, are respected by the locals.

However, there is no great comradery between Germans and Japanese as the Japanese tend to keep to themselves. They have their own "Japanese Club" with over 5,000 members, where they can catch up on the latest news and see videos of Japanese TV programmes. They also play majong, the Chinese "dominos", so popular with Japanese men.

The Japanese businessmen spend much of their free time in the club, or perhaps in a restaurant or bar. Except for the golfers, there seem few other possible entertainment. The women have regular meetings with each other, while the children are just as busy here

communicate with the locals, whose dialect isn't exactly the easiest. It may occasionally happen, for example, that in a downtown pub, a foreigner to these parts might wish to order half a chicken - a local speciality. His innocent request for "halven Hahn" is then presented to him as cheese with onion rings and bread. When this happens to an unsuspecting Japanese person, then it will normally be returned to the kitchen untouched; to most Japanese, cheese is rather too exotic.

The Japanese are generally not too keen on the German cuisine. They are not even attracted by "Sauerbraten" (stewed pickled beef) which is so popular in Rhineland and

as they are in their homeland, and therefore have little time for making friends with German children. There is a Japanese school in Düsseldorf-Niederkassel with 800 pupils. But the curriculum does not extend to the higher levels, and while an extension of classes is planned, the older children still have to attend the international school out at Kaiserswerth.

The "Düsseldorf Japanese" generally stay here for about three years. Most tend to find that this is too short to learn anything more than very basic German. This does tend to create misunderstandings when they wish to

Düsseldorf. Understandably enough, the Japanese prefer to eat in one of the 15 Japanese restaurants in the city. There they can get raw fish (Sashimi), Sukiyaki (beef fondue) and everything that the Japanese cuisine has to offer. For the price-conscious fan of Japanese food, it is advisable to visit these restaurants at lunchtime when the dishes are appreciably cheaper than at evening time. Insiders tend to plumb for the EDO (am Seestern 3), for its pleasant atmosphere. Those who are simply after the fine taste of the food might well choose the more plainly decorated Kikaku (Klosterstraße 38).

Unlike the German food, the beer, particularly the Düsseldorfer "Altbier" - the old ale, seems to go down very well with the Japanese. But while they like drinking, the Japanese are also known for having a low capacity for wine or beer. They can therefore get decidedly merry and even, in extreme cases, end up keeling over into the waiting arms of a German neighbour!

Most Japanese people like living in Düsseldorf. The thing that bothers them most is the regimented nature of everyday life, particularly apparent in the closing times of the shops. In Germany the shops close at 6.30 p.m. sharp, a fact which Düsseldorf's

about Germany is the indifference people show towards their relationships with others and the general unfriendliness. Closer acquaintanceship often changes this opinion, but the general unfriendly way in which people talk to each other still remains."

Abe Morihiro, director of his own trading company Abe GmbH, is married to a German and has lived in Düsseldorf for over ten years. He finds: "The general characteristic of the Germans seems to be their seriousness. But the Germans are friendly and life in Germany is very relaxed. In comparison to Japan, life in Germany is exceptionally easygoing." What Abe doesn't like is the weather,

Japanese simply can't get used to. Not to mention the weekends, when Germany's city centres practically die. In Japan, the weekends have always been *the* time to go shopping.

Another thing they find off-putting is the German *Nein* (no), so often so brashly used. Discourse is much more polite in Japan, they say. Hiroko Nakajima, a sculptress living in Düsseldorf, explains: "What I find negative

Left, a Japanese visitor to the city. **Above**, some Japanese like German food and drink.

and this indeed is a general complaint among the Japanese, who find it difficult to get used to the grey skies of central Europe.

Tomoko Yamamoto, a young lady who came to Düsseldorf on her own, answered without hesitation the question on what impressed her most about Germany: "The women!" she says the behaviour of women in Japan is so controlled; the women there are so programmed to respond to strict social mores, whether in language, gestures or mimicry, that she finds the human and spontaneous behaviour of German women "a breath of fresh air".

Officially, great efforts are made to promote mutual understanding. On the 700th anniversary of the city in 1988, the Japanese community donated to the city 400,000 Marks to enable two Germans a year to go and study in Japan. This was the second largest gift that the Japanese had given to the city. In 1975, they presented the capital with a 5,000 square metre Japanese garden which was installed in the centre of a park.

The municipal government is full of praise for the polite guests from the Far East, who have never presented any difficulties. But the Japanese hesitated about answering questions concerning problems of everyday

life. The men, who spend their whole day at work, obviously have it easier than the women who come into much closer contact with the German routine, where problems of language and understanding are part of their everyday life. A great help to them is the "Society for the Promotion of German-Japanese Relations" which organises language courses and arranges contacts between German and Japanese women.

A particular problem for Japanese ladies in Düsseldorf is that the clothes available in German shops are too big for them. Most women therefore have clothes sent from

Japan. They also have difficulties at the hairdressers because they often can't explain exactly what they want. The two Japanese hairdressers in Düsseldorf, therefore, do a roaring trade.

Until a few years ago, Düsseldorf was in the privileged position of being the chosen city of Japanese business in Germany. The municipal government, so keen to attract further Japanese enterprise to the city, must now cope with serious competition from other German cities, notably Frankfurt and Hamburg. But the supremacy of Düsseldorf is in no real danger yet. According to latest figures (February 1990), 326 Japanese companies have offices in Düsseldorf (252 in 1984). The trend for the Japanese to establish their own factories is on the increase. At the moment there are 17 in Greater Düsseldorf.

Ties between Düsseldorf and Japan have a long tradition. The first German Japan trading company was founded by a Düsseldorfer: Louis Kniffler settled in Nagasaki in 1859. Dusseldorf's development as the centre of Japanese business in Germany began in 1950. In that year the Trading house, Tokyo Boeki, established a branch in Düsseldorf and since then, many more firms have followed suit. Düsseldorf's position in the heart of Western Europe, its excellent communications links, as well as its proximity to other economic and industrial centres, makes it an ideal location for foreign investment.

Even if the Japanese have a powerful presence in the capital of North Rhine Westphalia, they still haven't succeeded in capturing the stronghold of local tradition - the Carnival. A few years ago, however, they nearly managed it as a Japanese girl was due to be crowned as the Carnival Princess. The idea was then thwarted by the conservative officials, who vetoed the proposal. The case was extensively covered by the national press and the attitude of the officials was an embarrassment to many German people, as the Japanese politely withdrew their princess. The Düsseldorf Carnival remains in German hands - for the moment anyway.

Left, welcome to one of the many Japanese restaurants in the city. Right, a meal being prepared at the table in the Teppan room.

EATING JAPANESE

Now that we are in Düsseldorf, it would seem a shame to miss out on one of the city's particular specialities - its Japanese food. With over 7,000 Japanese residents, the city contains the greatest choice of quality Japanese restaurants in all Germany, thus posing an exciting alternative to standard North Rhine Westphalian fare.

Amongst a galaxy of possible restaurants, a particularly popular destination for Japanese and Europeans alike, is the EDO. There are, in fact, three EDOs in Düsseldorf: one in the Kö Galerie on the Königsallee, another in Carsch House on Heirich-Heine-Platz, and another on the west bank of the Rhine between Oberkassel and Lorick at Seestern 33.

"Edo" is the ancient name for Tokyo and the restaurant on the other side of the river is a definite tourist attraction in itself. It is built in the *Sukiya* style. Entering the building, the visitor will immediately be impressed by the construction of the wooden roof and ceiling. The visitor will also be intrigued by the ferocious life-size model of the Samurai warrior standing in the lounge, likely to be the first Japanese face one sees upon entering the restaurant.

As with most genuine Japanese restaurants, there are two ways of eating at the EDO. You might have booked a table in one

of the *Tatami* rooms, where one sits cross-legged on the floor, or in the less intimate but more exciting *Teppan* room where you share the same table with a number of other guests and have a stool to sit on. Why not, indeed! Here, the food is prepared directly at the table; the table is the kitchen.

You are led through by a pretty Japanese attired in a striking kimono. If you have any niggling doubts about the adventure which lies ahead, these will soon be dispelled by glancing out at the calm Japanese garden with its bubbling waterfall and stream. Having relaxed with a suitable aperitif, which may well be the *Fujicolor* house cocktail, another kimono girl brings along the menu. You can choose either a la carte or combination menus like *Nagomi, Aoi, Miyabi* and

Irodori, and starters like *Sakura.* If you're not sure what's what, you can look at what the other people at the table are already eating and choose what takes your fancy. But almost before you have time to think, another girl slips a towel apron over your head, just to make sure you don't ruin any clothes. At the EDO, normal cutlery is a special request and most people eat with chopsticks. If you are not sure how to use these, instructions are given on its packaging.

Beer can be drunk with the meal and wine, too, if you want. A good choice of Rhine wines and *Altbier* is on offer. However, if you are eating authentic Japanese food, it would be a shame to drink anything other than authentic Japanese beer. Here at the EDO they have *Kirin,* brewed in Tokyo. After you've finished your starter, the cook comes to prepare your main course and takes his place amidst the bowls of fish, meat and vegetables which surround the hotplate. Having found out exactly what you want, he transfers your piece of meat (or fish) onto it and chops it into pieces just the right size for eating with chopsticks. Then, he concentrates on preparing the mixed vegetables - *Kisetsu-No-Yasai* - which he finely dices with an implement the size of a Samurai sword, nonchalantly smiling and talking to the other guests as he does so. Putting the vegetables to one side, he remains just as calm as he pours some fiery Japanese spirits onto the hotplate, instantly igniting the meat. The flames leap up just about as high as the ceiling. The meat is then transferred into a small bowl, the cook explains the sauces with which it can be eaten and then bows and departs, only to return when the next customer is ready for his main course. With the meat and vegetables you can eat *Gohan,* a fragrant warm, dry rice. But you can also eat cold rice and raw fish at the EDO.

Meal completed, the kimono girl duly arrives again to take off your apron. It is time for dessert and dessert is not eaten in the Teppan room. You will be escorted out to the hall and politely asked to sit at the low wooden table to which a selection of exotic Japanese fruit is brought. Then, to round everything off, why not be really brave, see the Japanese experience right through to the end and order a glass of real Japanese whisky!

As a boy I only knew Düsseldorf from books and stories. This city, it seems, was known as "little Paris", as the "writing desk of the West". The people in this Rhine city - so we say in the North - know how to live, they love elegance and luxury and every public holiday turns into a feast day.

I decided to move here some thirty-five years ago, at first provisionally, and then for good. I have been working as a journalist in the city for more than twenty years now, and have followed its evolution to a metropolis in detail. Its unprecedented rise to eminence culminates in several superlatives. I deem Düsseldorf to be the epitome of elegance in Europe. That sums it all up, the fascination that overwhelms the visitor, that causes him to rhapsodise about the diversity of the beautiful architecture and the dynamism of the population!

I should like to begin my stroll through Düsseldorf at the Rhine, the very place where Düsseldorf first nestled more than 700 years ago. In a wide curve, the unique silhouette of Düsseldorf unfolds on either side of the river. The district to the left of the Rhine bank - Oberkassel - is a jewel case of late 19th century and Art Nouveau houses, a virtual oasis within the metropolis.

From this verdant Rhine bank, Düsseldorf and its cosmopolitan architecture lies at one's feet. The post-war city planners have done a superb job in harmonising the historically evolved architecture - devastated during the war - with present-day construction concepts. The old Castle Tower, The Church of St Lambert, the Tonhalle and the official residence of the Minister President on the Rhine bank are symphonies in stone, petrified testimonials of old Düsseldorf.

Clearly visible from the Rhine bank are the highest buildings of this city, the Rhine Tower, the Wilhelm-Marx-Haus,

the Thyssen building as well as the sky-scrapers of insurance companies and other enterprises.

Düsseldorf has somehow managed to retain its unmistakeable features through exemplary city planning projects. Along the Rhine, the post-war bridges that join Düsseldorf with the hinterland have contributed to changing the face of the city considerably, and yet its originality has not suffered in the least. Now, as

before, the heavily loaded barges chug past the Rhine embankment on their way between Basle and Rotterdam. From summer to late autumn the white cruisers of the Rhine fleet moor along the embankment, inviting tourists for a cruise down the Rhine. Innumerable yachts and jolly boats all add to the atmosphere of this busiest of rivers.

The Rhine near Düsseldorf - how

Left, enjoying the sunshine on the bank of the Rhine. **Right,** showing the flag.

many century-old yarns could Old Father Rhine recount. Let's leave him be, for Düsseldorf with its unique parks, its monuments, its world-famous specialities is still to come. We can discover this city in many different ways; we can familiarize ourselves with its history, art and culture, its customs and economic diversity - and we would find an infinite variety in each case. Yet despite its dynamism and post-war expansion, Düsseldorf with its 600,000 inhabitants is still a kind of cosmopolitan village. It is its very self-containedness that is so fascinating and that evokes this feeling of well-being and familiarity after only a brief stay. Art, culture, trade and business lie cheek-by-jowl within a few square kilometres.

Right next to the Rhine embankment, is the Tonhalle, one of Germany's great concert halls. A ballctic lcap from thcrc is the Kunstmuseum (Museum of Art) in the Ehrenhof, with its multifarious collection of graphics, the State Museum of People and Science, the newly opened Goethe Museum as well as the Löbbecke Museum with its unique aquatic zoo. The jewel among these museums houses the Art Collection of North Rhine Westphalia. In this monumental building with its black, reflecting granite facade, priceless paintings by Picasso, Beckmann and, above all, Paul Klee are on display.

The biggest collection of Goethe memorabilia outside Weimar and Frankfurt is housed in Château Jägerhof, at the western end of the Hofgartenallee.

Between the Rhine embankment, Karlstraße and the Hofgarten are the city's theatres. Opera and street theatre triumph in the "Deutsche Oper am Rhein" and in the Düsseldorf Theatre. Visitors come from far and wide to Düsseldorf, to the "Mecca of Art".

Every metropolis is proud of possessing something unique. In Düsseldorf's case it is the Königsallee, colloquially called "Kö", the elegant boulevard of Düsseldorf. Intersected by a moat with beautiful old bridges and a Neptune fountain, one side of the Kö is an elegant shopping boulevard, the other a phalanx of banks. Chrome, marble and glass compete to form the elegant facades. It is a boulevard that wears its wealth lightly, and those aspects of life that beautify existence like jewellery, furs and porcelain are in abundant supply.

Rich and poor alike - the Düsseldorf population is proud of the "Kö" and the motto seems to be: "See and be seen". What a wonderful place for window-shopping. Come and enjoy the international flair, delight in the window displays and admire the elegant cars parked all around. Perhaps the most beautiful time to stroll along the "Kö" is in summer, when the numerous street cafés afford the possibility of enjoying a small repast on the sidewalk. Read your newspaper, cast an eye on the jet set people walking past.

What about Düsseldorf as a commercial city? While all the banks and company headquarters may confirm that first impression of Düsseldorf being the "writing desk of the West", the city's pre-eminence is actually due to its working class citizens primarily engaged in the production of steel, tubes, machinery and washing powder. It is not least due to Düsseldorf's advantageous geographic position that it became one of the centres of German trade after the war. Düsseldorf is the centre of one of the most densely industrialised areas of Western Europe. With increasing internationalisation of industry and the growing importance of the EEC, the interest of big enterprises has concentrated more and more on Düsseldorf. Nowadays more than 3000 foreign enterprises have subsidiaries in the city. Japanese industry has made Düsseldorf their second biggest overseas administrative centre after New York. Increasingly, industries from other South East Asian countries like Korea, India, Thailand, Taiwan and Singapore are opening subsidiaries too.

Düsseldorf has long been attractive for investment of foreign capital as well as in commodities, metals and steel products. Moreover, it has become one of the most important cities for industrial fairs and banking. With regards to the improvement of its infrastructure, Düsseldorf's post-war development has been exemplary. Both the construction of the exhibition site and the international airport promoted the establishment of new sales areas for industry and boosted the expansion of foreign trade.

Good flight connections within Europe, as well as to South East Asia and the Far East have enhanced Düsseldorf's reputation as an international centre.

Domestic Market in 1992, Düsseldorf is predestined to expand. The continual extension of the transport system is thus one of the main and most vital, tasks of the Government of North-Rhine Westphalia.

Düsseldorf evinces many superlatives that verify its international reputation and flair, but the economic aspect is only one aspect. On the one hand, there is a cosmopolitan flair, on the other, there is the ingrained traditionalism of its citizens. That is part of Düsseldorf too. The Carnival is one of the most joyous festivals in town. For three mad-

Fairs like Interpack, Drupa, Interkama, the Plastics fair and many others are the reason for an inflow of tens of thousands of visitors annually. The IGEDO is now the leading fashion fair in the world. Fashion, Fairs and the Airport - three calling cards of a metropolis that has acquired an international reputation as a service centre.

In view of the imminent European

Feeding pigeons in the Hofgarten.

cap days, the Düsseldorf population and more than a million visitors, celebrate the "meat farewell Festival" (thus the etymological explanation of the word Carnival) before the onset of Lent. But Carnival is not the only festival of course. There are also Riflemen's meetings in the rural districts and there is one of the biggest fun fairs along the banks of the Rhine.

And what would Düsseldorf be without its Altstadt? Without the "longest bar in the world?" Something would indeed be missing.

IN AND AROUND DÜSSELDORF

The city of Düsseldorf is a hive of activity, not only in business circles, but also in terms of cultural events and the arts. This coupled with its vibrant street life, partricularly in the Old City - the *Altstadt* - with its pubs, its street cafés, its fine restaurants, and all those wonderful (and expensive) shops, make it a fascinating place to discover. The pleasant atmosphere of Düsseldorf might in part derive from the Altbier which flows continuously from the taps and tends to level the social differences. Perhaps it also stems from the city's truly cosmopolitan nature. It may, too, have something to do with its fine architecture and sculpture, some of which has managed to survive all attempts at destruction and a great deal of which has been added anew. Impressive post war architecture, the manifestation of more recent economic and industrial achievements, jostles against ancient churches and dignified mansions, testimony to the glorious events of days gone by. Fine monuments honour the past heroes of the city. Theatres, art galleries and concert halls continue to display and perform the works of many renowned artists, not only from Düsseldorf, but from the world over.

So take a closer look at Düsseldorf, see its sights and experience what it has to offer. If you ever get tired, you can always relax in one of the many parks like the Hofgarten, the erstwhile royal gardens. You can even visit the city's suburbs; although many are now engulfed by the city, it is still possible to find outstanding architectural legacies from the past, including splendid country houses and fine examples of medieval moated castles. The suburbs were once villages and estates, and some of them were just as important as Düsseldorf.

They provide a fascinating glimpse into the region's past - as do several independent cities within easy reach, such as Neuss, Kaiserswerth and Ratingen. For those interested in the more recent past of the area, it is well-worth taking a trip to the Ruhr Basin, to the north-east, with its industrial cities, its many cultural activities and its wonderful beer; an area full of surprises. Or get right away from everything and take a trip to the Bergisches Land to the southeast, with its hills and lakes, abbeys and castles, and picturesque villages. Visit the towns where industry in Germany first started to flourish.

The city of Cologne, with its mighty Gothic Cathedral, is also easily accessible from Düsseldorf, about 50 kilometres up the Rhine. The Federal Republic's capital city, Bonn, is just a bit farther upstream. These and many other daytrips can be enjoyed by boarding a Rhine steamer. This is simple enough, for the river flows directly past the city.

Preceding pages, whoever shoots the golden *mosch* from its perch is the city's shooting champion; view from Oberkassel of the so-called "Mannesmann bank"; the Rhine promenade with the Castle Tower, St. Lambert's Church, and the Tonhalle. **Left**, Düsseldorf's most esteemed ruler Johann Wilhelm (Jan Wellem) astride his horse.

A WALK THROUGH THE ALTSTADT

Düsseldorf is a beautiful city and many illustrious personages have commented on this in well-turned phrases. One of the most qualified was Heinrich Heine, for he was born in the most beautiful part, the *Altstadt* of the "Dorf an der Düssel" (the village on the river Düssel). Initially, of course, the Altstadt - bounded by Heinrich-Heine-Allee and the Rhine, Ritterstraße and Wallstraße - was a small fishing village.

The erstwhile fishing village was granted the city charter in 1288, but in the course of the last 700 years, practically everything has changed. Floods, fires, plagues and, above all, the catastrophic destruction during the last war have altered the face of the city virtually beyond recognition. Yet great care has been taken to preserve what was worth preserving. Even if much has been irretrievably lost, the Altstadt still exerts some fascination, for one square kilometre contains everything the heart could possibly desire. No matter whether you prefer works of art or *dolce vita*, bustling shopping centres or peace and quiet, it is all to be found in the Altstadt.

The **Castle Tower** on Burgplatz - like some stony warden from ancient times - is all that remains of the enormous castle-estate that was once the residence of the Dukes of Jülich-Cleves-Berg. In the fourteenth century, customs fees were levied here. Between 1522 and 1559, Duke Johann III and, after his death, Wilhelm the Rich, had the castle converted into a tripartite palace, in accordance with the plans drawn by up Alessandro Pasqualini from Bologna. The palace was totally destroyed by French artillery in 1794 - but the tower survived not only this bombardment but also that of the last war. Today it houses the **Navigation Museum**, which docu-

Preceding pages, a pub in the Altstadt. <u>Left</u>, buskers are a common site in the Altstadt.

ments 2,000 years of Rhine shipping. On display is a model of Duke Johann Wilhelm's luxury yacht.

In the immediate vicinity is the east wing of what was once the **Elector's Art Gallery**, which was moved to the Pinakothek in Munich in 1805. People came from far and wide to see paintings by, among others, Rubens and Vanderwerf. Goethe wrote: "In the Düsseldorf gallery my predilection for the Dutch school of Art was satisfied in plenty. Many rooms were filled with splendid paintings of refreshing veracity, and if my vistas were not broadened, my knowledge was nevertheless increased and my fondness thereof enhanced."

Turning the corner, we come across the renovated facade of the former **Craftsman College**, which now houses the offices of the city administration.

Right in the middle of the market square is the **Statue of Duke Johann Wilhelm**, fondly remembered as Jan Wellem. Gabriel de Grupello started working on it in 1695 and it took him fifteen years to complete. The marble pedestal was designed much later by Adolf von Vagedes and executed by the stone mason Kamberger. There used to be a busy market here, but now only fruits and flowers are sold. In his book *Le Grand*, Heinrich Heine described Napoleon's victory parade through the city. In order to get a better look, Heine had climbed onto the pedestal. Suddenly he felt dizzy, and would have fallen off had he not thought he heard the bronze equestrian statue whisper: "Hold on to me!"

The market square is dominated by the **Rathaus** (Town Hall) with its Renaissance facade. It was most probably designed by Wilhelm the Rich's architect, Pasqualini. On the level of the second floor is a niche with the statue of Justitia, dating from 1749. Above that we see the city's coat of arms as well as those of the former Dukes. The bell, cast in 1545, still hangs in the tower. The facade was carefully renovated between 1958 and 1961. The walls of the ground

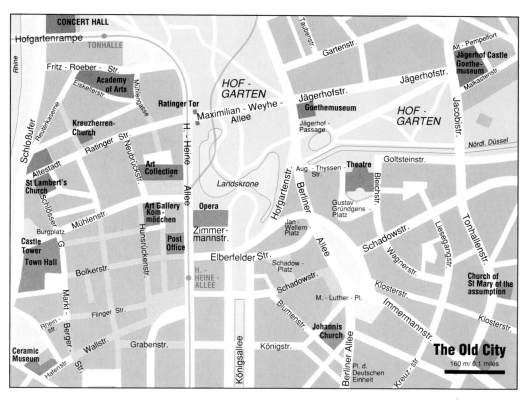

floor chamber are lined with cast iron plates on which the standard meter and the Prussian rod is marked. A few works of art are also on display: Peter Janssen's painting of the "Battle near Worringen" in the Jan Wellem Hall and a tapestry dating from the 17th century, with the panorama of Düsseldorf. Then there is the two metre high marble statue of Jan Wellem himself, visible proof of the court sculptor's artistry. The pedestal was made by J. Bäumgens in around 1780. In the adjacent Heinrich Heine Room, copies of Heine manuscripts are on display ("Lazarus" and "Loreley"). Note also the painted ceiling created by Domenico Zanetti.

The former **City Archive** building forms the western part of the market square, and at right angles to that is the building housing the Municipal Administration, built in 1956. Plaques on the walls commemorate citizens who have rendered the city some service. The facade facing Rheinstraße is decorated with a relief created by Jupp Rübsam, showing market vendors. Before the thoroughfare to the river bank is the bronze statue of the **"Gießerjunge"** (casting boy - 1932) and the bronze **"Gänsebrunnen"** (geese fountain - 1956). Crossing **Burgplatz** we come to the **"Radschläger Brunnen"**. These cartwheelers used to show off their skills in return for some small remuneration. These days there is a cartwheeling competition on Karlsplatz every year - just so that the tradition is not completely forgotten.

If we cross **Rheinstraße** we come to the oldest church in the Altstadt, the erstwhile monastery **Church of St. Lambert**, which was built when Count Adolf of Berg granted the village a city charter in 1288. As the parish grew, so the church became ever more splendid and today it still looks much like it must have looked in the 14th century. The Dukes are buried in the vault of the church. The baroque ornamentation dates from the reign of Phillip Wilhelm and his son Johann Wilhelm. The tower

was struck by lightning in 1815 but the locksmith Josef Wimmer managed to save the church from total destruction by sawing off some burning beams. A plaque to commemorate this daring deed is seen on the west face of the tower. Two years later, the tower was re-roofed but the tension on the wood was so great that the beam construction was twisted in the process - all still clearly visible.

The **Treasure Chamber** can be reached via a spiral staircase in the smaller tower. More than one hundred exhibits are on display - one of the largest collections of clerical vestments, crucifixes and monstrances in the whole of North Rhine Westphalia. A relic of Staufen origin dating from 1170 and a one metre high "Sweden monstrance", donated by Duke Philipp Wilhelm in 1662, deserve special mention. Priceless works of art may be found in the church itself: the Gothic font, the tomb of Duke Wilhelm the Rich who died in 1592, the carved confessionals, the stone figure of St. Christopher, the gilded figure of

K.H. Seemann named his bronze sculpture *Auseinandersetzung* - "the dispute".

the Virgin Mary, and the vesper picture dating from 1395.

If we leave the church and walk down **Lambertusstraße**, we pass the Lambertus school, and eventually come to a small square. Here where **Ratinger-straße** leads into **Liefergasse** is the **Kreuzherrenkirche** (the Church of the Crusaders), originally situated outside the city walls. There used to be a cloister here and extensions were effected right up until the 18th century. The "crusaders" gave refuge to pilgrims as well as looking after the poor. In 1888 the walls of the cloister were pulled down and the church served as warehouse, stable and was finally converted into an office building. Extensive restoration work was carried out between 1960 and 1968. Fragments of frescos dating from the early 16th century were uncovered and restored. The Kreuzherrenkirche is now used as a church once again as the chapel of the St. Ursula Grammar School.

The St. Ursula nuns came to Düsseldorf in 1677 and a convent was built for them by Michael Cagnon, the Elector's architect. The baroque building was destroyed during the last war and has been replaced by a modern building. The **Palais Schaesbert** in **Ursulinengasse**, named after the duke's chancellor, was originally part of the convent. At one place in Ursulinengasse, the course of the 1288 city walls is marked in the pavement.

Walking along **Ritterstraße** towards **Mühlengasse**, one passes **house No. 30**, in which Gottfried Esser first created the famous Düsseldorf mustard, locally known as "mostart". Opposite - now a post-war building - the poet Christian Dietrich Grabbe lived and wrote the play "Napoleon or the Hundred Days". **Mühlen-gasse** eventually leads to **Ratinger-straße**. At the corner is the beautiful portal **Ratinger Tor**. (See also "In and around the Hofgarten").

Walking down Ratingerstraße in the direction of the Altstadt, one passes **house No. 45**, where there is a commemorative plaque to the theatre direc-

Düsseldorf is proud of its attractive women.

tor and poet Karl Immermann, who died there. **Neubrückenstraße** leads to **Grabbe-platz** where we find the **"Kunstsamm-lung Nordrhein West-phalen"** - the North Rhine Westphalian Art Collection. The elegantly curved facade, rendered with black, marble slabs, reflects the towers of St Andrew's Church. The plans for this stark yet impressive building were drawn up by the Danish architects Dissing and Weitling. The collection on display is mainly concerned with 20th century art. One part of the collection is devoted to pre-World War II art - cubism, fauvism, expressionism, *Blaue Reiter*, surrealism, Bauhaus, *pittura metafisica*, constructivism and the Dutch "*de Stijl*". The other half concentrates on postwar, primarily American, art. Paul Klee had been a professor at the Düsseldorf Academy from 1931 - 1933 and in 1960 the state of North Rhine Westphalia and the *Westdeutsche Rundfunk* financed the acquisition of a Paul Klee collection, which is also on display - together with

works by Julius Bissier.

In the late 1960s, the **Kunsthalle**, opposite, was built in accordance with the plans by Brokes and Beckmann. In front of the entrance we see the almost four metre-high bronze "**Habakuk**", a creation by the painter and sculptor Max Ernst. This is a huge copy of a tiny (52 cm) original. To the right of the entrance in **Hunsrückenstraße** are the Four Caryatides by Wilhelm Albermann. Above the entrance is a relief by Karl Harting and on a platform a statue: "**The great fetish**", created by the Swedish sculptor Carl Frederik Renterswärd.

In the immediate vicinity of the Kunsthalle we come to one of the most interesting churches of all: **St. Andreas** (St Andrews). In 1619 the Duke summoned the Jesuits to Düsseldorf and a church was built for them. Construction started in 1622 and took seven years. Note especially the splendid stucco work. This was the time of the 30 Years War, in the course of which many cities were devastated. Düsseldorf survived,

Sleeping it off.

largely because of the diplomatic skills of the Ducal rulers. Naturally - given such a history - there is a fair amount of eclecticism. The styles range from baroque to the present day. The marble **High Altar**, for example, was created by Ewald Matare and was erected in 1960. Dating back to the 17th century are the side altars, the pulpit, the confessionals, the painting of the crucifixion by Johannes Spielberg, the frescos in the sacraments chapel, the pewter sarcophagus of the Elector Johann Wilhelm in the mausoleum where seven members of the Electoral family have found their final resting place. Special mention must be made of the five one metre silver statues (St. Andrew and the four Jesuit saints) that form part of the church treasure, the gold and silver thread embroidery, the breastplate with the emaille coat of arms of Duke Wolfgang Wilhelm, the silver Mount Calvary, which was created by the Cologne goldsmith Johannes Post in 1687. This and the relic of Saint Erentius are

donations by the Ducal family.

Turning into **Andreasstraße,** we see on the left hand side the bronze **Martinssäule**, a column created by Reinhard Graner, and erected in 1965. On the right is a wing of the Jesuit college and to the left is the Protestant "**Neanderkirche**", which can also be entered from Bolkerstraße. Similarly situated is the Protestant **Berger Kirche**, which can only be reached through a gate of house No. 18 in Wallstraße. It seems that in the predominantly Catholic Rhineland, the "reformed churches" had to be hidden as far as possible.

Running parallel to Andreasstraße is **Mühlenstraße**, where a house with neo-baroque facade containing a memorial for the victims of National Socialism stands. The documentation on display gives a heart-wrenching summary of the twelve years under Hitler.

Strolling through the Altstadt, we pass **Kurzenstraße No. 15**, where the painter and art academy director Peter Cornelius was born. **Bolkerstraße No. 53** is the birthplace of Heinrich Heine. The poet Hans Müller Schlösser, who wrote "Tailor Wibbel", was born around the corner, in **Rheinstraße No. 10**,

When walking through the old city centre, it's worthwhile glancing upwards occasionally. For example in **Flingerstraße** you'll see the beautiful gable roof of the house "**Zum goldenen Helm**" or in **Markstraße** the **Glockenspiel**. Walking through **Zollstraße** we come to the Rhine and the obelisk with its four clocks and the water-level mark. This obelisk was erected around the turn of the century, purely for decorative purposes. Almost exactly opposite we see von Breek's eight metre high granite column with a two metre high heraldic lion with a golden anchor. Finally mention must be made of the bronze group "**Auseinandersetzung**" (dispute) - two life-sized men. It was created in 1980 by the sculptor K.H. Seemann. Looking at these two characters one would wish that all the world's disputes could be carried out in a purely verbal manner.

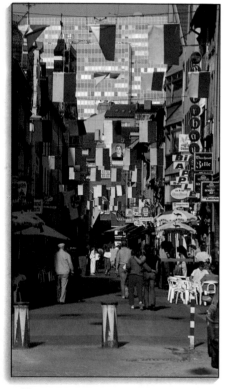

Left, decorations for a major fair in the city. **Right**, one o'clock and time for Tailor Wibbel to show his face.

TAILOR WIBBEL

"Streichle den Wibbel ein kleines Stück und Du wirst sehen, es bringt Dir Glück!"

(Stroke Tailor Wibbel just a bit and luck will come, he'll see to it)

This encouraging invitation is written on a plaque affixed to the Wibbel monument - hence the pointed beard of the bronze statue has been rubbed till it is quite shiny. The statue is now situated in a niche of the wall above the Schneider Wibbel Stube in the Schneider-Wibbel-Gasse in the heart of the Altstadt. With a whimsical grin on his face, Tailor Wibbel, the folk hero of Düsseldorf and eponymous hero of a comedy written by Hans Müller-Schlösser, bends over his work.

Eight hundred times the author himself played this role and innumerable actors have subsequently performed the play. It has been adapted for the screen several times and Müller-Schlösser even wrote a sequel: "Wibbel's resurrection" - which was not quite as successful. So he adapted the play into an opera libretto, which was subsequently set by Marc Lothar and it enjoyed a certain vogue for a time.

The basic plot of the play concerns Anton Wibbel, who is sitting in a pub, no longer quite sober, fulminating against the authorities - at the time when Napoleon's forces occupied the city.

Wibbel is denounced and is about to be dragged off to prison. Fin, his resolute wife, hits on the idea of cajoling one of her husband's apprentices to go to prison in his stead. Zimpel is the good lad's name and, replete with his master's papers, he is incarcerated.

After a short time the unfortunate Zimpel dies and is buried as "Tailor Wibble". As far as the authorities are concerned then, Wibbel is dead. This somewhat ludicrous story was turned into a witty folk comedy that has lost none of its acerbity.

In 1912, when the author submitted his manuscript, the dramaturgs of the Theatre were highly dubious about the whole venture. The director, the legendary Lindemann, did not want to premiere the play in the winter months in order not to alienate his regular public, so it was not performed until July 14th, 1913.

It was an immediate success and many other theatres subsequently performed the play - much to the author's surprise.

Shortly before he died at the age of 72 he wrote that although he was now old, his tailor had retained his youth and "will probably survive me" - quite true.

Above the statue there is a large clock and at 11 a.m., 1 p.m., 3 p.m., 6 p.m. and 9 p.m., the shutters open and Tailor Wibbel pops out, accompanied by the strains of German folk songs.

The play is a classic - not only in Düsseldorf but throughout Germany. And if you're strolling through the city of his birth - do yourself a favour and wait for him to appear.

THE LONGEST BAR IN THE WORLD

The revered local poet Hans Müller-Schlösser once wrote: "The Düsseldorfers have always enjoyed a good swig and if you hail from this region you can take your drink too." But, of course, not everyone who strolls through the square mile that constitutes the "Old City" is a native son. No, the fame of the "longest bar in the world" has spread far and wide. That's why the local breweries like the **Uerige**, **Zum Schiffchen Füchschen** and **Zum Schlüssel** serve half of their total output in Düsseldorf itself. Approximately 30,000 litres in one weekend.

The brewery-owned pubs are crowded at nights. You'll find the craftsman having a drink with the professor, the student will sit next to the production line worker, the general manager next to the pensioner. *Altbier* works wonders in levelling out the social differences.

The *Köbes* is the very soul of the Altbier pubs. Don't think that he's merely a "waiter" - he'd resent that. And he'd make sure you knew he resented that. He might also just ignore you - until you were positively parched. What a lamentable fate if you're sitting next to full kegs of beer. But take heart, none of the men in their blue shirts or green aprons is hard-hearted. Sooner or later one will come up to you and explain the rules. Then he'll serve you a glass of ALT beer, the local brew, because he'll presuppose that that's what you wanted to order in the first place. It is interesting to watch how such a man holding his tray of full drinks aloft will weave his way through the throng, take your order with stoic patience without writing anything down and will actually serve you in due course.

The boisterous mood is, of course, in direct proportion to the amount of beer consumed, and the more the beer, the greater the noise. But the *Köbes* has good hearing. He'll never shout back, he'll

just gesture to indicate that he has understood. Of course the local breweries don't only serve beer. They also serve the special snacks that go with it. The menu is sometimes printed in the local dialect and, with the condescending air of a Father Confessor the *Köbes* will explain what is meant by *Blootwoosch met Ölk* or *Ferkeskoppsülz met Bolter*. Naturally everything is eaten with *Mostert* - the world-famous mustard of this region. All this is part of the ALT beer routine, just like the *Köbes*. The Mostert increases your thirst and provides the good foundation for the alcohol, otherwise you'd be under the table after a few glasses...not that anyone would really notice. You would probably wake up though when the cleaner sloshes a bucket of water over your head the next morning. And that might be unpleasant.

Left, the Altbier never runs dry. **Right**, there are many places to sit outside and enjoy your beer - not only here on Burgplatz.

During the day-time the little streets and alleys of the Altstadt are a fashionable shopping area. A slight breeze from the Rhine wafts the smell of beer away. Everyone goes about his business as if they had never heard of bars and pubs being around. But, once the sun has set, it's back to the bar. Not only the brewery pubs are the "in" scene. There are more than 200 pubs of all kinds in the Altstadt and, all of them together constitute this remarkably long bar - the longest in the world, or so it is claimed. Any special recommendations would be impossible - objectivity doesn't work here. Just use your own common sense. Take your time, have a look and decide for yourself. Naturally, the longer you linger in the Altstadt, the greater the sample that can be taken in.

Just two little hints. Do you know what *Trab-Trab* is? It is stewed, pickled horse meat and one of the specialities at **Zum St. Maximilian,** Citadellenstraße 8. That's not all they serve, of course. There is seafood too, for example. On the first floor you'll find the elegant **Walliser Stuben**, where Swiss specialities are served.

Another recommendation in the Altstadt is the **Weinhaus Tante Anna**. The motto engraved in one of the ceiling beams is: "*Ein kluger Zecher steckt sich fein den Schlüssel vom Haus schon morgens ein*" (approx.: experienced drinker that you are, forget not your key before venturing far). The door to the restaurant will only be opened if your apparel is deemed suitable. Someone peeps through the spy, just to make sure. Once inside you can revive your flagging spirit with...well, spirits, or wine or whatever you care to drink. There's a choice of 160 different wines, apart from the ubiquitous Altbier or a good Pils. The restaurant serves food until midnight - so, if you're in town don't forget to look in. The description of its interior would fill volumes. Suffice to say then that you can enjoy an olde-worlde atmosphere, without getting the feeling that you're sitting in a museum.

Just as in every other pub in town, there is a place to stand and drink in the Uerige.

You'll see quite a few things that might ill accord with impressions you have so far gained from the city. You'll see punks, bag ladies, drug and alcohol addicts - the carbuncles on the thick skin of prosperity. Much is done to try to contain the problem - but to little avail in the long run. And if the statistics say that the annual per capita consumption is 240 litres Altbier - that includes these particular groups as well.

Yet merriment and joie-de-vivre is part of Düsseldorf life and a certain slothfulness is also evident occasionally. "Don't worry - be happy" is very much the motto. After all, it's a respectable city - so as an inhabitant there's something to be proud of too.

Radiating self-assurance, the locals join the strangers in the bars...ever willing for a little chat. Of course there are some special secret haunts too, bars only known to the locals where tourists rarely venture.

The mark of quality. With the city's fairs attracting about 1.8 million visitors annually, it's always a bit of a crush in the bars. Except of course in summer - more beer gushes from the taps and more people decide to guzzle in the fresh air - and the *Köbes* rush hither and thither. There's a statue for just about everybody who is anybody in this city - but, inexplicably, none for the *Köbes*. But they'll take it in their stride, so to speak.

There are, of course, some first-class restaurants - if not in the Altstadt, then in the immediate vicinity. In Bilker Straße 30 is the **Orangerie** or the **Naschkörbchen** in the Königsallee, or **The Düsseldorfer** in Hotel Holiday Inn. If you really want to treat yourself, go to the **San Francisco** in the Hilton Hotel.

Then there are two restaurants which are always specially mentioned as being in the top category in Germany: the **Victorian** in Königsstraße and the **Schiffchen** out in Kaiserswerth, if this isn't too far for you to go. Here you'll find equally good service and a kitchen that specialises in the finest quality French cuisine.

"ZUM UERIGE" - A LIFE-ENHANCING PUB

"Straight across from the *Uerige*", or "not far from the *Uerige*"! You'll hear that again and again if you ask your way around in Düsseldorf. The brewery "*Zum Uerige*" is something of an institution. For all those who want to get to know the "longest bar in the world", Berger Straße 1 is simply obligatory. Here you'll find that original, inimitable *Altstadt* atmosphere that has given so much pleasure to so many people all over the world. Shiny, scrubbed tables, the patina from generations of beer-guzzlers on the wood-panelled walls, the oak kegs. It's your genuine brewery pub.

This part of the city is almost 600 years old, and, as in times of yore, Berger and Rheinstraße are a-bustle. During the last war, practically all the old houses here were destroyed or severely damaged and were later rebuilt - as was the case with the "Uerige".

Nevertheless the corner house on Berger Straße retains its tradition. For at least 250 years it has served as inn, wine house and, eventually, as a brewery.

The brewery part began on 4th January 1862 when the brewer and publican Wilhelm Cürten bought the inn "Zum Bergischen Hof" complete with backyard buildings, stables and courtyard for 19,000 Thaler. On 12th June he applied for a licence to start brewing operations and the backyard and cellar below the courtyard were duly converted. The beer was pulled in the small rooms of the house and was carried out to the neighbouring houses.

It was around that time that Wilhelm Cürten came to be known by the nickname of "uerigen Wilhelm" - the word "uerig" in Rhenish dialect means something like "scowling". And Wilhelm Cürten was anything but amiable. He was plain bad tempered, in fact. But his brewing art and the good beer made up for this and the Düsseldorf burghers liked to pop in for a drink at the "Uerige".

Naturally the history of the past decades has left its mark on the "Uerige". In 1911 the pub had been expanded to 80 square metres. 6,000 hecto-litres of beer were served that year (1911 was a pretty hot summer). Then came the First World War and the opening hours had to be curtailed because hops and malt were rationed. Jean Keller, at that time owner and publican, initially refused to brew less potent beer. He resorted to brewing as much as officially allowed, opening the pub for a few hours a day and closing it again when all the beer had been drunk. Of course, ultimately, he had to give in and started brewing diluted beer. Yet the regulars struck up a new ditty: "The Uerige and Hindenburg, they'll both keep going."

Much the same thing happened during the Second World War. Again hops and malt were rationed and the "Uerige"

The waiters in the Altstadt pubs are known locally as *Köbes*.

started issuing ration cards: 10 litres of beer a week. On 23rd August 1943 the front part of the house was devastated, and in April 1944 the brewery was completely destroyed.

Rebuilding started immediately after the war and Rudolf Arnold, the new owner, was soon able to start a modest sort of service again. By 1954 everything was back to some sort of order. Expansion work continued and was completed on 16th October 1974 when the "*Brauhaus*" was opened in celebration of Arnold's 85th birthday.

Thus far, five generations have been in charge of running the brewery. The art of producing "*dat leckere Dröppke*" (the tasty brew) as the Düsseldorfers call it, is still firmly rooted in the tradition of old Wilhelm Cürten.

Every morning it is the same old routine. By the time the Altstadt has bestirred itself and woken from its drowsy slumber there's already hustle and bustle at the "Uerige". Josef Schnitzler, the "baas" (landlord) of the Uerige has been up and about since about 6 a.m. The tall head brewer and his wife, Christa, have been in charge of the brewery since 1976. Both make very sure that the traditional standards are maintained - despite all modernisations. Besides the beer itself, it is the atmosphere that accounts for the popularity of the pub. Here all social differences are levelled. Snobbish cliques are taboo.

The first regulars start arriving around 10 a.m. For years they have started their day with a glass of *Uerige* and a sandwich. Housewifes pop in after their shopping spree and old-age pensioners have a quick rest. Every hour more and more people arrive for a quick drink *in* the pub - and, if the sun is shining, for a quick drink *in front of* the pub. "Dat leckere Dröppke" tastes quite good in the fresh air as well. Businessmen and tourists mix with the locals. It's a bit tricky finding a place to sit, mind you, although most people don't want to sit down anyway; they just want to have a good time and a pint.

The noise level increases in direct proportion to the number of beers and the chalk marks on the wall. The hassle of the office and the toils and tribulations of existence are discussed, raucous laughter issues from every nook and cranny. Once the tap has started flowing, it doesn't stop. Up to thirty thousand litres of beer are consumed in the course of a good weekend.

There's food on sale too. But unless you're a local, you'll have a bit of a tough time fathoming out the menu. Try ordering "*Uerige Blotwoosch met Ölk on Brot*" or "*Ferkesbrode met jedönstete Appel on jeschmorte Ölk, kalt*". Should you feel queezy at the thought, there is a translation on the menu card.

Perhaps, if it's your first time, you'll feel a bit startled when you walk in. Why are all these people standing around, holding a glass of beer? Once you have shoved and pushed your way inside, take care that you're not rolled flat by one of these huge oak kegs that seem to roll down the passage with risk to life and limb. The place where you're standing will most probably be the general thoroughfare. Of course, you'll have gathered that all you can order here is beer or apple juice. Don't bother asking for a beverage card. The *Köbes* might find a few choice epithets for you.

Once you've collected a few of those chalk marks on the wall, you'll really start getting into the swing of things. You'll have struck up a conversation with your neighbour, you'll be on first name terms with your *Köbes* and any troubles you might have will have long since been swilled down your gullet. Next time you come to Düsseldorf, you'll be back in the *Uerige*, and you'll try to find a place to stand - probably in that same throroughfare. Perhaps that's why the beer mats carry the motto:

"*E Gläske Bier schmeckt immer jot on jöft Dich neue Läwennsmoot.*"

("The lion's roar you'll never fear Just drink a glass of Uerige beer.")

THE DÜSSELDORF ALTBIER

In 1516 Duke Wilhelm IV of Bavaria imposed the Purity Law for beer - valid to the present day. Yet by this time the art of brewing in Düsseldorf was already a long-standing tradition. Of the two main fermentation processes, top-fermentation and bottom-fermentation, the former gradually prevailed. Here the yeast rises to the top during the fermentation process, which takes place at the temperature of 15-20 degrees celcius, and is relatively quick. A bottom-fermented beer uses a different yeast that sinks during fermentation, at the lower temperature of 4-9 degrees.

A brewery expert, Georg Staudigel, member of the "Society for the History and Bibliography of the Brewing Industry" has the following explanation the developments in brewing around Düsseldorf "First let us recall that until the rise of the cold bottom-fermented process in the 15th century, only top-fermented beer existed. Bottom-fermented beer gradually replaced the older variety and by the end of the 19th century the transition was virtually complete." Except, of course, in the area around the Lower Rhine. Here the climate was too mild to brew bottom-fermented beer. After several unsuccessful experiments, the old method was re-introduced. Hence the term *Altbier*.

Barleymalt, hops, water and yeast are the ingredients stipulated by the Purity Law. Almost all breweries cultivate their own yeast. If one believes the advertising, Altbier must be the healthiest drink in the world. Each glass of beer contains more than 1,400 grains of barley, and it is said that the high hops content has a tranquillising effect, and that it also improves your digestion and metabolism.

Of course the locals don't only drink beer brewed in Düsseldorf. Equally good beer is brewed in Cologne, Krefeld, Korschenbroich and Mönchengengladbach. Yet 150 years ago, a double taxation rate was levied on beer imported from other cities. The result was that landlords, each of whom brewed his own beer, watered it down if the ingredients were too expensive - frequently the case when the harvest was bad. A police regulation then stipulated that beer could be sold at a higher price. A supervisor was thereupon appointed to inspect the brewing kettles and made sure that everything was in order.

Even today there are "home breweries", some of which may be seen in the pubs themselves. The brewing process is as follows: "To brew Altbier, germing barley is converted into malt. During this malting process the grain starch is converted into sugar. The resultant "green malt" is dried. After the dried malt has been bruised, water is added and the mixture - known as mash - is heated. In this process more and more starch is converted into sugar. The mash is then filtered and is now known as wort. A third ingredient, hops, is now added. Hops provide the aroma, the smoothness and the bitter-fresh taste. They also ensure natural durability. The wort is boiled with the hops, filtered and cooled. Now comes the most important part when the yeast - in the case of Altbier the top-fermentation yeast - is added. The fermentation process begins and part of the malt sugar changes into alcohol. Carbonic acid is released which gives the beer its bubbly freshness and frothy head. After the main fermentation, the yeast is skimmed off. The so-called *Jungbier* continues to ferment, whereupon it is filtered again and, after about four weeks, it is ready for bottling or kegging".

Altbier thus brewed is called *Vollbier* with a wort content - before fermentation - of 11-14 percent. 12 percent means that in 1000 g. wort, before fermentation, there is 120 g. extract, i.e. malt sugar, protein, minerals and vitamins. The alcohol content, in turn, is about one third to one quarter of the wort content, as the extract consists not only of malt sugar, and only a part of the sugar is converted into alcohol during fermentation.

That may read like a detailed description - but there is a lot more to it than that. But if more were generally known, perhaps a lot of people would simply brew their own. The breweries of Düsseldorf wouldn't like that at all.

Above, a chalk mark for every pint and a piece of sober advice: "Eat, drink - but don't talk about politics". Right, curbside encounter.

Its bridges, its architecture and the Kö are indeed elegant; the commercial power the city wields is undoubtedly impressive. Quaint are its pubs and breweries. But descriptions of Düsseldorf don't end there, for the spicy thing about the city is undoubtedly its Löwensenf, the world-famous mustard that not only improves a simple sausage but also gives a refined Entrecote the incomparable taste of fine cuisine. Löwensenf is like its city: plain and yet at the same time noble.

Theodor Esser had already founded Germany's first mustard factory as early as 1726 in the house of "Stadt Venlo" on Ritterstraße. Soon the product became famous and his market share grew rapidly. In 1781 the business was inherited by the palace's caretaker, Johann Cornelius Bergath, who soon had to ward off sharp competition from Cologne: it was claimed that genuine Düsseldorf Löwensenf was actually produced there. This gave a fresh impetus to the rivalry

Löwensenf was created exactly 85 years ago in France. The fact that it is now a genuine product of the Rhineland is thanks to the Treaty of Versailles which required all Germans who wished to keep their German nationality to leave French Lorraine. Otto Frenzel was no exception. He was the owner of the "First Vinegar and Mustard Factory" in Lorraine. With a great deal of diligence and expertise, he had already established a reputation as a manufacturer of first-rate products. He had no difficulty in choosing a new location for his factory: Düsseldorf, with its great mustard tradition.

between the two cities on the Rhine. But the mustard business of Adam Bergrath, Johann Cornelius Bergrath's son, flourished and he had his monogram and Düsseldorf's anchor printed on all mustard pots. This remains Bergrath Mustard's emblem to this day. The title of Purveyor to the Court was conferred upon the company in 1778.

From the beginning of the 19th century, Düsseldorf's mustard industry really began to boom. New factories sprang up and the fame of the product grew. It was often mentioned in contemporary literature. Heinrich Färber began his "Historical Walk" through the older part of Düsseldorf with the following line: "We are so pleased to be able to talk about Düsseldorf's most precious product, for it is in a way the speciality of our city, Düsseldorf's mustard." Düsseldorf's mustard is also proverbial: "To bring mustard to Düsseldorf", quoted by a Rhenish dictionary, means to do something unnecessary.

When Otto Frenzel arrived in Düsseldorf, the city was already known as the "Mustard Metropolis" of Central Europe. So he had to come up with something special in order to stand his ground. But Frenzel had a trump card up his sleeve: the recipe for Düsseldorf's world-famous "Original Löwensenf".

Whether with fish or meat - the fine spicy taste of mustard should not be lacking. And if "Düsseldorf roast beef with mustard" is on the menu, then the guest can rest assured that the cook has used nothing but Düsseldorf's Original Löwensenf, no matter if the restaurant is on the Kö or the Ku-Damm in Berlin.

Mustard has become an integral part of the city's culture and jokes abound. In 1934 Hans Müller-Schlösser even entitled his collection of witty yarns "et Mostertpöttche" (that small mustard pot). The association of Düsseldorf's Carnival Song Writers joined forces under the name "Die Mostertpöttche" (The Small Mustard Pots). Members of the

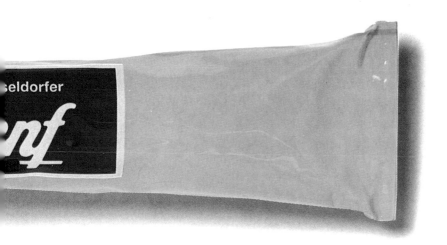

After initial difficulties the Löwensenf "extra" finally managed to make a name for itself, thanks to Frenzel's recipe and his determination to bank on quality. The factory had to be expanded and modernized as early as 1928. The reputation of Frenzel's earthenware pots and his jars with the head of Düsseldorf's lion extended far beyond Germany. Löwensenf is now exported to all Western European countries, Canada, the United States, Africa, Japan and Australia.

Above, the famous Düsseldorf mustard: Löwensenf.

"The Mustards" society turned up at postwar Carnival festivities wearing a grayish blue mustard pot as a helmet. At the parade on Monday before Lent in Düsseldorf, the carriage with the large "Mustard Pot" has been part of the procession for years.

Meanwhile, the city's importance for mustard in Germany and Europe has not diminished. The Löwensenf has such a good reputation and such a significant market share that this success has been passed on to two other Löwensenf varieties: the "medium" and the "Bavarian Sweet", both of which are genuine products of Düsseldorf.

THE KÖNIGSALLEE

For all those who like shopping, or even just window shopping, a stroll down the Kö, Düsseldorf's world renowned boulevard, is an absolute must. Study the people. The ladies in their smart outfits, perfect hair-dos, caked in jewellery and loaded with money. Or the Yuppies, marching along with their briefcases, no time to stop, no time to smile, as they earnestly dash to another appointment. Then the more relaxed pace of posh old ladies, arm in arm and browsing, constantly glancing at the window displays. And no sooner have they said "Oh, I like the look of that", then they disappear inside the shop for a closer inspection.

But people like you and me can also browse, and maybe even buy, on the Kö.

The elegant boulevard: The Königsallee is one kilometre long and runs between the Hofgarten in the north and Graf-Adolf-Platz in Friederichstadt in the south. It was built at the beginning of the last century, along the line of the old city fortifications which had been conveniently razed to the ground in 1801 by the French.

The Königsallee is in fact two streets with a total width of 85 metres. They are separated by the the old defensive ditch. The boulevard was completed in 1804 and subsequently landscaped by the Court architect Caspar Anton Weyhe. The ditch was filled with water and trees were planted on either side; so although the Kö first went by the name of *Mittelallee* this was soon changed to "Chestnut Avenue". Its importance increased dramatically in 1840, when Friedrichstadt first appeared on the map.

The boulevard was given the name Königsallee as a result of a mishap which one day befell the Prussian King Friedrich Willhelm IV. The story goes that as he was walking along the street he was struck on the coat by an apple which had been thrown by one of the

Preceding pages, the Neptune Fountain provides the Königsallee canal with fresh water from the River Düssel. **Below**, the Kö is not the only expensive shopping area in town.

crowd. The city fathers debated long and hard about how to find an honourable way out of this unfortunate event. Chestnut Avenue became Königsallee, the King's street.

Today the water channel, some 580 metres long and 32 metres wide, does not run the whole length of the Königsallee. Its northern end is marked by Theodor-Körner-Straße and the famous statue the **Triton Group**, one of the hallmarks of Düsseldorf. It was created in 1902 in accordance with the design drawn up by Fritz Coubillier, a student of the Academy. It is probably the most dynamic statue in the city; Neptune lunges his triton towards the fish which spews forth real Düssel water. There are swans contentedly paddling up and down the canal.

The 120 chestnut trees and 85 plane-trees lend the Kö its special character. In 1985 the Kö was given a face-lift; the new lanterns which are designed to look like old gas lamps, as well as the bollards, the clocks and the telephone kiosks, were all specially designed to enhance the elegant surroundings.

But it was the economic boom of the fifties and sixties of this century that transformed the Kö into a truly international boulevard. On the west side, according to the experts, 15 percent of the total export trade of the Federal Republic is negotiated. The head offices of numerous banks are situated here, along with the **Trinkhaus Gallerie** which was built in 1974 and the **WZ Center** which was completed in 1980. The latter is a modern multi-storey shopping centre with a number of noble boutiques, antique shops and restaurants. The focal point of the complex is the fountain "**Begegnung und Dialog**" (meeting and discussion) by the Swiss sculptor André Bucher. It consists of two vertical bronze pipes. The building can be entered either from Trinkhausstraße or via the entrance to the *Düsseldorfer Nachrichten* newspaper offices whose beautiful *Jugendstil* portal with gold writing on a blue background is very hard to miss.

Düsseldorf's jewellers enjoy an international reputation.

Most shopping is actually done on the other side of the Königsallee, on the eastern Kö which, with all its glamour and elegance, displays all the latest fashion whichever way you look. It isn't for nothing that Düsseldorf has established a wide reputation as the *Modestadt* - fashion city of Germany. Opened in 1986, the **Kö Gallerie** was named "the best shopping centre in Europe" by the "International Council of Shopping Centres".

A shopping spree: With wallets and purses bursting at the seams, cheque books and credit cards at the ready, let's start our shopping spree at the southern end of the Kö. In need of a new pair of glasses, I take a look at **Preuss**, the opticians, where Cartier glasses are a snip at DM 1,000. Then I pop into **Modeparadies für die Dame** and purchase a fine cotton handkerchief for a mere DM 18.

In the bookshop **Claus Linke** there are all the books about Düsseldorf you could ever wish for. The jeweller **Wichelmann** has a particularly fine selection of watches.

For feet that need pampering, **Fausto Santini** sells the very finest Italian shoes. Leather bags and belts too. **Paschen's** offers a wide range of watches, bracelets and necklaces; Dior, Seiko, Les Must and Cartier, Dupont, Longines, Maurice Lacroi and Dugena. I plumb for the diamond bracelet for DM 39,000. Next door, at **Barbara Freres**, there is exclusive apparel for the young. I continue past the **Kinderladen**, cross over **Bahnstraße** and casually stroll in through the glass doors of **Slupinski**. There's an exquisite Russian sable fur coat which rather takes my fancy, for DM 148,000.

At **Schlüter** you can find fashion for young ladies. Smart jeans, lots of glitter and colourful stones. Fake medals and logos. What about a nice jacket? At **Villeroy and Boch** you can marvel at the precious glasses, the fine porcelain, everything for the poshly-laid table. Shall I? No, on second thoughts, I'll go

Cartwheeling has a strong tradition in Düsseldorf.

for the French earthenware - not quite such a catastrophe if it shatters.

You can get shirts, jackets, trousers and fine shoe polish at **Uli Knecht**. If only I had the money - there are such wonderful things to buy for the kitchen at **Casserole**! I walk on, past the furs of **Jindo Pelzen**. I already have my sable, thank you very much. In the next window, that of **Selbach**, I discover the most beautiful hand-knitted cashmere cardigan I have ever seen. The shop assistant tells me it costs DM 3,698. The leather jacket for my son would set me back a further DM 3,498, wrapped. I decide not to go for the cardigan, and move on to **Rodier**, where I content myself with a coat for the rather more modest price of DM 900.

My attention is suddenly diverted as I stroll past **Königsallee 82**. A small window, hardly noticeable, is set into the wall, and within, golden light pours onto gleaming golden bracelets and a chain, no, what am I saying, a necklace, which simply takes my breath away. A

fine piece of craftsmanship, but there is no price-tag: next to the window on a metal plaque is written **Georg Horneman, Goldsmith, 2 floor**. I decide to resist the temptation and continue along the Kö as far as **Herbert Stock**, men's wear. Here in the window, on its background of blue silk framed in dark oak, something with which I am not at all familiar catches my eye. I ask the assistant what it is. A collar link is the the answer, a replica from the twenties, of the kind that a former Federal President is supposed to have worn. I decide to take it, useless though it is, but it only costs DM 45. What a bargain!

The attractively decorated display window of **May and Adlich** lures me in through the door. I look around. There's a pair of socks with funny teddy bears on for DM 34 for my daughter, a pair of yellow rabbit boxer shorts for her friend and some gaudy turquoise boxer shorts for my son. The cat can play with the ribbon with which everything has been so nicely wrapped.

Outside once again and I am standing in front of a gleaming black facade where renovation work is in progress. I continue. At the **Auctioneer's**, there are horses, bears and dragons in the window. There is an auction every afternoon. But the public, who have turned up in great numbers, don't seem to be all that interested in the carpet now going for DM 1,700.

Standing outside the jeweller **H. Stern**, I am captivated by all those gleaming stones in their priceless settings. They sparkle in all colours of the rainbow. Next door is **Prange Comfort**, where sore feet can slip into a pair of shoes for DM 360. Only the best here, and those who are really having problems can rub their feet with a special foot balm, also on sale.

At **Burberry's**, I invest in an umbrella for DM 268. I only fondle the cashmeres, but take a can of air freshener for DM 28 and a golden Burberry teddy bear for DM 78. Directly adjacent is the Lufthansa office, the screen in the window indicating that the flight from Chicago has been delayed.

Past the next crossing is the shoe shop **Regina Schuhe**, with the music of Ramazotti, Rod Stewart and others blaring away. This shop is an experience not to be missed. I am attracted by a pair of purple boots for DM 249. They are of shiny material, and look incredibly impractical. At the next jewellery shop, **Niessling**, I find a pair of platinum cuff-links for DM 7,900. I only have a brief look in the next arcade. Children's wear, fine silk and lace ladies underwear, shoes for him and her, clothes for the sportsman and sailors' fashion by Captain McArthur. I decide on a golf bag for DM 2,500. The young shop assistant says he's wild about Hamburg. What can I say to that? At the **Seidenhaus Schmidt**, which I already know from Frankfurt, I purchase a silk scarf for DM 239.

Suddenly I feel watched. A young man is staring at me - from a photograph - alluding to the presence of **René**, the

Waiting for the green light.

146

hairdressers, up on the first floor. Next door, men are standing outside the **Commerzbank**, studying the display boards inside. One leg in front and the other behind, presumably to provide extra stability should they discover that the value of their shares has dropped!

At around mid-day, I am finally standing in front of the **Kö Galerie**, a sparkling concoction of stone, brass and glass. I am told that you can find everything here, but only the finest: chocolates and fudge, caviar and cakes, ham and fish, balloons, ice-cream, cheese, an infinite amount of fashion clothing, tea, vitamins, keys, jewellery and fruit, coffee and musical boxes, tights in hundreds of colours, tobacco and pipes, bangles and beads, buttons and bows.

If your maxim is "better to be fit than fat", then a visit to the **Kö-Thermen**, is to be recommended. There are saunas and squash, a swimming pool, as well as golf and jogging on the roof. And who does all the advertising for this recreation centre? None other than Michael

Groß, Germany's very own swimming superstar, from Offenbach.

In the noble Kö Galerie, I proceed to buy ham, homemade noodles, exotic fruit, a nice bag of sweets tied with a bow, and fresh chocolates. DM 100 for the lot, naturally without the tights, which would have cost a further DM 125. Back on the Kö, I take a peek inside the jeweller **Weiss** and almost get tempted to go for the chic earrings on display. The shop next door sells carpets and all kinds of bronze figures. There are wonderful antiques at **Eva Schuelte**, and I fall in love with a glass decanter. It is very old and valuable - DM 2,500.

In **Eichoff**, I discover a pair of jeans for DM 259 and a velvet jacket to match for DM 1,290. And then yet another jewellery shop.

Despite my hunger, I only look through the door of the **Benrather Hof**, where Düsseldorfers are busy devouring fresh *Reibekuchen* - potato pancakes - together with a glass of Altbier.

Here, even a policeman can't resist the ladies' charm.

I cross **Steinstraße**, only glancing at **Schröer Shoes**, and then stop in front of the jeweller **Kuck**, fascinated by what is going on in the window: there's an adult man brushing away minute specs of dust with a fine paint brush, without even touching the expensive articles on display. I then proceed to leave **Mara**, the shop next door, with a stylish wide-rimmed hat which I bought for DM 195.

In the meantime, the day has drawn on a little and the shadows of the warm autumn sun are beginning to get longer. At **von Eicken**, people are sitting inside and outside, eating oysters. In the window of the **Galerie Paffrath**, I admire a little oil painting from the last century. There's a little sign at the door that says the shop is closed until 3 o'clock. What a pity. I continue past **Van Cleef & Arpfel's**, another jewellery shop. At **Douglas**, I acquire a little bottle of perfume for almost DM 300. From the window of the **Kö Café of Otto Bittner** baskets and crates of fruit made of marzipan tempt me to enter. Sadly the café is full. At **Pelzer**, a carpet shop, I buy a little elephant and duck, extras for the sofa costing a total of DM 29.90.

What I see in the next shop is very fragile: a table made purely of crystal for the horrendous price of DM 70,000. The wares on offer at **Palm Tobacco** are safer to handle: comical lighters for smokers and collectors. The photographs hanging up in the **Lichtburg** remind me of the fact that I haven't been to the cinema for a long time. Instead of bread and cheese or oysters, I spoil myself with 100g of cream fudge, for DM 7.50.

Fuchs and Creven have handmade sets of pokers and tongs for the fireplace for DM 1,344. There are further displays of shoes, menswear, paint and jewellery. At **Lipsia Mode**, the lure of a red knitted blouse for DM 895 was simply too strong to resist.

Out on the pavement, five charming young French girls talk among themselves, pointing out the displays, discussing, nodding and laughing as they continue on their way, evidently very

The newly renovated Kaufhof at the Kö. One of the oldest and largest department stores in the city.

happy with the fashion on offer in the "village" on the Düssel. I pass **Gucci** and also manage to avoid entering the jeweller **René Kern**. But at **Hörhager & Laimböck**, selling fashion clothes for both men and women, I decide to buy a silk suit for only DM 259. The sporty pullover for him, applied with a posy logo "King Arthur and the Knights of the Round table" costs much more, DM 1,600 to be exact. At **Langhardt**, I purchase a fine black leather briefcase for DM 359. There is a bookshop right next door, which, I discover, even sells APA Guides!

The assistant at the private jeweller **Hans Münstermann** (1938-1988) packs into neat little boxes the dainty silver picks I have just bought to help me eat all the different types of cheese I have at home. There are the ones with a little silver goat on for the goat's milk cheese (DM 196), those with a sheep for the sheep's milk cheese I have from Greece (DM 169), and the ones I shall probably use most often, which have the larger silver cow to hold on to (DM 353).

Now I am just about at the end of my tether. I just have a look at another pair of shoes, marvel at the fine, delicate ladies underwear on sale at **Haita**, and finally invest in a fancy anorak for DM 1498. Having passed the Royal Danish Consulate, I also decide to pass, for today at least, on a visit to the Trinkhaus Galerie and the WZ Center. Find out what's there for yourselves, back on the west side of the street. I hail a taxi and have it drop me back at the Holiday Inn. I shove my way through the doors, stagger into **The Düsseldorfer** where I end up sipping mustard soup from a hollowed out apple, accompanied by a fine glass of Champagne! What a day! If I add everything together I discover that I am DM 292,159.40 worse off than I was when I started my spree.

I would love to have spent *so much money*, but, to tell the truth, I actually only purchased the socks, the boxer shorts, the ham, the sweets and that elegant pair of tights. Never mind!

The Kö festival attracts thousands to a feast of lobster and champagne.

CITY OF FASHION

Residents of Düsseldorf are generally not all that keen to hear the catchword "city of fashion". It sounds as if they had nothing else on their minds but new clothes - of the finest sort, of course.

Yet the fashion business, the life with fashion, is an integral part of the city. You come across this phenomenon mainly on the Königsallee, that luxurious bridge between the oldest and the modern part of the city where you can find everything that is stylish and expensive. From pendants by Cartier to evening gowns by Yves Saint Laurent; from silk ties by Italian designers to chincilla. There is stiff competition between major stores and it is worth looking out for bargains even before important seasonal sales.

The neighbourhood too is influenced by the standard of the Kö. In this fashion competition, even department stores (Kaufhof on the Kö, Carsch-Haus at Heine-Platz, Karstadt on Schadow-straße) offer more classy items than junk, with cashmere for everyone.

No wonder one comes across a remarkable number of elegant people strolling around the city. But when you have the impression that Düsseldorf has become one whole cat-walk - and when all tables in the upper class restaurants are booked for small groups of perfumed, elegantly dressed clients - then there is no doubt about it, Igedo is in town: the fashion show, the world's largest clothing market.

It was in 1949, the year the Federal Republic was founded, that 24 manufacturers joined forces and formed a community of interests for ladies' wear (Igedo). They had the models smile for the retailers for the first time at the old fairgrounds at Ehrenhof.

Today the exhibition halls of the "Neue Messe" (the new fair) are not big enough to accommodate this major fashion show. 200,000 buyers from 70 countries order clothes and accessories for approximately 9 billion Marks in the course of one year. Reason enough for Igedo's organizer Michael Kronen to increase the number of annual trade shows to eight. At the "Fashion Promotions", a new show introduced in 1989, dealers get to see what will be fashionable next autumn as early as December. Düsseldorf - the trendy city. This, of course, also inspires the creative. A few of the most celebrated German fashion designers work in Düsseldorf.

Beatrice Hympendahl came from Kiel to the Rhine and found enough demand for her unconventional designs in the lively Kö-society. It goes without saying that she is one of the top ten designers to display her work at Igedo's designer show. Her colleague, Uta Raasch, prefers a show of her own - in the "Weißen Haus" on Emmericher Straße. Ladies from Hamburg to Munich like to wear her casual, elegant look. The Italian designer Tristano Onofri has also settled in Düsseldorf. He sells his beautiful, classic designs in his own shop on Theodor-Körner-Straße.

Ready-made clothes of the best quality - for some ladies even that is not good enough. They prefer something unique, something that has been designed exclusively for them. Hanns Friedrichs and Lore Lang with their wonderful, antiquated fashion houses still belong to the guild of high-class tailors. Any woman can be a beauty - as long as she wears the right dress. The couturiers and their clients believe in that. Of course, beauty has its price. But you never talk about money. After all, moneyed aristocracy always oblige.

Those who have made it in the fashion business are the stars of the world of elegance. Many young, talented people in Düsseldorf dream of the day when they will get a chance. There is a long waiting list for the renowned fashion school in Castle Eller. And yet after completing this highly desired training, not too many get into big business like ex-fashion school pupils Brigitte Haarke and Brigitte Kyra.

Exclusive collections are generally too expensive to make, and the market is limited. Only a few young people can afford designer fashion. Most tend to buy smart mass-produced articles, for example by Esprit, whose German head office is also located in Düsseldorf - the city of fashion.

Above, elegance in marble and brass: the Kö Gallery, since 1986 the jewel of the Königsallee. Right, Igedo makes fashion. The world's biggest fashion fair takes place several times a year.

At the northern end of the Königsallee the Kö Passage is a pedestrian subway which leads through to the **Hofgarten**, a large park which forms the northern boundary of the old city centre. Access can also be gained via the **Ratinger Tor** which is situated just to the west of the park at the point where **Maximilian-Weyhe-Allee** and **Ratinger Straße** intersect. The gate is flanked by two small Classical temples (one of which, incidentally, houses the **Hella Nebelung picture gallery**) with facing Doric columns. They were built between 1811-1815 by Adolph von Vagedes.

The park itself, which now covers 26 hectares, was planned around 1770 by Nicolas de Pigage, the architect of Benrath Chateau. During the reign of the elector Carl Theodor, who commissioned the Hofgarten, the city budget was frequently in a highly precarious condition and the planning of the Hofgarten can thus, in retrospect, be regarded as one of the first labour-providing measures. On completion it was immediately opened to the public.

During the Napoleonic era, the adjoining fortifications were pulled down so enabling the park to be expanded westwards. The costs were partly borne by Napoleon himself, who always refered to Düsseldorf as "mon petit Paris". In 1803 Maximilian Friedrich Weyhe, a landscape architect, came to Düsseldorf and set about the extension the Hofgarten, diversifying and increasing the stock of trees and planning extensive meadows to create a jewel of German landscape architecture.

Dotted around the park are a number of sculptures. The **Heinrich Heine Memorial**, one of many such tributes to the city's most famous son, is situated on the **Napoleonsberg**, a hill from whose summit Napoleon viewed the city on the occasion of his visit in the autumn of 1811. The memorial consists of a small flight of steps with a portrait medallion of the poet as well as the bronze statue "Harmonie", which the French sculptor Aristide Maillol designed in 1944. This was presented by the "Arts Association of the Rhineland and Westphalia" on the occasion of the 160th anniversary of the poet's birth in 1957.

The "**Aufsteigende Jüngling**" (rising youth) created by Georg Kolbe is another memento to Heinrich Heine. Not far from here is the sculpture "**Röhrender Hirsch**" (belling stag) by the Düsseldorf artist Pallenberg, who specialised in animal sculptures. We come across a whole collection of Pallenberg works again if we pay a visit to the Löbbecke Museum.

Henry Moore's impressive sculpture "**Reclining Figure**" can also be found in the Hofgarten. The classicistic memorial for the victims of the 1864/66

Left, "Eyes Right"; a marksmen's procession during the *Kirmes*. *Right*, the statute of Art Academy director Peter von Cornelius.

and 1870/71 wars was donated by the city council. In the immediate vicinity is a Peter Rübsom memorial to Gustav Gründgens, the famous actor and theatre director who had a decisive influence on the post-war Düsseldorf theatre and established its international fame.

The "**marble bench with cats**" behind the **Theatre** was designed by Peter Behrens in 1904. In this section of the Hofgarten we also find the bronze statue of the poet Karl Leberecht Immermann (1786-1840), the founder of the Düsseldorf *Musterbühne*. Originally the statue stood in a corner of the old Municipal Theatre, next to a statue of Felix Mendelssohn, which was melted down by the Nazi's because of Mendelssohn's Jewish origin. Louise Dumont (1862-1932) was a supremely gifted actress and theatre directrice. To commemorate her, the architect Hentrich designed a memorial stone complete with a bronze bust by the Milanese sculptor Ernesto de Fiori. The Hofgarten version is a copy - the original is in the Dumont-Lindemann Archives located in the former **Hofgärtnerhaus**.

An impressive statue on the southern edge of the Hofgarten, facing Corneliusplatz and Königsallee, is that of the painter and Art Academy director Peter von Cornelius. An unadorned stone with the head of the composer Robert Schumann nestles in a leafy bower nearby. Then we come across a sandstone monument of Maximilian Fredrich Weyhe, the afore-mentioned landscape architect. Here he is on his pedestal, holding plan and pen. This statue was created in 1850 by the Cologne artist C. Hoffmann. Unfortunately the years have visibly taken their toll.

Standing by the **Runde Weiher** (a pond) one can't help but notice the triton that seems to be playing with a water-spurting hippopotamus. This statue was created by J.C. Hammerschmidt between 1889 and 1900. The green patina on the statue has given rise to the nickname "**Gröne Jong**" (green lad). Looking past this sculpture one can see

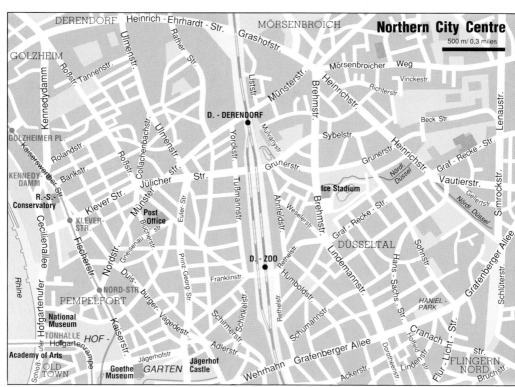

Schloß Jägerhof. On one's way there, in a little recess on the right, is the **Stephanie memorial**. Princess Stephanie was a daughter of Count Karl Anton from the House Hohenzollern-Sigmaringen. She devoted her short life to trying to assuage the poverty of the poor, who, in turn, revered her as a virtual saint. Eventually she became Queen of Portugal but died, only 22 years of age, in 1859. At the insistence of the populace, the city administration commissioned Julius Bayerle, a pupil of Wilhelm von Schadow, to design this memorial. Even now she is venerated in Düsseldorf and on Stephanie's Day the riflemen's clubs commemorate her with a ceremony.

The Baroque **Château Jägerhof** was designed in 1758 by Johann Josef Couven and Nicolas de Pigage. Having taken five years to build, it became the official residence of the Bergische Foresters and Hunters. The Counts also used it as a hunting lodge. Napoleon resided here when he stayed in Düssel-

dorf in 1811. Ten years later Prince Friedrich Wilhelm Ludwig of Prussia, the commander of the local infantry divisions, made it his headquarters. Subsequently the château served as the official residence of the Lord Mayor. It was severely damaged during the last war but the facade has since been restored to its original state. Internally it has been modernised. It now houses the **Goethemuseum** - 35,000 Goethe-related exhibits are displayed in 11 rooms. One room is entirely devoted to Goethe's famous treatise on colours. Also on display are original manuscripts, busts, coins, letters, pictures - by Goethe himself - proving what a visually-orientated, versatile designer he also was. There is also a library with 17,000 books. Alongside the collection in Weimar and Frankfurt, the Düsseldorf Goethe collection is the most important. The Kippenberg foundation donated the collection to the city of Düsseldorf in 1950. Also on display is a fine collection of Meißen porcelain as well as furniture

and silver, dating mostly from the 18th century.

At the foot of the **Ananasberg**, created from the rubble of the former ramparts, we find the **Fairy-tale Fountain**, designed by the French sculptor Max Blondat. Copies can be found in Odessa, Denver, Zurich and Dijon.

To the south of Schloß Jägerhof is the "**Malkasten**" (paint box) - which is not merely a house, it is an institution. Its tradition goes back almost 150 years. In 1848 some students of the Art Academy met to try to combat the ossified conservatism of the Academy. This "Malkasten" became the spiritual home for the younger generation of painters. In 1860 the artists moved to a new home - the former domicile of the Jacobi brothers - which was acquired by the "Malkasten" Association. Thereby hangs a tale. The house had been subdivided and was up for sale. In view of the importance of the Jacobi brothers for the city of Düsseldorf, this sale had to be prevented at all costs. The "Malkasten"

organised a lottery of pictures and the King of Bavaria, politicians, affluent artists like Andreas Achenbach and even Prince Albert of Saxony (the consort of Queen Victoria) donated sufficient funds for the Malkasten to acquire the building and grounds. Up to the present day it is a centre for independent artists. The building was gutted in the Second World War but rebuilt from 1950-1954. The gardens are quite splendid and are open to the public. In the house is a permanent sales exhibition of modern art and rooms may also be hired for conferences as well as official and private functions.

Who were the Jacobi brothers? Friedrich Heinrich Jacobi was a philosopher and one of the founding members of the first Free Mason Lodge in Düsseldorf and Johann Georg Jacobi was a poet. Their home became a meeting place for the most illustrious members of society - Wilhelm and Alexander von Humboldt, Spinoza, Kant, Mendelssohn, Graf Goltstein, Herder, Wieland, Baron von Hompesch zu

A Mack fountain (1988) on the Platz der Deutschen Einheit. Heinz Mack was a member of the "Group Zero".

Bellheim, to mention just a few. The most prominent visitor was undoubtedly Johann Wolfgang von Goethe, who later remembered the Jacobis thus: "When I returned to my friend Jacobi, I enjoyed the overwhelming feeling of a spiritual bond...how much goodness, beauty, heartwarming work has he carried out. And thus we bade farewell in the blessed knowledge of eternal union, without the premonition that our endeavours might separate us, as is so often the case in the course of a lifetime."

In **Prinz Georg Straße**, north of the Jägerhof is the Catholic **Church of St. Rochus**. It was destroyed during the war but rebuilt in 1953. The neo-Romanesque tower was retained and integrated into the modern steel construction, which was designed by the architect P. Schneider-Eisleben. The interior of the church is remarkable as well. It was designed by Ewald Matare, a professor at the Düsseldorf Art Academy. Especially of note is the huge figure of the resurrected Christ, which was completed in 1940/41. The Cologne congregation that had commissioned it refused to accept because they considered it too abstract. The bronze crucifixion on the facade of the tower was designed by Bert Gerresheim. It was created for the Catholic Assembly held in Düsseldorf in 1982.

The **Löbbecke Museum** is named after a pharmacist and natural scientist Theodor Löbbecke (1821-1901) whose widow donated her late husband's collection to the city. With the interest that accrues from the foundation the collection is kept up to date. Naturally the collection has since increased substantially - so much so that in the 1970s the city invited architects to submit plans for a new building to house the collection, which now includes an insectarium and an aqua-zoo. The Löbbecke Museum is in **Rotterdamerstraße** near the **Nordpark**.

To the south - in the triangle formed by **Fischerstraße** and **Sittarderstraße** - there is the **Golzheimer cemetery**,

"Reclining figure in two parts" by Henry Moore (1969) in the Hofgarten.

where many illustrious people who contributed to the importance of Düsseldorf in the 19th century lie buried. The poet Immermann, the painters Rethel and Schadow, the landscape architect Maximilian Friedrich Weyhe, the composer Burgmüller have all found their final resting place here.

In the vicinity is the **City Hall** - note especially the steel construction of tapered prisms.

Of special importance is the **Kunst-museum** (Art Museum), which is housed in the **Kunstpalast** complex. The entrance is in **Inselstraße**. The two bronze statues were created in 1926 by the sculptor Ernst Gottschalk. On the northern part of the complex we see the enormous "Aurora" by Arno Breker. On the facade which faces the Hofgarten is the inscription: "Ars aeterna vita brevis" (art is eternal, life is short). The museum is one of the most diversified in the Federal Republic. There is a fine display of glass objects as well as German painting of the 19th and 20th cen-

turies and European art from the Middles Ages to the present day. There is also a collection of drawings, textiles and a huge library. The **Robert Schumann Hall** - ideal for recitals and conferences - is also housed here.

Towering over everything is the **Tonhalle**, the former planetarium. This huge circular building, with a diameter of 50 metres, was built in 1925/26 and since 1977 it has been used as a concert hall, with a seating capacity of 2,000. It is considered to be one of the most perfect examples of Art Deco architecture. In the "green vault" of the building (so-called because of the green ceramic tiles) part of the collection of glass from the Kunstmuseum is on display.

In front of the main entrance is a rondel with fountains. Here there are fragments of the monument Jupp Rübsam erected in 1927/8 to commemorate the end of the first World War. It was removed by the Nazis in 1933 because it was deemed too "unheroic". Today, a memorial to the

The Tonhalle, the erstwhile planetarium.

dead of the 39th artillery regiment stands in almost the same place.

At the foot of the steps to the **Oberkassler Bridge** is the gilded statue of Pallas Athene, designed by Johannes Knubel in the 1920s. In 1985 Bert Gerresheim created the sculpture of Saint Nepomuk, the patron saint of bridges. It also commemorates the Polish priest Jerzy Popieluszko, who was murdered in 1984. The two groups of planets (Saturn and Venus, Jupiter and Mars) recall the time when the Tonhalle was still used as a planetarium.

To the south in Fritz Roeber Straße, is the **State Academy of Arts**. Paul Klee taught here, as did Ewald Matare. The first directors were Peter von Cornelius and Wilhelm von Schadow. Not only the classical arts are taught here however. Artistic treatment of modern substances like plastic and medial art like films and video are also part of the curriculum. Initially the Academy of Arts was housed in the palace, but this burnt down in 1872. Seven years later the Academy found a new home in a Victorian-style building. A frieze bears those names of painters and sculptors who were of special importance for the 19th century; Dürer, Holbein and Raffael are just three such personalities.

"**Rheinpark**" is the name of the long strip of green between the Ehrenhof and the Theodor-Heuß Bridge. The shady park is sandwiched between the Cäcilienallee on the east and the high tide protection wall which runs parallel to the Rhine on the west. The main road is flanked by chestnut trees affording shade in the summer. Here there are also a number of contemporary works of art like Karl Hartung's "**Plastische Säule**" (1960) or Friedrich Werthmann's steel tin construction "**Diabolo**". One limestone sculpture is called "**Rheinschiffer um 1850**" (boatman around 1850) and noteworthy is also the green, steely "**High Water Serpent**".

Returning once more to the Hofgarten, we come to the elegant **Hofgärtnerhaus** (from 1804-1808 the home of the landscape architect Weyhe), which now houses the **Dumont-Lindemann-archive**, the theatre archive of the city. On display is an impressive collection of exhibits all relating to Düsseldorf theatre history. Starting with Dumont and Lindemann, the founders of this archive, to the legendary Gustav Gründgens of contemporary theatre productions. Photos, stage designs, including those of the late Jean-Pierre Ponelle, costumes, stage accessories, cast lists, reviews and also the puppets created by the Zangerle family, the founders of the Rhine Puppet Theatre. A veritable eldorado then for all who are interested in the theatre and opera.

The **Filminstitut**, Prinz-Georg-Straße 80, is also worth a visit. On display are old projectors, original film scripts, historic cinema posters and - the special attraction - an old Wurlitzer, dating from 1930. The Film Institute was opened in 1977 and every two years it awards the Helmut-Käutner prize of Düsseldorf for new film productions.

A metal serpent guards the flooded Rhine.

Just imagine you're strolling through Düsseldorf port and you find a shiny nail. Pocket it quick! Walk towards the Rheinturm. You can't miss it, it's 234 metres high. When you walk down Kaiserstraße, look in the **Hans Mayer Gallery** - you'll recognise it, it's the white-washed building. Ring the bell next to the name plate Uecker and have your nail autographed. If there is no reply, the artist might just have popped over to the seafood restaurant "Maassen" for a bouillabaisse.

Continue your walk in the direction of the Rheinturm, but turn right shortly before you get to the old, brick, customs court, on a level with the RTL Studios. Cross the large car park and the adjoining Stromstraße, order an aperitif in **Robert's Bistro**, and consult your Düssel-dorf APA City Guide on what it says about the port.

Right now the **Rheinhafen** (the port) is the City Fathers' pet project. A redis-covered district simply waiting for city planners and speculators to get going. A small part of it is about to be turned into a media centre - so we're told at least. Quite undoubtedly, things have really started to get going since the lease on a few hectares of the total 175 hectares expired a short while ago. A bit of working out has been prescribed for the port - to get rid of excess flab - and hence an entire area is being opened up to speculators.

A health cure if ever there was one, and a successful one, too, it seems. The abandoned warehouses and offices ex-ude an almost gravitational pull on gallerists, photographers, advertising agencies and artists. One by one they come to suss out the area, and some even consider renting an entire storey. There's not exactly a shortage of space, after all. "Lofts aplenty", in fact. In the immediate vicinity a number of restau-rants and bars have opened up. The

slogan very much seems to be: "On-ward Christian Yuppies".

Don't fret, you inner city landlords, see the silver lining rather than the clouds. Those guys that come to the port to be seen have been ignoring the inner city area for quite some time now.

For some strange reason, the Düssel-dorf population never used to think much of the area. The port was shifted farther and farther up river until, in 1896, it nestled here in the Rhine bend. Of course it isn't nearly as big as the neighbouring Duisburg port - the biggest inland port in the world - but, together with Düssel-dorf-Heerdt and Düsseldorf-Reisholz, it is one of the most important inland ports in Europe. State-of-the-art cranes, a superlative rail network, more than a score of suction plants for the loading and unloading of fluids, more than enough grain elevators, high capacity

Left, the Rhine Tower. Its lights form the largest decimal clock in the world. **Right**, Ratinger Straße, meeting place for punks and hippies.

storage tanks and a brand-new container terminal all make Düsseldorf port the perferred discharging area for ships throughout Europe, primarily from the Benelux countries and Great Britain.

A typical, flourishing port, then. No kinky bars anywhere around. No red lights, no - or very few girls saying: "Hello sailor, feeling naughty??" And if you see some fat seagulls hovering around, they are probably pigeons from the nearby **Church of St Martin**, pretending to be seagulls just to get at the fresh fish titbits. The church was built between 1894 and 1896. It was gutted during World War II and was rebuilt in 1952. The **Old Church of St Martin** in Bilk dates from the 11th century. It is the oldest building in Düsseldorf.

But we were talking about fish. At the time when the port was still in the inner city there were plenty of small seafood restaurants - with whimsical names like: "The Golden Salmon", "The Three Herrings" and "The Dried Cod". *Tempi Passati*. All that is left of the city port which was levelled in 1810 are a few old walls that reappeared when the underground carpark was built - a bit like the re-emergence of Atlantis.

The **Rheinturm** (Rhine Tower) and the adjoining **Landtag** (The North Rhine Westphalian parliament building) are built on what used to be the port basin. For years the State Administration had been on the lookout for a suitable site - and their collective beady eye had lit on the Rhine embankment. But, no planning permission was forthcoming. When the city fathers in Düsseldorf continued to procrastinate, the powers that be threatened to move to Cologne. That did the trick. Hurriedly the basin of the old Berger port was filled with tons of rubble and, lo and behold, the outcome was a round building, made up of concave and convex circles which interlock. The architects Eller, Moser and Walter explained that it symbolised the idea of democracy. The complex structure of the building can perhaps best be appreciated from the viewing platform of the

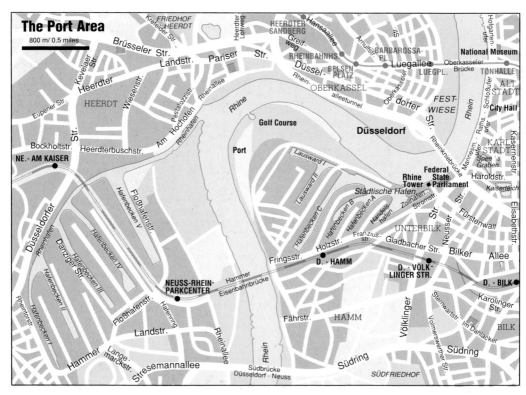

The Port Area

800 m / 0.5 miles

Rheinturm. Since the completion of the Landtag in 1987, new buildings have sprung up like beads on a string, jutting farther and farther into the port area. These include the studios of West German Radio and Television (WDR), the local TV station.

The days of the old **Zollhof** (customs hall), undoubtedly the most beautiful building of the port area, and, at present, home to artists and their studios, are numbered. Teams of architects are already preparing their blue-prints. If the conservationists don't get their way, the Zollhof will have to make way for a media building - future home of an advertising agency as well as audio and photo studios. The view the media crowd will be afforded is spectacular: the new marina and the Landtag. And should the heavy-duty highway disappear underground, as the Landtag plans, the view will be simply priceless.

For people like you and me there is still the somewhat euphemistically named **Rheinpark Bilk** - a strip of green along the Rhine embankment. This stretches from north of the Rheinknie-brücke and past the Landtag and the Rheinturm to the port entrance. There is even a suitable industrial memorial in the park: a restored Rhine crane. A century ago it was used for the discharge of chests and crates from Holland and England.

The practical, but architecturally inconsequential bridge, via which one can reach the east area of the port and the adjoining Rhine meadows, has been open to the public since 1989. The golf enthusiasts like it - it is a shortcut to the **Lausward**. The Lausward was once the site of the first Düsseldorf racecourse until the expansion of the harbour necessitated the location of a new site out at Grafenberg. Today, sport has returned and the Lausward has become one of the few municipal golf courses in West Germany. It is a nine-hole course and, for a moderate fee, you too can try to reduce your handicap. But it tends to be very crowded at times - the Japanese

The North Rhine Westphalian parliament building sits on reclaimed land.

appear to have taken a special liking to it. Whether it is the ideal site for a golf course is a moot point. Right next to it there is a coal-fired power station, providing a setting more appropriate to the Ruhr than to the noble administration city of Düsseldorf.

If you don't simply want to retrace your steps, you have to walk back through the seedy part of the port. The southern part - far enough from the water - has a pad where junior can practice driving Dad's car.

Inland ports are anything but exciting. You can breathe a sigh of relief once you've hit Kaistraße, where you first found that brand new nail, if you remember.

The owners of all those expensive cars parked illegally in the vicinity are doubtless sitting in the seafood restaurant "**Maassen**" - if the Gallery Mayer hasn't organised a vernisage, that is. "Maassen" is a name with great tradition in Düsseldorf. The seafood restaurant "Die drei Häringe" (The Three Herrings) dating from the 17th century is part of the "Maassen" dynasty too.

The "Maassen" in the port is the most popular seafood restaurant in Düsseldorf - not because the seafood served is necessarily the best, but because of the fish-market atmosphere. You order at the counter. Eventually someone will scream your name and you will get your food. The motto seems to be: the best service is no service. The more brusquely you are treated, the more at home you will feel. If you are lucky, you will get a place by the window, overlooking the water. But don't dispair - the fish chalked up on the menu slates most definitely cavorted in other waters.

One of the first in the port, when others were still pining for the city casemates, was Mayer, the gallerist. (The casemates - former storage vaults by the embankment - are remnants from times of yore). Hans Mayer, who started out in the 1960s as a furniture consultant and eventually became a gallerist, hit the jackpot when he refashioned an old storage vault into a gallery. The present gallery is an offshoot of his famous gallery in the Art Gallery.

Now…, put away the City Guide and devote yourself to culinary matters. Just peruse Robert's menu. Basically everything is recommended. After all, Robert when he still ran a restaurant in Oberkassel, was one of the few cooks in Germany who had been awarded a star.

By the way, how did you get to the port in the first place? With the 834 bus from the Main Station? Or by car from Graf Adolf and Kavallerie Straße? Or did you travel in style on a steamer setting out from Kaiserswerth?

In any case, when you turn back, just compare your watch with the biggest decimal clock in the world. Although it is indeed very large, you may miss it. After all, who would suppose that the round lamps that blink all the way down the side of the Rhine Tower are parts of a clock? Checking the time is quite simple, although many locals still haven't caught on to the principle and furtively gaze at their own wrist-watches if they really want to know how late it is.

But it really is very easy: Count from top to bottom. How late is it now? 22.35 and 46 - no 47 seconds. So: two lights at the top, blank, two lights, red light, three lights, gap, five lights, red light, four lights, gap, six lights - no seven lights. The Rheinturm, frequently - and wrongly - considered a TV tower, is in fact a telecommunications tower of the German Post Office - a Post Office Tower.

The building was completed in 1982. It is 234.20 metres high. Inside the base of the tower the shaft is glazed with an enormous mirror with an engraved map of the world with digital world times. At a dizzy 174.50 metres there is a high-class, revolving restaurant called the "Top 180". A little farther down, at 166.25 metres, is a viewing platform. On a clear day, you can even see the mighty spires of Cologne Cathedral from here. Düsseldorf by night is not exactly New York, but it is pretty spectacular nonetheless.

The Rheinkniebrücke with a view of the harbour area and the power station.

164

BOATING ON THE RHINE

There is no end to the sights in Düsseldorf. But whether you walk up and down the Kö, stroll through the alleys of the older part of the city, tour two or three museums, go on a shopping spree through the department store "Kaufhof", take a walk down the Heinrich-Heine-Allee and through green parks - you are always on foot. Though it's all very interesting, it's actually quite hard work.

Then suddenly your gaze falls on the broad river that silently and peacefully flows past Düsseldorf towards the North Sea. In the hustle and bustle of the city, you long for peace and tranquillity. All aboard! Throw your stress overboard and give your nerves - and your sore feet - a break. Here on board the *White Fleet*, the cruise ships with 5 stars, you can rest and relax.

And where does this journey take you to? Upstream or downstream? The Passenger Shipping Company of the Rhenish Railway Company offers several suggestions: On the first Saturday of the months of June, July, August and September the relaxing journey takes you from Düsseldorf-Rathausufer at 9.30 a.m. to the Hohenzollernbrücke in Cologne. It costs 20 DM per person.

You get off the ship at this point and find yourself once again in the hustle and bustle of a big city. Shops are open till 4 p.m. on the first Saturday of the month, so you have the opportunity to go on a shopping spree.

So, this is the holy city of Cologne. Since your ship will put out to sea at the Hohenzollernbrücke at 5 p.m. you will have exactly three hours to get to know the city. Cologne has approximately one million inhabitants and is known as the city of churches, the city of art and of the eau-de-Cologne. Walk down Hohe Straße, a colourful shopping street - different from the Kö and a shopping experience of a special kind.

Of course, you will have to visit Cologne's Cathedral which is situated opposite Central Station (also see pages 172-173). You can hardly miss it. Beside it you will find the Roman and Germanic Museum with its remarkable collection of unique treasures from times past. And next to that you will come across the Wallraf Richartz Museum and the Museum Ludwig (see page 174). So you don't have to walk all that far to see the beautiful things that Cologne has to offer.

Before you go back on board your ship, take a walk through Cologne's older part, situated directly on the Rhine and visit one of the typical pubs. Order a *Kölsch* and relish the aromatic beer before finally saying good-bye to Cologne.

Passenger ships will take you down the River Rhine to Duisburg, the world's largest inland river port, every Wednesday from the beginning of July to the end of August. The ship leaves from Düsseldorf's town hall bank. The journey takes you past Kaiserswerth and Krefeld-Uerdingen to Duisburg. Once you arrive in Duisburg, you will go on a tour of the Duisburg Ruhrort Ports for an hour (see pages 159-160). From the end of March to the middle of October, a ship will take you from Düsseldorf's old town to Kaiserswerth where you will have enough time to visit the ruins of the famous Imperial Palace and the Cathedral of St Suidbert (see pages 155-156).

The river you glance at from Düsseldorf's riverbank has a long journey behind it. It rose in the St. Gotthard Massive in Switzerland, worked its way to Lake Constance in the course of millions of years, passed between the Vosges and the Black Forest, crawled through a narrow valley of the Rhenish Uplands where today people from all over the world admire the romantic Rhine from land and water. When the Rhine finally flows into the North Sea it has travelled over 1,300 kilometres from the Swiss mountains and passed through five different countries.

The "Köln-Düsseldorfer Deutsche Rheinschiff-fahrt AG" offers day excursions from Cologne or journeys lasting several days on luxurious ships from Cologne, Basle, Amsterdam or Rotterdam. There is no other way of getting to know the river better than on board one of these comfortable ships of the White Fleet.

Left, Düsseldorf's landmark: the Castle Tower is all that remains of the Dukes' castle which burnt down in 1794. Above, pleasure steamers ply between Zons and Kaiserwerth from spring to autumn.

Taking the centre of the Altstadt as your point of bearing, the south of the city starts just beyond Hafen and Wallstraße. The district from here southwards to the Schwanenspiegel and Kaiserteich is known as **Karlstadt**, after the Elector Carl Theodor, on whose orders it was built. He didn't believe in doing things by halves. The city was to be considerably expanded and fortifications were, of course, prerequisite. The Elector's architect, Michael Cagnon, drew up plans but when he died in 1700, his successor, Jacob Dubois, only half-heartedly put them into practise. There were suggestions to change the name of the city to "Düsselstadt". Only very few of Carl Theodor's grandiose plans could be effected during his lifetime and when he died, development came to a virtual standstill.

Around the middle of the 18th century the original plans and drawings were dug up again and a further expansion was attempted - urgently if necessary because the city was bursting at the seams. The Chancellor, Graf von Nesselrode, wrote detailed instructions regarding this expansion, some of which are still in existence. He insisted that development be carried out in a controlled and ordered manner and gave strict orders for geometric planning. Thus, by 1796 the streets had been numbered and around 1800 they were given the names some of which were not changed to the present day.

In 1792 street lamps had been installed, tended by two specially appointed lamp lighters. Officers and physicians, artisans, merchants and officials now settled in Karlstadt. In 1800 Johann Moritz Schwager wrote in his essay, "Notes on a journey": "A new district of Düsseldorf, Karlstadt, has been developed since I was last here. Such splendid buildings, such regular streets I have never seen before." Even now, walking through this district one can trace the stylistic evolution of the architecture.

Karlplatz, now a permanent market square, was once flanked by linden trees. Only two facades - house No. 3 and 4 on the west side - still look as they did when they were first built.

You can reach the Schwanenmarkt via **Bilker Straße**. Here and in the adjoining streets there are galleries and antique shops, noble residential houses with many an idyllic courtyard. A case in point is the house of the Court Adviser Johann Wilhelm von Zantis - No. 5 - in which a collection of old city plans is displayed. In house No. 4-6, on the other side of the street, is the Düsseldorf Authors' Association. Its purpose is to help up-and-coming authors to get their works published and to organise readings. Here is also the office of the **Robert**

Left, a wall painting in Bilk, a part of the city which the speculators are busily trying to get their hands on. *Right*, Church of St. Martin.

Schumann Society and the Robert Schumann research centre.

On the right side of the street is the **Palais Wittgenstein**, No 7-9 (named after Prince Alexander von Sayn-Wittgenstein who resided here) housing the Municipal Culture and Education Centre as well as the Institut Francais. In the same house is the **Rheinisches Marionettentheater** (puppet theatre), run by the Zangerle brothers. The beautiful wrought-iron gate with its vine leaves and grapes was specially designed for the wine merchant Eduard Houth. Since the renovation of the house in 1974 Hermann König's bronze statue of "Daphne" has been the focal point of the courtyard. The **Düsseldorf Clara Schumann Music School** is right next door - No. 11.

The two houses No. 12-14 on the left side were built around the end of the 18th century. For many years house No. 14 was the city residence of the Count of Salm-Reifferscheid and his family, where Luise Hensel, a famous local poet, was employed for a time as a governess. The **Theatermuseum** was located in the adjoining house until 1988. It has since been moved to the Hofgärtnerhaus. Subsequently both buildings were joined and the **Heinrich Heine Institut** has since moved in. The collection includes about 5,000 volumes dealing with the life and work of the poet, his correspondence as well as his original manuscripts. There are also pictures and statues dating from his time as well as furniture. Of the twelve rooms, eleven house the collection, the twelfth is a reading room open to the public.

Opposite the Heinrich Heine Institut, a commemorative plaque has been affixed to house No. 15, surmounted by a relief with the heads of Robert and Clara Schumann. The Schumann family lived here for some time. Here Schumann wrote his violin sonatas, the cello concerto and the "Rhenish" symphony.

After crossing Bastionstraße, one comes to a Palais on the left named after its former occupant Baronvon Eynatten.

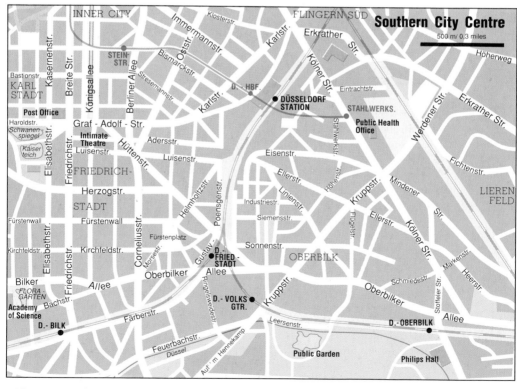

A little farther down the street the facades of houses No. 36 - 42 including the **Kolpingshaus** - former digs for working men - are indicative of the simpler form of architecture of Karlstadt.

The **Schwanenmarkt** marks the Southern end of Karlstadt. Bert Gerresheim's controversial **Heine Memorial**. was installed here in 1981 to mark the 125th anniversary of the poet's death. The sculptor himself stated that the memorial, which recalls the death mask of the poet, should be a "question mark", a "physiognomic picture-puzzle landscape". The square was designed in 1831 by Adolph von Vagedes, who was also responsible for the **Schwanenspiegel and** the **Kaiserteich**, two small lakes on the opposite side of Haroldstaße to the south. The buildings surrounding the two lakes are in Neo-gothic, Art Nouveau and Classicistic style. At the other side of Ständehausstraße, we find the **Ständehaus** (guild hall) for many years the seat of Local Government, until it moved to the new government centre on the Rhine. The mighty Neo-baroque fountain **Vater Rhein und seine Töchter** (Father Rhine and his daughters) occupies the square in front of the Ständehaus. This fountain is considered the classic example of the monumental style prevalent at the time of Kaiser Wilhelm. It was designed in 1897 by the two sculptors Jannsen and Türhaus and is intended as a reverence to the Imperial Rhine provinces.

Moving back to the north-west, between Bilkerstraße and the Rhine bank, is the **Zitadellen quarter**. Here the **Palais Nesselrode** on Schulstraße deserves special mention. It was completed in 1792 and, until it was destroyed in 1943, was considered one of the most beautiful houses of the Royal residence. Only faded drawings and old photos recall its former splendour. As the external walls survived the bombing, it was rebuilt in the 1960s and the **Hetjensmuseum** is now housed here. Laurenz Heinrich Hetjens donated his priceless collection of historical ceramics to the city. The

Schwanen-spiegel and Kaiserteich, oases in the heart of the city.

collection expanded all the years and now numbers some 10,500 items from all over the world. Modern artists are also afforded the opportunity to exhibit their works. The museum arranges courses and affords professional advice to collectors. There is also a concert hall. A guided tour of the museum in English is offered.

A stone's throw from here is the **Parish Church of St. Maximilian**. It was originally a Franciscan monastery church, dedicated in 1740. The industrious monks also built schools, refectories, and breweries. These buildings were partly damaged or destroyed during the last war. The church itself is still a sightseeing attraction: the altar painting in the choir as well as the other Baroque paintings, the two rows of choir stalls dating from the 17th century or the lectern dating from 1449. It was commissioned by the Abbot of the monastery in Altenberg.

Late-Gothic tapestries with the Coat of Arms of the founders are also from Altenberg. Especially noteworthy is the statue of the Virgin Mary, supposedly originating from the studio of Gabriel de Grupello. The choir stalls for the laymen, the wonderfully carved pulpit, both made between 1735 and 1742 and the Baroque organ deserve special mention. Constructed around 1750 by Ludwig König, an organ builder from Cologne, it is the same instrument that Felix Mendelssohn and Robert Schumann used for their concerts in the city, though it has been renovated. The original stucco work under the organ loft is also worth closer inspection. The stucco work in the summer refectory depicts scenes from the life of St. Antonius of Padua.

Next door to the church is the **Heimatbrunnen**, a fountain designed by the sculptor Karl Heinz Klein. The artist here depicts the history of the city from 1288 to 1982, when the city had finally been reconstructed after the ravages of war. Included in the depiction are portraits of five citizens that are of special

A memorial to the Jewish community and their synagogue, which was destroyed in the "Kristallnacht" of 1938.

importance for Düsseldorf: Louise Dumont, Arthur Schloßmann, Wilhelm Marx, Fritz Henkel and Heinrich Heine.

In **Zitadellenstraße** there are also a number of houses that deserve special mention. The **"Maximilian Volksschule"**, an erstwhile monastery school founded in 1673, extends along the left side of the street. "Volksschule" means primary school, but it was far more than that. Here oriental languages, physics and jurisprudence were taught. Opposite is the late-classicistic facade of house No. 3. The two neighbouring houses both date from the 17th century. At present No. 7 houses a Polish Art exhibition: "Ars Polona Galerie". House No. 17 is remarkable not least for its Rococo door.

The corner house on **Bäckerstraße** was built by the architect Michael Cagnon between 1692 and 1698. Passing down this street one soon comes to the gate of **Palais Spee**, which now houses the **Stadtmuseum** (city museum). The von Spee family were loyal servants of the Elector for generations. He rewarded them by raising them to the ranks of the nobility. They seem to have known how to make best use of their influence, for in the 18th century files they are registered as owning several houses and sites. The impressive Palais as well as the surrounding gardens and the "*Speeschen Graben*", all that is left of the citadel, are a point of repose in the hectic city. A plaque has been mounted above one of the gateways that lead to the courtyard. It commemorates Admiral Graf Maximilian von Spee, his two sons and 1,000 sailors and officers who died during a naval battle off the Falkland Islands in 1914.

The Stadtmuseum was founded in 1874. It is the oldest of its kind in the Rhineland and houses an extensive collection of almost 40,000 exhibits - coins, graphics, paintings, furniture, weapons, apparel and historic photographs.

The bakeries that baked the bread for the troops based in the citadel were, of course, located in Bäckerstraße and

There is market six times a week on Karisplatz. You'll find anything from local fruit and vegetables to French ducks. The market is closed on Sundays.

Bäckergasse. In the 18th century this area was a favourite residential area for the nobility and the affluent.

To the south of here, there are many high-rise administration blocks including the **Horrionhaus**, the official seat of the Minister President of North-Rhine Westphalia. Beyond the road going over the **Rheinkniebrücke**, is the *Landtag*, the new building of the State Administration, the government of North Rhine Westphalia. It was built by the Düsseldorf architects Eller-Moser-Walter and Partners. To get a good view of the port area, the river and indeed of the whole city, step into the elevator of the 180 metre high **Rheinturm** - the Rhine Tower. By the banks of the Rhine, not far from the foot of the Rheinturm is an old Rhine crane. There, near the old yacht harbour, is also the new Broadcasting House of the WDR (West German Radio and Television).

More than a millenium ago, the area to the south and south-east was a Royal estate with a church. Its first mention dates from A.D. 799 - "Villa Bilici" - nowadays known as **Bilk**. The old farm houses have long since had to make way to industry. The University has been located here since 1965, but the **Old Church of St Martin**, built around 1150, is still a witness to the times of yore. The turbulent times have done their worst and what still remains of the historic interior has been renovated beyond recognition. Until 1943 the observatory of the astronomer Johann Friedrich Benzenberg, which was built exactly a century before, stood here. All that is left now is the memorial of the "*Sternwartemal*".

We come full circle with the districts **Friedrichstadt** and **Unterbilk**. Here the **Kapelle der Vierzehn Nothelfer** (Chapel of the Fourteen Saints) is worth a visit. It dates from 1734, but pilgrimages to St. Christopher and the fourteen saints are known to have taken place as early as 1658. The Elector Carl Phillip donated some relics to the church. That is why there is a relief showing his

Elegant Art Nouveau houses on Berger Street.

electoral crown and his initials C.P. on one of the gables.

A short distance away is a pedestrian bridge across Werstener Straße. Crossing over we come to the south entrance of the Stoffeler cemetery, since 1879 the third biggest municipal cemetery. The **Südpark** extends to the right of the cemetary. It was designed for the Federal Garden Fair in 1987. The area to the north of the cemetery and the Botanical Gardens of the University form a 90 hectare park. At the southern end of the Südpark is the **Phillipshalle**, a congress hall which seats up to 4,600 people.

To the north-east the two urban districts Oberbilk and Friedrichstadt merge. Special mention must also be made of Friedrichstadt's **Floragarten**. Designed in 1875 it was taken over by the city in 1904. The Festhaus and the Palmgarten in the Floragarten were destroyed during the last war. Now the **Haus der Wissenschaften** (House of Sciences) is the focal point of the park, which also sports a small lake with a little island. Near the north bank is a statue group of "Adam and Eve".

Let us conclude our little tour of the parks with **Fürstenplatz**. This square has not changed much since 1884. Only the **Industriebrunnen** (Industry fountain) has been moved here from its former site in Kaiser-Wilhelm Park. The huge statues of the Industriebrunnen were designed by Fritz Coubillier, the basin of the fountain below the tools was designed by G. Nestler. The "message" of this impressive fountain is that Düsseldorf is not only a city of Art but of Industry as well.

The Neo-romanesque **Church of St Anthony** on the east side of the square dates from the turn of the century. It was built by the brothers Wilhelm and Paul Sültenfuß. The Neo-gothic **Parish Church of St. Peter** to the west between the Fürstenwall and Kirchfeldstraße is, of course, less monumental but more elegant. Designed by Caspar Clemens Pickel it was built between 1895 and 1898.

It is worth queueing up for some delicious fish at Maassens.

To the South of Düsseldorf lie the suburbs of Wersten, Reisholz, Hassels, Hothausen, Itter, Himmelgeist, Benrath, Urdenbach, Garath and Hellerhof. In 1929 Benrath, the "rich bride", was fused with Düsseldorf, the remaining districts were the "dowry", so to speak. Even today there is a well-known dividing line in the South of Düsseldorf: the so-called *"Benrather Linie"*, a dialect frontier that separates the middle and lower German dialects.

Benrath and its *Ritter von Benrode* (Knight of Benrode) is first mentioned in 1222. Castles and palaces were built on the "clearing" that the German word "roden" implies.

Benrath Château: The first castle at **Benrath** was built in 1662. Johann Lolio, called Sadeler, built it on commission of the second wife of the Palatinate Count Philipp Wilhelm. All that is left is the orangery, which now houses the Further Education Centre. To supersede the old moated castle, the Elector Carl Theodor instructed Nicolas de Pigage to design a new building. The result is perhaps the most famous Rococo château on the Lower Rhine. The pond at the front is flanked by the separate single-storey east and west wings, their curved facades directing one's attention to the one-and-a-half storey main building at the centre. It actually looks fairly modest from the outside. Only once you get inside the building that you can begin to appreciate the full magnificence of Rococo art; the marble floors and intricate stucco work and fine frescos adorning both walls and ceilings.

The park extends to the south of the building. Down the middle runs a 700 metre long water-filled moat, flanked by avenues of trees. To the west, a

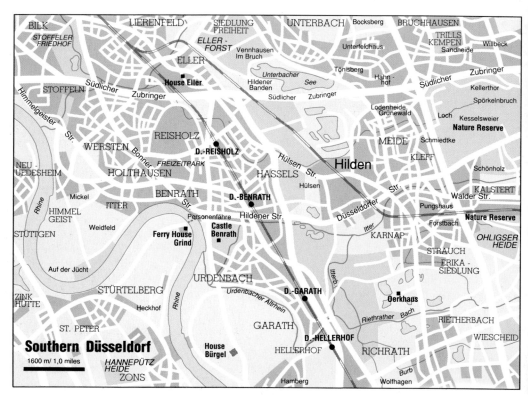

woodland park area extends almost as far as the banks of the Rhine.

In 1911, at a cost of 1.5 million Goldmarks, the citizens of Benrath bought the palace back from the Prussians, who had acquired it in 1815. In 1945, the château was severely damaged by a bomb, but has now been fully restored to its former splendour and is well worth a visit. Today it is used for civic receptions as well as by the North-Rhine Westphalian Government. One of the the most recent Heads of State to come here was Michail Gorbachev.

The Düsseldorf "dowry hunters" were less enamoured with the splendour of the castle when they fused the area with Düsseldorf in 1929 than of the vast industrial area in **Reisholz**. Even in those days there were more than 52 plants and enterprises employing more than 12,000 people. The *Rheinwerft* (Rhine wharf) in Reisholz was also much frequented. Hermann Heye, the son of the founder of the *Gerresheimer Glashütte* and co-founder of the Reisholz Industrial area,

had called the railway station there, in wise premonition, "Düsseldorf-Reisholz" although, at the time, Reisholz still belonged to Benrath. Today, workers' housing and factories lie cheek-by-jowl in Reisholz.

Holthausen has a similar structure. At the end of the 18th century there were fewer than two dozen houses surrounding a pond. At the time the little hamlet was called Langeweyer. The name Holthausen (or Holzhausen) is first mentioned in 1817 and has since been frequently confused with the older Holthausen near Düsseldorf-Stockum to the north-west of the city.

The centre of southern Holthausen was for centuries the Rittergut Elbroich (Elbroich Estate) which was built in the Middle Ages. Today it houses a charity clinic for the rehabilitation of senior citizens. **Elbroich Park** is also open to the public.

In 1899 Fritz Henkel acquired his first plot of land in Holthausen. Today his grandson, Konrad, is the Chairman of an enterprise that covers a quarter of the suburb's area, providing work for 13,000 employees. The international Henkel group also has its headquarters in Holthausen (see page 197).

The senior employees of the industries based in Reisholz, Holthausen and Wersten have always preferred to live in the wooded district of **Hassels**, first mentioned in 1288. The name Hassels is etymologically based on the word "Haselholt" - "Hasel" refering to hazelnut and "Holt" to wood. Today this district is overshadowed by the historically more important neighbouring regions Eller and Benrath, where in the last few years new residential areas have been developed, within easy reach of the city but at the same time close to the huge areas of green and woodland that lie to the east.

Apart from the industrial areas this region of Düsseldorf has its idyllic spots as well, such as Himmelgeist, Itter and Urdenbach which lie adjacent to the right bank of the river.

Himmelgeist is first mentioned in A.D. 904 as "Cellula in Humilgiese". It once belonged to the monastery at Kaiserswerth. It was here that Margravine Jakobe of Baden stepped ashore from the Rhine to marry the heir Johann Wilhelm in 1585.

Itter is well-known because of its old Church of St. Hubert, much in demand for romantic wedding ceremonies. It dates from the 11th century.

Urdenbach has always been the overflow basin of the Rhine. The fertile soil was constantly flooded, providing a rich farmland. Meanwhile the number of farmers has declined. Instead every year visitors come for the traditional *Schürreskarren Rennen,* a wheelbarrow race. Even Düsseldorf's Mayor participates, as he hails from Urdenbach.

The deep south: Where there's a South, there must be a "deep South". Düsseldorf has two districts, which are not only situated in the midst of verdant pastures but are also the site of architecturally important and internationally famous

municipal housing projects. Few districts have given rise to so much debate as **Garath**, where a new project was commenced in 1958 to cope with Düsseldorf's population overspill. Praise comes from city planners who come from far and wide to study the remarkable housing concept, the leisure time facilities, the controversial architecture of the **Burg Kirche** designed by Gottfried Böhm.

"You don't know Garath - let me weep. You must have spent your life asleep" rhymed a local - perhaps to combat the idea that Garath is nothing more than a grey housing area. On the contrary, the local inhabitants have developed their own regional awareness and there are now a lot of recreational facilities in Garath.

Garath used to be a little hamlet nestling around Schloß Garath. In the Middle Ages the Garderode family lived here. At the end of the 14th century it belonged to the Knight of Kalkum. The most important Lord of the Castle was Albert von Burgsdorff (1857 - 1919) who founded the world-famous "Garather Hühnerfarm" (chicken farm) at the turn of the century. At the time there were only 170 inhabitants but - to quote an advertisement - 50,000 chicks were born annually. An especially fertile chicken breed was imported from the area around the Niagara Falls.

Meanwhile Garath has had to cede the title of Düsseldorf's most southern district to a "pink butterfly" - the symbol for "living in green Hellerhof". **Hellerhof** has become the dream area for those citizens that can afford to buy their own home. Every wing of this symbolic butterfly represents one step towards the development of this region. Hellerhof used to consist solely of an estate called "Hoff zu Hellendail", first mentioned in 1440. As was the case with Schloß Garath, the city of Düsseldorf bought the "Altheller Hof" which now houses a riding school and equestrians can enjoy riding along a 13 kilometre network of paths.

There is plenty of countryside around Düsseldorf. Right, one of the first Persil advertisements.

HENKEL - WASHING WHITER THAN WHITE

Rapid growth and investment abroad, technological innovation, and an ever-increasing awareness of environmental problems are some of the major keys to the success of the multinational chemical concern Henkel Enterprises and all its subsidiary companies worldwide.

It is a success story which started way back in 1876 when, together with only three employees, Fritz Henkel began producing his "Universal Washing Powder" in the city of Aachen in 1876. Realising the better communications and closer proximity to markets this would provide, Henkel duly moved his factory to Düsseldorf, started operations at various premises near the city centre, and then, as the firm grew, moved out to Holthausen in the south, which is where the firm is still based today.

As early as 1878, Henkel's Washing Soda, consisting of 23 percent liquid glass, 57 percent chrystallized soda and 20 percent anhydrous soda, was launched. Fritz Henkel wrote that "A high quality and inexpensive detergent can be produced by mixing liquid glass with calcine soda and this can be sold in powder form". Mankind had been striving to produce cheap and effective washing agents for hundreds of years. Suddenly, here was the answer! But developments didn't stop there.

The company continued to expand and develop new product ideas. By 1907 the firm had 100 employees and was ready to launch the product by which it is famous today, the first ever automatic washing powder which Henkel christened Persil. The product was named after its two primary ingredients, perborate and silicate. Suddenly here was an all-in-one washing powder containing its own bleach. The soft soaps and curd soaps which had been used for washing clothes right up to the beginning of this century were now out of date. No more need for slaving away in the scullery; Persil did the whole job, whiter than white.

Henkel has continued to maintain its positon at the forefront in the development of washing powder, washing-up liquid and other detergents, many of which have been market leaders for a very long time. They are household names.

The company is very conscious of the new environmental awareness which has recently been forcing industry to change its ways. The first major development came as a result of the outcry over the disastrous effects that washing powder was discovered to be having on the environment, largely through the high concentrations of phosphates which appeared in waste water. As there was no cheap way of eliminating these once the water arrived at the treatment plants, a substitute had to be found. Once again Henkel led the field. The company ceased the production of detergent containing phosphates in 1988. Other companies followed suit and today most washing powder and liquid is free of phosphates.

A further threat to the environment came with the production of washing liquid sold in plastic containers. The increasing problems created by undegradable refuse led Henkel to introduce a refil pack out of thinner, more degradable plastic, thereby reducing waste.

Successful TV advertising campaigns have been at the forefront of the company's marketing strategy. This is now pitched at the environmentally conscious and hence concentrates on other aspects apart from the ability of its products to wash "whiter than white". An industry which has been responsible for so much pollution now exhorts the public to be more careful. It is the public which is left with the bad conscience.

Today, Henkel is not just a manufacturer of washing and household cleaning products. These only account for some 33 percent of all production. The giant chemical combine has a total product range of some 8,000 items in many branches of the chemical industry; fats for treating leather, paint and glue, pharmaceutical products, industrial adhesives and cleaners, hair colour and wallpaper paste, shampoo and a variety of products for body care. The firm has taken over many other successful companies, and together with its subsidiaries is now active not only in Germany, but in most other Eurpean countries, in Mexico and South America, Australia and Japan. The present Chairman of the group is Dr. Konrad Henkel, the grandson of the company's founder.

AROUND THE AIRPORT AND THE DÜSSELTAL

The story of Düsseldorf airport begins on 19th September 1909, when Graf Zeppelin's first airship, the Z III, landed on Golzheimer Heath. Twenty years later the airport was officially inaugurated, when the Deutsche Lufthansa opened three regular flight routes: Berlin, Hamburg and Geneva.

Shortly before the end of the war the airport was totally destroyed in a bomb attack but was reopened in 1949. Since that time it has been expanded considerably. The old, almost quaintly romantic, airport lounge has long since been replaced by a huge, ultra-modern building. About 9,000 people work here to ensure maximum efficiency for an annual passenger volume of some 10 million.

Düsseldorf is the biggest charter airport in the Federal Republic, and second in size only to Frankfurt. It is of vital importance for the export-orientated Rhine/Ruhr enterprises, servicing 26 cities with 12 million inhabitants. Some 35 airlines and 30 charter airlines regularly fly to Düsseldorf, and occasionally 50 other airlines. Eight hangars, 49 depositories, an air freight centre and 50 forwarding agencies transport more than 70,000 tons annually. Düsseldorf airport covers 618 hectares and a major share of the profit that *Düsseldorf Flug-hafen GmbH* makes is used to finance environmental protection measures.

"Harmony in aluminium and concrete" enthused the experts, and passenger comment concerning its functionality is predominantly favourable. The layout of the buildings affords the smoothest possible transfer from one place to the next. Even at full capacity - daily passenger volume 45,000 - there are few difficulties. About 800,000 spectators come to the observer's platform on the roof of Flugsteig B annually, to watch the take-offs and land-

ings. Guided tours of the airport are also available on demand.

The service available to passengers and guests is impressive. The huge restaurants with a seating capacity of 1,000 are on the fourth floor of the terminal building. There is a grill restaurant, cafe, self-service; there are coffee bars, cafeterias and snack counters scattered throughout the airport. The suburban railway below the terminal links up with the railway network of the Deutsche Bundesbahn. The luggage conveyor belts in the pedestrian tunnel go right up to the terminal. There is also a bus service. Line 727 will take you to the Main Station, Line 153 to Essen, Line 759 to Ratingen and Line 072 to Krefeld, as well as a special bus service when fairs are held in Düsseldorf.

Lohausen: The airport lies in the immediate vicinity of Kalkum, Licht-

Left, the River Düssel, which gave Düsseldorf its name. Right, the château at Kalkum, which is close to Kaiserswerth.

enbroich, Unterrath and **Lohausen**. Lohausen is particularly closely associated with the airport: two farms had to make way in 1969 for the extension of the airport, as did the so-called "Ickt", a medieval fortification. The earliest mention of the village dates from the 11th century. For more than 550 years (1235 - 1798) the Calkum zu Lohausen family resided in the castle. At the beginning of the 19th century, Heinrich Balthasar Lanz, a merchant who had earned a fortune in the German colonies, acquired the site and had a manor house built in the park. The landscaping of the 16 hectare gardens was carried out by Joseph Clemens Weyhe, the son of the Düsseldorf landscape architect Maximilian Friedrich Weyhe. We come across the Weyhes - father and son - everywhere in Düsseldorf.

In the centre of Lohausen is the **Parish Church of Our Lady of the Assumption**, built 1899 in the then customary brick style. On entering the church one can't fail to notice the statue of the virgin Mary. It was donated by Theodor Lanz and, as he was also passionately fond of hunting, he had the beautiful statue framed by antlers. Note also the black columns with Neo-franconian capitals as well as the supra-mounted arabesques.

Kalkum: The Düsseldorf suburb of **Kalkum**, originally named Calichheim, was first mentioned in the 9th century chronicles. The lords of Calichheim were a pretty rough lot and in the 14th century they even waged war against the powerful city of Cologne. After 1500 the Lords of Kalkum were the Winkelhausens, who had the medieval buildings destroyed and replaced by a baroque manor house with three corner towers. In 1739 the Counts von Hatzfeldt took over and from 1806 - 1814 Maria Anna Countess von Hatzfeldt had extensive alterations and expansions of the grounds carried out. The architect Georg Peter Leydel designed a castell-like quadruple palace in pure classicism. The ground floor rooms are still in the original style:

Düsseldorf Airport. The observation platform includes a small aircraft museum.

inlaid floors, stucco ceilings and marble fireplaces. Occasionally art exhibitions are presented and the Ministry of Culture organises receptions here. Again we encounter a Weyhe, this time the father, Maximilian Friedrich, who was given instructions in 1808 to plan a landscape garden beyond the moat that surrounds the palace. He succeeded admirably. The palace courtyard was built in a circular fashion, linden trees were planted in regular intervals, continuing down along the linden tree avenue.

Here lived the voluble Sophie Countess von Hatzfeld (1805 - 1881), who had the effrontery to rebel against her tyrannical husband. She is regarded as one of the first supporters of women's emancipation and by demonstrating that women have their own political judgement and mental independence, she managed to get a divorce in a spectacular court case ruling. A commemorative plaque in the courtyard affixed on the occasion of the centenary of her death, is inscribed: "Far ahead of her time, she fought for liberty as well as political and mental independence". Ferdinand Lassalle, twenty years her junior, was her lawyer in court. There were rumours at the time that they were more than just good friends. Perhaps their social inequality prevented them from marrying. Be that as it may - in the grounds of the palace there is a black marble bust of Lassalle in a pavilion near the eastern wall of the gardens.

Lassalle founded the so-called *Allgemeine Deutsche Arbeiterverein* (German Labourers Association) which later became the Social Democratic Party, and, in contrast to his contemporary, Karl Marx, he tried to achieve humanitarian improvements solely in a peaceful manner - knowing full well that this would be a long process.

Beyond the palace walls, only a few steps from the pavilion, there is the Romanesque **Parish Church of St. Lambert**. The basilica was probably built in the 13th century and resembles other churches in the Düsseldorf area

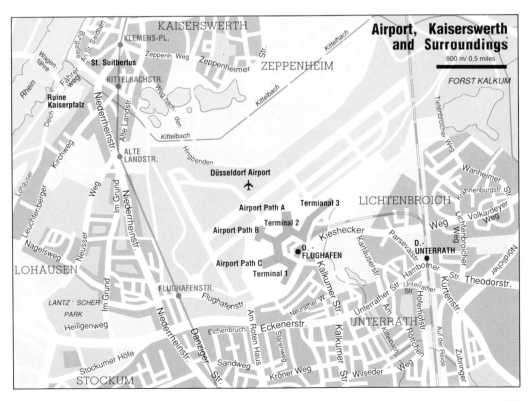

(Himmelgeist, Wittlaer and Bilk). There is a legend: Three sisters from the Kalkum line inherited a fortune when their parents died, with the injunction that each should build a small church.

One of the three sisters was blind and was cheated by her sisters when the fortune was distributed. When she noticed, she prophesied: "Your churches won't last, but mine will." It took a few hundred years before the prophesy was fulfilled. The other two basilicas were destroyed during the last war, whereas St. Lambert's was only slightly damaged. For many decades the church was also the burial site of those ruling Kalkum. Worth studying is a window in the north side of the nave and a marble epitaph to the infant Johann von Winkelmann, who died in 1609. The paintwork dates from 1915 and the other windows are post-World War II.

Düsseltal: Don't expect the valley through which the River Düssel flows to be particularly idyllic. The river that gave Düsseldorf its name meanders everywhere; through the zoo, below the Schloßallee in Eller, feeding a few ponds on its way to the Rhine, then goes underground and pops up again around elegant Königsallee, only to disappear again after 900 meters. The municipal water authority alone knows the exact course.

About 150 years ago there was a 300 metre wide valley in the north of the city. At this time the little stream was still a river - and quite a splendid one, especially when the snow melted in winter. Today the river has been tamed to a rivulet and houses and offices are built there. But the ecological value of the Düssel is well-known and the Water Authority looks after it well. While the river has been given back its "natural" bed in several places, a complete renaturisation is totally impossible due to cityscape through which it flows.

So much for the Düssel, which now no longer has a valley but a city. And in this city there is a suburb called **Düsseltal** (Düssel Valley). It was integrated into the city area one hundred years ago and

The marksmen also gather in Düsseldorf's suburbs - here in Lohausen.

was administered by Flingern, another suburb. Grafenberg and Derendorf, tiny hamlets, were part of it. In 1707 Trappist monks asked the Elector Johann Wilhelm for permission to settle in the Düsseltal. Seven years later the Elector allowed the monks to expand the monastery into an abbey, which was, however, secularised in 1803. Some of the installations were later taken to the Theodor-Fliedner-Kirche (a protestant church) in Kaiserswerth.

In 1822 Adalbert Count von der Recke-Volmerstein founded the *Rettungsanstalt Düsseltal* - an orphanage. Here the orphans were apprenticed to learn a craft. The pietistically orientated Count also endeavoured to convert young Jews to Christianity - but virtually nothing is known about his success. Leopold Freund, who joined the association after he left school and tried to familiarize himself with the new teachings wrote in his biography: "I went to the spiritual rejuvenation services and listened to the Sunday sermons, but all this only increased my desire to leave the Düsseltal and stick to the belief of my forefathers."

The **"Hungertürmchen"** at the intersection of **Max Planck** and **Sohn Straße** is all that is left of the Abbey. It is a dainty, baroque brick building with a conical roof. The cemetery also served as burial ground for the orphanage. Here the two infant daughters of the founder are buried. The entrance to the cemetery is in Klopstockstraße.

In 1874 a stock company bought the buildings to convert the site into a zoological garden and entrusted the garden architect Hillebrecht with the project. A fake castle ruin was built, a big restaurant with a garden, a few lakes - fed by the Düssel. In 1880 a "trade and art exhibition" was held here, which attracted more than one million visitors. Subsequently the area became a fashionable residential area. Düsseldorf's first tram had its terminal here. When the company began to get into financial difficulties at the turn of the century, the zoo was acquired by the city, with the support of a private foundation. The stock of animals did not survive the First World War and the zoo itself was destroyed in the Second World War. Now it is a normal public green.

The **Eisstadion** (ice stadium), built in 1936, but thoroughly modernized since, holds 10,000 spectators - not nearly enough, according to the fans. Whenever a key match is announced, the streets are innundated with fans wearing the red and yellow colours of the "Düsseldorfer Eis Gesellschaft". When the puck is swished into the opponent's goal, the whole stadium turns into a virtual cauldron. And if the armoured players of the "DEG" face the "Kölner Haien", then enthusiasm reaches almost frightening proportions.

There are two interesting churches in the Düsseltal. The **Protestant Church of St Matthew**, built by the two architects Heinrich Roßkoten and Karl Wach, takes pride of place. A building deemed avantgardistic at the time of its construction in 1930/31, it is asymmetrical inside with a separated choir. Next to the steel-girdered nave there is a bell tower made of yellow sandstone and red clinker. One year after completion, Arno Breker's supra-life-sized bronze statue of the church's patron was installed outside the church.

The **Catholic Church St. Paul** was built by the architect Josef Kleesattle between 1910 and 1913. It was designed as a five-nave basilica. After a bomb attack in 1943 only the entrance facade remained. When the church was rebuilt in 1952-54, the facade was integrated into the new building. Heinrich Campendonk designed the impressive windows. With the help of donations, valuable works of art were acquired and prominently displayed to create an impressive contrast to the otherwise stark, whitewashed surroundings: a French Madonna statue and a statue of Jesus dating from the 14th century. These and other donations make a visit to St. Paul's worthwhile.

AROUND GRAFENBERG

The racecourse: If people in Düsseldorf talk about Grafenberg, they would not normally be referring to the exclusive residential area adjoining an extensive area of woodland in the suburbs of the city. For **Grafenberg** is also the home of an institution which in 1989 celebrated its eightieth birthday and which has long since established itself with an international reputation; the racecourse of the Düsseldorf jockey and race club. And the meetings held here are often international events, attracting world famous horses and their jockeys and thousands of spectators too, keen to try their luck on the tote.

Due to extreme difficulties caused by the rolling terrain, a great deal of hard work had to be done before the course on the Grafenberg could be innaugurated in 1909. But the first president Wilhelm Pfeiffer, his deputy Lieutenant Lucius and the businessman Johann Janssen, were successful in completing what had at first seemed an impossible task.

The construction of a new racecourse was necessary because the original course at Lausward had been expropriated by the city in order to accommodate the much needed expansion of the harbour facilities. Impractical though it was, an area of land on the Grafenberg was offered as a new site and it is thanks to the efforts of the above-mentioned pioneers that Düsseldorf's racecourse now lies in such a beautiful setting.

Racing fanatic and banker Pfeiffer, who eventually became honorary president in 1929, built a stand here right at the beginning. But then, on an October evening in 1911, fire broke out in the kitchens, destroying the entire structure. A replacement stand was ready for the beginning of the following season, in 1912, the same year that the first tea house was opened.

A second fire once again reduced the main stand to ashes in 1917. This time,

In the paddock at the Grafenberg racecourse.

due to the First World War, its reconstruction took somewhat longer. A make-shift shelter had to be built to protect the spectators before the permanent stand could be completed. It was inaugurated in 1921, and still stands to this day - though somewhat overshadowed by the new main stand, completed in the jubilee year 1989.

"Racing in Düsseldorf would never have become as important as it is without the tireless efforts of personages from industry and the administration who were always there to add new impulses to the wonderful traditions of Grafenberg", reminded Businessman Enno Albert on the occasion of the jubilee. He recalled a long list of illustrious past presidents:

There was Lord Mayor Dr. Robert Lehr, who later became Home Secretary of the Federal Republic. Then came Ernst Bischoff, founder of the Mydlinghoven stables and long time chairman of the Technical Commission. Then the industrialist Curt von Berghes,

the Lawyer Paul Wenzel and, from 1946, Hans Baron von Schlotheim who had himself been a successful jockey in his time. Following on from Baron von Schlotheim in 1959, Lord Mayor Walter Hensel took over the position for a further twelve years. Before Peter Bühring-Uhle took up the reins of President in 1988, from 1971 Consul Herbert Liesenfeld had skilfully guided the fortunes of racing at Grafenberg.

While the Grafenberg course was always there, changes have always had to be made, to keep up with the demands of modern racing. This was not at first so necessary, as steeplechasing always had priority and a first rate course had already been layed out for that purpose in 1909. But over the years, the flat course was always perfected, until today when it has become a course of international standard.

The distinguishing feature of the course is the "*Berg*", the hill, whose steep gradient has often sorted out the winners from the losers, even 1000 metres

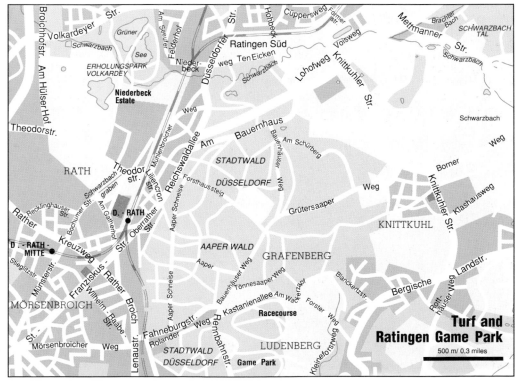

before the finishing post. The whole raceground now covers a total of 43 hectares. It is surrounded by the Grafenberger Forest, a particularly beautiful area. Lying on the edge of the Bergisches Land and within easy reach of the city, the Grafenberg racecourse is said to be one of the most attractive places to visit in the whole of Germany.

The Game Park: The Düsseldorf Game Park lies right next to the course. It is a public park which was established before the Second World War. Through well-maintained and easily accessible paths, the park offers a rare glimpse of some of the game indigenous to German forests. Deer and stags graze freely, while fencing ensures that the wild boar are kept at bay. The animals to be found here include 60 fallow deer, 10 red deer, about 60 sows and their piglets, two wild cats, two raccoons, four foxes, two grey geese, three swans and 12 turkeys.

The animals live for the most part in their natural habitat, even if they have now become accustomed to all the visitors and demand the occasional titbit. The Game Park covers an area of 40 hectares and, apart from the animals, it contains some very valuable woodland. Some of the trees are 250 years old. The Park is therefore not only a favourite place for a day out, but it also has an important educational role to play. It isn't often that one sees so much flora and fauna so near a city. Entrance to the park is free and and it closes at 6.00 pm in winter and 7.00 pm in summer.

Ratingen: To the north east, beyond the Düsseldorf district of Rath, lies the historic "city" of Ratingen. It is one of the oldest cities in Germany with a rich and varied history. The city celebrated its 700th anniversary in 1976. The city charter certificate, signed by Duke Adolf von Berg on 11th December 1276, has been preserved to this day and is kept in the city's historical archives.

Due to its location at the intersection of a number of important and very ancient trade routes, Ratingen always attracted settlers, traders and missionar-

"D" for Düsseldorf.

ies, crafts and industry. In times of war too, the soldiers of whichever power happened to be on the advance, would also take up accommodation within its walls. Over the centuries the fortunes of the city have changed continuously. Its history is marked by long periods of prosperity, followed by destruction, decline and upheaval, from which it has always risen again.

The Ratingen of today is a modern city with a population of about 100,000. Surrounded by forests, fields and pastures, it is the only "independent" city which exists between the State capital Düsseldorf and the vast conurbations of the Ruhr Basint, with all its seven million inhabitants. Through this favourable situation as well as its proximity to the Rhein-Ruhr Airport and to the Düsseldorf fair and exhibition site, Ratingen has become an exceptionally attractive location for business and industry. The advantages of good communications combined with its beautiful location in the forested fringes of the

Bergisches Land have further added to its appeal.

There is direct access to Ratingen from three Autobahns, as well as via S-Bahn - the district lines - from Düsseldorf and Essen. Ratingen has a great deal to offer in terms of cultural and recreational activities. The municipal theatre provides seating for 640 people. There is a municipal museum and a city hall with a concert hall for 1,300 people. There are modern indoor and outdoor swimming pools. The town is home to the most modern ice-skating rink in Europe. Ratingen does not lack much in the hospitality sector either. There is everything from the modern first class hotel to the cosy inn.

Despite developments, Ratingen has never completely lost its medieval character, and in recent years countless ancient monuments and buildings have been restored. The city thus attracts tens of thousands of visitors annually. Much admired is the **Church of St. Peter and Paul**, one of the oldest basilicas on the

Rolling countryside near Hubbelrath, where one of the most famous golf clubs in Germany can be found.

Rhine, whose towers date from the twelfth and thirteenth centuries. It is situated adjacent to the old **city wall** which has three imposing towers dating from the fifteenth century.

A few minutes away from the church, in a very picturesque meadow, by the river lies the historic moated castle "**Haus zum Haus**". In the 14th century this was the seat of the Lords of Ratingen. Here too, in 1783, Johann Gottfried Brügelmann constructed the first machine-driven spinning mill in the continent. He soon built up a whole factory complex which he called "Cromford", and the clever businessman had his workers - mostly young children - producing gloves, socks, stockings and hats.

The Mansion, a castle-like building designed by no less than Nicolas de Pigage, was built to cater for important visitors. The English garden was designed by the famous Maximilian Friedrich Weyhe. Johann Gottfried Brügelmann died in 1802 at the age of 52. His home "Cromford" is situated in

the Angertal near Ratingen.

Another popular place to visit is the miniature town "**Minidomm**", near the motorway intersection of Breitscheid. Here it is possible to see small-scale replicas of Germany's most beautiful and interesting buildings.

A further attraction of Ratingen is the **Blauer See** (blue lake) with its open-air theatre. The high point of each season is the annual Karl May Festival held in the autumn.

Festivals: The people of Ratingen know how to celebrate. Their inherent jolly spirit is linked to their feeling for traditional culture. Marksmen's festivals are held seven times a year in the town centre and other areas, attracting thousands of visitors from surrounding towns and cities. The most important festival takes place in the city in the first week of August.

But it isn't only the marksmen's associations which celebrate here. The various carnival societies also boast a long tradition going right back in the Middle Ages. It is therefore only natural that the "crowning of the Carnival Prince" is one of the high points of Ratingen's cultural calendar.

The city of the "Dumeklemmer": In the High Street adjacent to the town hall, there is a fountain at the base of which is a sculpture of three cheerful lads stretching out their thumbs towards the onlooker. The existence of this edifice is thanks to an event which took place here in the Middle Ages. When Bishop Suidbert visited Ratingen to convert the populace, the locals slammed the city gates in his face and succeeded in trapping his thumb! It is said that since then all Ratingen folk have been born with a "flat" thumb. Certainly the inhabitants still like to call the city by another name - "*Dumeklemmer*" (thumb trapper).

The "trapped" Bishop is honoured to this day by a restaurant bearing his name - the **Suitbertus Stuben**. It is to be found in the High Street, inside what is perhaps the most beautiful medieval half-timbered house in the city.

192

Neuss is one of the oldest places on the Rhine and one of the oldest cities in Germany. Two thousand years ago the Romans erected the legion's camp "Novaesium" here, at the mouth of the Erft on the Rhine and by doing so they laid the foundations for a steadily growing settlement. Versatile and extensive trade relations by water and land made this city particularly significant as early as the Middle Ages: Neuss was granted Hanseatic rights in 1475. Of the many monuments of the past, the Quirinus Cathedral (the city's landmark), the Obertor and the *Zeughaus* are particularly special sights which are well-worth visiting.

The cornerstone for the **Quirinus Cathedral** was laid in 1209. The cathedral, which was completed hastily in the style of the late Romanesque, became a leading symbol for the self-confidence of the city and its residents. The relics of the Holy Quirinus are still preserved here today.

Alleys and streets around the Cathedral form a district with a special character. Many of the small houses of the Biedermeier period have been renovated with loving care. Thus, cast-iron capitals, arches and stucco rosettes have been restored to new lustre.

The visitor will notice a niche over the high, pointed portal of the **Obertor**, adorned by the statue of the Madonna. In 1475, during a siege of the city by Duke Charles the Bold of Burgung, the Obertor was renamed "Liebfrauentor". Later a wooden statue of Saint Quirinus held vigil for a long time beside the Obertor. It was acquired by the museum in 1906 and is now in the city's historical collection situated on the second floor of the gate's building.

A further impressive monument is the **Zeughaus**, which looms over Neuss' market place with its characteristic silhouette. The former Franciscan Church,

the cornerstone of which was laid in 1637 by the Elector Ferdinand, was used as an arsenal between 1826 and 1864. From that time on the name "Zeughaus" has found its way into common regional linguistic usage. It means warehouse.

The visitor will find a district typical for Neuss in the area of the **Hamtor** and **Neustraße**. Anyone, who has preserved his sense for ambience, will not only be overwhelmed by its bustling activity but also by its characteristic atmosphere of peace and long-standing tradition.

The **Church of St Sebastian** was built between 1718 and 1720 in the style of the Dutch Classicism. It has left an impressive mark on the city's main street to this very day. Seven slender stone pilasters with projecting capitals stand against the crimson brick facade. Through broad windows the light enters

an interior which has been redecorated recently in a way that would accord its significance.

Up until the devastation of World War II, the town centre was characterized by residential buildings of the 17th and 18th century. One of them has outlived all threats of destruction, the "**Haus zum schwatten Roß**", better known today as the "schwatte Päd" (black horse). The exterior of this building, presumably built by the lay assessor Rembold Breuer around 1604, displays a series of remarkable details: iron wall anchors which bear witness to the art of regional smithery and among other things a sign on the house whose theme, a black horse, refers to the name of the house. Hidden in the triangle formed by the streets Klarissastraße, Michaelstraße and Zollstraße, the visitor will come across the back of the house on Michaelstraße 76 which was built in 1609. The strictly geometrical half-timbering impressively testifies to this method of construction, traditional also in the city's development.

Two delicate portals afford entry into the interior of Neuss' former **Franciscan Monastery**. The building became a secondary school in 1803 and housed a grammar school from 1852 to 1889. The resident's pride and passion for collecting items occasioned the first collection of documents relating to town's history in 1845. The documents were kept in this monastery. Thus, with the help of the Prussian king, an important museum came into being at a very early stage.

The **Harmtor Madonna** is one of the regional curiosities which the residents of Neuss are very fond of. The Harmtor consists of two pointed arches of the older inner city wall which have survived. A statue of the Madonna was found here during excavations in 1961. It is now displayed in a small oriel of the Harmtor.

Another Madonna adorns the entrance to the **Marienburg Convent** at the Glockhammer. Until its dissolution in

1802 the two-storey Baroque building housed a branch of the "canonesses regular" (a religious order of nuns following the teachings of Saint Augustine) which was established in 1439.

Rheinstraße 16 is the former residence of Mayor Jordans who held office from 1685 to 1756. Preserved in its original state, it is similar to later buildings of the Napoleonic era. Franz Joseph Jordans was "maire" of his city and later deputy prefect of the "Arrondissement Krefeld".

A relief of great artistic value adorns the entrance of the archiepiscopal governor's residence at **Münsterplatz** built in 1597. It shows the adoration of the three Magi, also a popular theme in Rhineland after Archbishop Reinald von Dasse had brought the relics of the "Three Wise Men from the East" from Milan to Cologne.

The monument made by sculptor Josef Hammerschmidt to the memory of **Theodor Schwann** was unveiled on 6th June, 1909. It stands beside the building

A masksman displays his medals at a *kirmes* in Neuss.

of the main post office, at the start of the pedestrian precinct. The research work done by this scientist, who was born in Neuss on 7th December, 1810, is considered epochal. As the founder of cellular science Schwann was greatly acclaimed throughout the world. He died in Cologne on 11th January, 1882.

The Island of Hombroich: Neuss offers a special attraction for those keenly interested in the arts: the museum "**Island of Hombroich**". You can get there either by public transport from the central station or by car travelling on the Köln-Neuss motorway and taking the Neuss-Reuschenberg exit.

What exactly is the Island of Hombroich? Well, one thing is for certain; it is a definite treat for all art lovers. Six buildings built in a way similar to sculptures are partly hidden in a park and meadowland designed with loving care by landscape architect Dr. Bernhard Korte. The buildings were planned by Erwin Heerich. There is also the house of artist Anatol Herzfeld, and a collec-

tion of his works are on display. Two older buildings are also worth mentioning: a studio and an apartment house as well as the so-called "**Rosa Haus**" where ancient to contemporary works of art are exhibited. There is also a small exhibition room where aquarelles by Paul Cézanne are on display. The actual museum, the **Labyrinth**, houses several collections.

Gotthard Graubner's highly individual display brings the exhibits to life. Ritual objects of the Maori and from Africa are set off against European works from the twentieth century. Khmer sculptures and Chinese statues from the Han Dynasty are juxtaposed alongside paintings by Gotthard Graubner, sculptures by Jean Fautrier and Erwin Heerich. Paintings by Francis Paccabia and Gerhard Hoehme are contrasted with sculptures by Karl Bobek and Fritz Schwegler.

Main highlights are collections from the early Chinese periods of the Han, the Tang and the Ming Dynasties, the Khmer art and works from the the 20th century

Quirinius Cathedral in Neuss, from the 13th century.

by artists such as Hans Arp, Lovis Corinth, Ives Klein, Bart von der Leck and Kurt Schwitters.

This brief account of the museum clearly demonstrates that the Island of Hombroich is more than just an ordinary museum. The whole display is rounded off by musical and literary contributions. The Island of Hombroich, which has chosen "art parallel to nature" as its motto, is open all year round.

Theatres and Restaurants: There is an enormous variety of cultural facilities in town, including the **Rheinische Landestheater**. The reputation of the concerts held in the Zeugenhaus extends far beyond Neuss. European music from the Renaissance all the way to contemporary music is performed. "Musikalischer Frühling" (musical spring) and the international "Tanz-woche" (dance week) are two other popular events known throughout the country.

Yet Neuss does not solely live off its history and culture. The city has a sound, well-structured economy that is keenly aware of the advantages its location offers and knows how to put them to good use. Nissan, Canon, Toshiba, 3M and British Leyland are only a few of the international companies that have established themselves in Neuss.

Even the district round about has a lot to offer. The District of Neuss was restructured during the District Reform of 1970/1975. This reform not only resulted in the inclusion of the city of Neuss into a district (Neuss did not belong to any administrative district since 1913) but also in uniting 33 small communities to form eight towns: Dormagen, Grevenbroich, Jüchen, Kaarst, Korschenbroich, Meerbusch, Neuss and Rommerskirchen.

Neuss, with approximately 409,000 inhabitants, is the tenth largest administrative district in the Federal Republic of Germany. It is in close proximity to Düsseldorf, Cologne, Mönchengladbach, Krefeld and Duisburg. Within a radius of 60 kilometres there is the Ruhr District in the east and the city of Aachen,

The museum "Island of Hombroich".

the Netherlands and Belgium in the west and the south-west.

Dormagen: Dormagen with its 56,000 inhabitants is a modern industrial town in green surroundings. The international enterprise Bayer with its oil chemistry is the main employer, providing one in every six residents with work. In contrast to all the industry is the wild-life sanctuary "**Tannenbusch**" (encompassing an area of 100 hectares) with a botanic path through the woods, a geological park, a biological museum and numerous other recreational facilities. Its reputation extends far beyond the town of Dormagen. The far-flung tract of woodland, the Rhine meadows and the Zons Heath welcome visitors all year round who come to rest and to hike.

Zons: One of the best-preserved examples of a medieval fortified town, is only five kilometres away from Dormagen town centre, and some 20 kilometres south of Düsseldorf. The ancient town of **Zons**, which was built around 1370 to 1400 to defend the area and

Sheep on the Rhine Meadows.

impose customs, is often referred to as the "Rhenish Rothenburg", and its touristic appeal is certainly no less. The largely preserved fortification presents itself as a sturdy rectangle of solid walls and encompasses an area of 300 by 250 metres. The north-east corner of the town is dominated by the imposing six-storey high, square shaped **Rhine Tower**, which provides an imposing gateway to the city. On the side facing the town there is a relief depicting St Peter. Other landmarks of the city include the **Juddeturm** with its cupola roof and the **Church of St Martin.** Between the corner towers on the Rhine side, there are two more turrets. The defensive capabilities of the town were further strengthened by small watch cabins attached to the walls.

The **District Museum**, many well-preserved buildings from the past, cafés and restaurants are situated within the town walls and welcome tourists who come to visit and to stay. In the summertime, open-air theatre is performed on the stage located in the south-east corner of the city. Theatre companies from the region's major cities and towns come to perform.

A good overall view of the city can be had from the Rhine Dyke between the city walls and the river. A little farther to the north, there is the quay for ferries to and from Düsseldorf.

Some eight kilometres south-west of Zons, at the other side of Dormagen and the Autobahn lies the Premonstratensian **Abbey of Knechtsteden**. It was built in the 12th century and is one of the most important Romanesque edifices on the Lower Rhine. The restored basilica with its triple nave, the octagonal tower that rises above its east transept and the Missions Museum, today part of the abbey, are open to the public. Of particular interest is the huge fresco in the western apse showing Christ flanked by Peter and Paul. The man at Christ's feet is Albert von Sponheim. It was he who commissioned the painting upon the abbey's completion in 1160.

Grevenbroich: Grevenbroich with its 59,000 inhabitants is the second largest town in the District of Neuss. The brown-coal opencast mining to the south of the town has left its marks on the country-side. Two of the world's largest thermal power stations are also located here. Sugar-beet is one of the most important crops in this area. The remains of the **Castle of Grevenbroich**, the Premonstratensian Monastery in Langwaden and the ruins of the Castle of Hülchrath are sites of great historical interest.

The Commune of Jüchen: The Commune of Jüchen is made up of 26 small and large towns and villages that chiefly concentrate on farming. It encompasses an area of 72 square kilometres and has 21,000 inhabitants. The villages and towns of this commune have a remarkable past. The oldest settlements date back to prehistoric times. The location of the so-called "Villa Jucunda" to the west of Jüchen is known to date from the Roman Period. The **Castle of Dyck** is situated in the commune between Damm, Aldenhoven and Steinforth. It is a picturesque late-Baroque moated castle with a manor-house and two castles at the front. The park is designed in the style of the English landscape gardens, contains rare plants, and trees which are over 200 years old. The collection of weapons was gathered from the arsenal of the Princes of Salm-Reifferscheidt and is today one of the most valuable in Europe.

The **Monastery of St. Nicholas** is in close proximity of the Castle of Dyck. It used to be a simple forest chapel. Today the tomb of the Prince and the old Count of Salm-Reifferscheidt-Dyck and Krautheim is situated in this monastery.

Kaarst: Today Kaarst has 40,000 inhabitants, and is known as the town of resettlers. The majority of the houses were built only within the last decades. Be that as it may, Kaarst was actually founded as long ago as the 5th century by the Franks. The Celts had already settled in Büttgen (a part of the town) in 100 B.C. The small Romanesque ba-

Brown coal excavations are digging deeper and deeper into the landscape.

silica, which has been restructured and rebuilt many times in the past, is well worth a visit. The nave was torn down in the middle of the 19th century and was replaced by a brick building. In 1963 the Romanesque building could finally be "exhumed" from the subsequent renovations and extensions and was reconstructed on old foundations. The three-storey west tower built around 1150 has been preserved. It is roofed with an octagonal slated pyramid.

Korschenbroich: The town of Korschenbroich was created from five formerly independent communes and has approximately 28,000 inhabitants. It is a well-liked commune and a popular destination for excursions. Despite its rural character many business enterprises have settled here. Metal-working plants, building contractors, a brewery, textile factories, clothes manufacturers and gravel pits are a few of the most important industries.

The **Castle of Myllendonk**, an impressive brick building with Gothic and Baroque elements, is located in the Niers Lowlands in the town area. The **Castle of Liedberg**, which was built in the 14th century, is in a part of town also called Liedberg. **Fürth House** is situated to the east of Liedberg. Surrounded by a moat, it is a beautiful building dating from the 16th/17th century. It is primarily a half-timber construction with brick infils. Fürth House is the last example of a moated castle in the Rhineland built in the half-timber technique.

Meerbusch: Meerbusch is one of the most sought-after residential areas in Greater Düsseldorf with a population of some 50,000. Again, due to its favourable location, many industries are located here as well. The **Dyckhof in Büderich** is one of the old manor-houses which are today classified as a historical monuments. Its architecture is of great interest. **Gripswald House** in Ossum-Bösinghoven is a simple, two-storey brick building from the 16th century.

The **Castle of Pesch**, which is also situated in Ossum-Bösinghoven, used to be the lordly residence of a big landowner and was built in 1906. It reflects the opulence of the local gentry at the turn of the century.

The Commune of Rommerskirchen: The Commune of Rommerskirchen has 11,200 inhabitants and encompasses a total area of 60 square kilometres. Even in early history it is mentioned as a settlement. Numerous archaeological finds from the Romans and the Franks have been discovered. The oldest secular monument in Rommerskirchen is the **Castle of Anstle**, which was probably built in the 12th century. The moated castle was converted into a Baroque château in 1772. Several old village churches in the area are testimony to the high quality of ecclesiastical architecture of times past.

Over 50 castles and citadels make the District of Neuss an interesting area for those interested in history. There is plenty of scope for cyclists and hikers too, and indeed anyone who wishes to discover the area's unspoilt charm.

Sculpture in the park of Hombroich island.

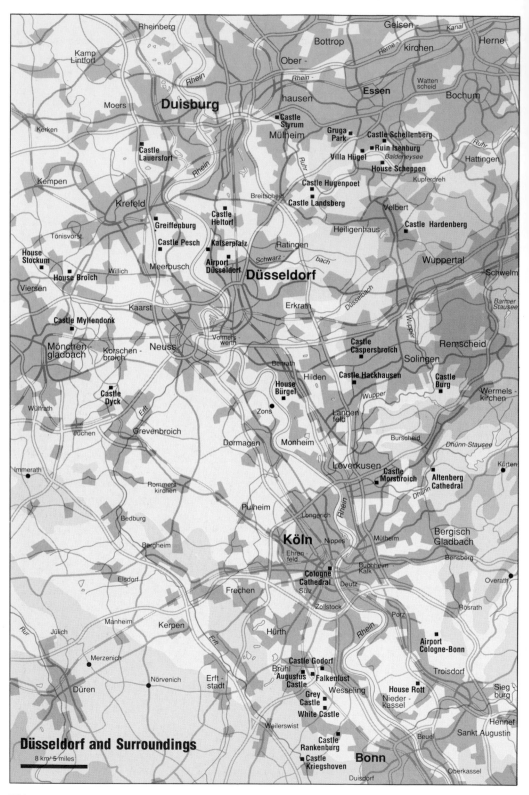

Düsseldorf and Surroundings

8 km / 5 miles

Rheinberg
Kamp Lintfort
Gelsen-kirchen
Herne
Kanal
Bottrop
Ober-
Essen
Watten-scheid
Bochum
Moers
Rhein
hausen
Duisburg
Mülheim
Gruga Park
Castle Schellenberg
Ruin Isenburg
Kerken
Castle Styrum
Villa Hügel
Baldeneysee
Hattingen
Castle Lauersfort
Rhein
Ruhr
House Scheppen
Ruhr
Kempen
Castle Hugenpoet
Kupferdreh
Krefeld
Breitscheid
Castle Landsberg
Velbert
Tönisvorst
Greiffenburg
Castle Heltorf
Heiligenhaus
Castle Hardenberg
House Stockum
Castle Pesch
Kaiserpfalz
Ratingen
Schwarz-
bach
Wuppertal
House Broich
Willich
Meerbusch
Airport Düsseldorf
Düsseldorf
Schwelm
Viersen
Kaarst
Erkrath
Düsselbach
Barmer Stausee
Castle Myllendonk
Volmers-werth
Wupper
Mönchen-gladbach
Korschen-broich
Neuss
Benrath
Castle Caspersbroich
Remscheid
Solingen
Hilden
Castle Hackhausen
Castle Burg
Wermels-kirchen
Castle Dyck
Erft
Grevenbroich
Zons
House Bürgel
Langen-feld
Wupper
Wülfrath
Juchen
Dormagen
Monheim
Burscheid
Dhünn-Stausee
Kürten
Immerath
Rommers-kirchen
Leverkusen
Castle Morsbroich
Altenberg Cathedral
Dhünn
Pulheim
Bedburg
Longerich
Rhein
Bergheim
Köln
Nippes
Mülheim
Bergisch Gladbach
Bensberg
Elsdorf
Ehren-feld
Buchheim-Kalk
Overath
Rur
Mänheim
Jülich
Kerpen
Frechen
Cologne Cathedral
Deutz
Sülz
Rösrath
Merzenich
Zollstock
Porz
Airport Cologne-Bonn
Düren
Nörvenich
Erft-stadt
Hürth
Erft
Castle Godorf
Brühl
Augustus Castle
Falkenlust
Wesseling
House Rott
Nieder-kassel
Troisdorf
Sieg-burg
Grey Castle
White Castle
Hennef
Weilerswist
Castle Rankenburg
Castle Kriegshoven
Bonn
Beuel
Sankt Augustin
Oberkassel
Duisdorf

The **"island" on the Rhine: Kaiserswerth**, which has been integrated as part of Düsseldorf since 1929, is about 10 kilometres north of the city centre. It is generally considered to be the most interesting of all Düsseldorf suburbs, having retained most of its historically evolved characteristics. Nowadays it is difficult to imagine that it was once an island. During the course of centuries the section of the river that separated the island - the *"Werth"* - from the mainland dried up.

The English church historian, the venerable Bede, who died in 735 A.D., wrote that the Anglo-Saxon missionary Swidbert built a small church on this island, dedicated to St. Peter. Suidbert, sent to convert the *Bukterer*, had become embroiled in a militant dispute between this tribe and the Lower Saxons. He escaped to the banks of the Rhine. The Franconian custodian Pipin and his wife Plektrud afforded him protection and gave him the island in the Rhine. Suidbert thereupon built a Benedictine monastery. According to legend, the exceedingly successful missionary was canonized by Pope Leo III in the presence of Charlemagne.

In honour of the saint, the island was known for a time as Suitbertswerth. Between 824 and 864 the church was repeatedly destroyed by heathen Normans. When it was rebuilt approximately a century later, it was dedicated to St. Suidbert. After a further one hundred years - 1050 to 1072 - Henry III and his son, later Henry IV, converted the small church into the present Basilica, still standing on Stiftsplatz. The tower was removed in 1243 by Count Gernandus - for strategic reasons, as he claimed, and he promised to rebuild it in "calmer times". A proof of his well-intentioned but never realized plans is still visible in the form of a tablet affixed to a wall on the west side. The full text

reads: "Anno Domini 1243. Gernandus, fearing imminent war, has had this part of the church razed and has had the tower forcibly removed, so that it may not be a landmark that overwhelms the castle. In more fortunate times it will be rebuilt in better stone." To confirm this, a relief of a hand raised in solemn oath can be seen over the western portal of the church. It is not known why neither Gernandus nor his descendants carried out the vow.

The centuries passed and there was a major upset in 1702 during the Spanish war of succession, when the basilica was severely damaged - in the same battle that brought about the complete destruction of Barbarossa's Imperial Palace, (see below). In the 1870s, extensive renovation work was carried out on the basilica, during the course of which the two east towers were rebuilt. To-

Preceding pages, the Lower Rhine Plain near Düsseldorf. Right, a typical landmark of the Lower Rhine area.

gether with the two western towers they were a clearly visible symbol of Kaiserswerth until their destruction by artillery fire during World War II. Despite the fact that there are no towers now, the Basilica is still an imposing sight. Also the triple-naved interior with its wide transept and tripartite choir in Romanesque style is impressive.

One of the most precious objets d'art is the **St. Suidbert Screen**. It is on display in the relique chamber in the choir. It is a splendid piece of craftsmanship, influenced by the so-called "Cologne school", of great importance for goldsmith art in medieval times. Several generations worked on this screen. It was completed around 1330. The screen contains reliques of St. Suidbert and his companion, St. Willeikus. Twice a year, on the first Sunday in July and the Sunday after the 3rd September, the memorial day of canonisation, the golden screen was ceremoniously paraded through the streets of Kaiserswerth. Meanwhile this custom has been dis-

continued in order not to jeopardize the work of art. On the occasion of the 1250th anniversary of Suidbert's death the church was accorded a rare distinction. Pope Paul VI granted it the title "Basilica minor".

Nearby, the **Kaiserpfalz** - the Palace of Barbarossa - dates back to a fort built by the Emperor Heinrich II. It played a vital role in German history. By the middle of the 13th century no less than 57 imperial decrees had been issued here. It was also the site of a spectacular coup. The Archbishop of Cologne, Anno von Köln, kidnapped the future Emperor Heinrich IV, at that time a twelve-year-old prince whose mother, Anno thought, had a baneful influence on him. He was taken by ship to Cologne and the Imperial insignia, which were kept in the chapel, were taken at the same time. Nothing remains from this time.

In 1174 Emperor Friedrich I, known as Barbarossa because of his red beard, granted Kaiserswerth the charter as the customs levy city of the *Reich*. The

The ruins of Barbarossa's Imperial Palace in Kaiserswerth.

building was duly expanded: black basalt and strachyet were primarily used. The foundation walls are 580 metres thick. A letter from Philippopel which he wrote to his son in 1189 enquiring how construction work was progressing shows how dear this fort was to him. On walking through the ruins we notice that bricks were also used for construction work. But these date from a much later time, when further expansion work was carried out by the Archbishop of Cologne, Salentin von Isenburg. An invoice dating from 1576 proves that 35,000 bricks were used in the construction work. The end of the war of succession in 1702 was also the end of the proud palace. The victorious imperial troops blew up the mighty fort.

In the centre of Kaiserswerth is the idyllic market square, replete with chestnut trees. Stolid ancient houses encircle this square. Equally picturesque are the houses around **Stiftsplatz** with the Basilica. On the north side of this square is the birth place of the Jesuit priest Friedrich Spee (1591 - 1635) famous for his opposition to the notorious "witches" persecution.

Krefeld: Travelling north-west, we soon come to Krefeld, a genuine Prussian city. First mentioned 800 years ago, it was granted a city charter in 1373 and became renowned for its textile industry which started in the 16th century when Menonite refugees introduced weaving to this region. Frederick the Great further encouraged this trade by granting Krefeld a virtual monopoly. Thus Krefeld soon prospered. The Prussian influence can be seen everywhere. The houses are built in "Weaver-house style" - the dimensions being double the width of the weaving looms. French and English competition was fierce but Krefeld nevertheless managed to consolidate its fame as a "city of velvet and silk". The textile museum affords detailed information on this development as well as displaying textiles from all over the world. Apprentices and textile engineers still study the skills of the

Before it was destroyed by the French in 1702, the palace was an imposing site.

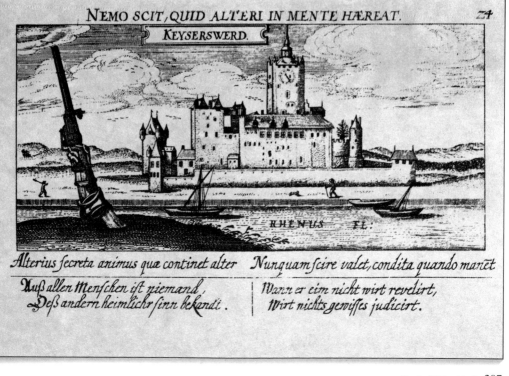

NEMO SCIT, QUID ALTERI IN MENTE HÆREAT.   74

KEYSERSWERD.

RHENUS   FL:

Alterius secreta animus quæ continet alter   *Nunquam scire valet, condita quando manet*

Auß allen Menschen ist niemand,   *Wann er eim nicht wirt revelirt,*
Deß andern heimlicher sinn bekandt.   *Wirt nichts gewisses judicirt.*

past. In the house by the **Andreasmarkt**, 20,000 objects are on display, the biggest such collection in Germany. But also the **Kaiser-Wilhelm Museum** in a Neo-Renaissance building on **Karlsplatz** is worth a visit. On display are works of art from Gothic times to the present day.

Ludwig Mies van der Rohe built the houses **"Lange"** and **"Esters"** on **Wilhelmshofallee**. Both are now museums of contemporary art. Railway enthusiasts will appreciate the **"Schluff"** train pulled by the venerable locomotive Fürst Bismarck XV, which runs between the recreation area **Hülser Berg** and **St. Tönis**.

Should all this have whetted your appetite, you can have a fine meal at the **Koperpot** in Rheinstraße, or **Gasthof Korff** in Kölner Straße

Duisburg: A few kilometres to the north-east of Düsseldorf lies Duisburg. What, you may ask, is the connection to Düsseldorf? Answer: the **"Deutsche Oper am Rhein"** - the regional opera company - one of the most important opera houses in Germany. The company commutes regularly between the two cities, an exemplary fusion of two theatres. Famous artists and conductors appear here and a substantial number of artists that started out from here have since become world famous.

Gerhardus Mercator, the famous mathematician, geographer and cartographer, was not really a native of this city but he lived here for more than forty years. He was born in Flanders, studied in Löwen, where he acquired artisan skills, viz: copper etching and the assembly of scientific appliances. In 1569 he drew the first viable map for seafarers. His masterpiece is the great Atlas which he himself engraved. When he died in 1594, his pupils continued his work. One of them drew the map of medieval Duisburg with its city wall, showing the island-like parts of the city in the Rhine. But history began much earlier in Duisburg.

In 883 A.D. Norman knights spent the

Left, the "Silk Weaver", a symbol of the town of Krefeld. Right, displaying wares at the Flax Market in Krefeld.

winter months here. Before they passed on in 884 they burnt down the city of Thusberg as it was then known.

The only fire now is that in the furnaces, which still give Duisburg the reputation of being the centre of the steel industry. Duisburg also has the world's largest inland river port. 60 million tons are loaded and unloaded here annually. That is a greater volume than many international coastal ports. Trade also has a long tradition. As early as the 15th century the city became a member of the *Hanse*, that legendary medieval association of cities which developed, above all, due to the necessity of protecting oneself from marauding bands of robbers and pirates.

During the last war the old city centre was almost totally destroyed, but meanwhile a lot of reconstruction work has been carried out. One case in point is the **Dreigiebelhaus**, the oldest building in the city, dating from the 16th century, where artists now live. In **Oberstraße** there are remnants of the **city wall** dating from the 14th century. About 200 years older is the **Collegiate Church**, situated in the suburb of **Hamborn**. Part of the original cloister still exists.

One of the most notable municipal museums is the **Niederrheinische Landesmuseum** (State Museum of the Lower Rhine) in the **Immanuel Kant Park** housing an exhibition especially devoted to Gerhardus Mercator. As the Romans founded a number of settlements and cities along the Rhine, the collection also includes various exhibits dating from that time.

A further interesting exhibition is to be found in the **Old Town Hall** in the suburb **Ruhrort**. On display are exhibits showing the development of river shipping. Beginning with the primitive log ship we can follow the development to the radar-driven barge and push tug assembly. Children will enjoy the diorama displays especially. The **Museum der Deutschen Binnenschiffahrt** (The Museum of German Merchant Shipping) is situated in **Dammstraße**.

The museum Haus Lange and Haus Esters, built by Mies van der Rohe. A mecca of modern art.

Art lovers should not miss the **Wilhelm-Lehmbruck Museum**. On display is a virtually complete collection of the sculptures of this internationally famous artist, also famous as a painter and etcher. Wilhelm Lembruck was a member of the Prussian Academy of Arts. His most famous sculpture is the "kneeling woman" dating from 1911. It is now on display in front of the museum. Contemporary art and pictures dating back to the beginnings of expressionism are also on display.

Duisburg also has an internationally famous zoo. The enterprising director managed to acquire some small whales called Jacobitas, which are found in the South Atlantic. These cute mammals as well as the dolphins and white whales have been trained to perform numerous acrobatic stunts.

Although geographically Duisburg is part of the Lower Rhine, it is still considered part of the **Ruhr**. Within the city confines the Ruhr merges with the Rhine at the **Ruhrort**. The Ruhr is not really a famous tourist region, yet nevertheless it has much to offer. The Ruhr is an area full of surprises, full of contrasts, full of diversity. Coal is juxtaposed by High-Tech, industrial areas and one of the most important Higher Education areas of Europe, where science and research fuse, where the development for the next decades is planned. The Ruhr has more than 10,000 sports grounds, making it the biggest physical recreation area in Germany. More than 100 museums recall the past. In this area there are more theatres than in New York or Paris. The Ruhr is home to 16 Symphony Orchestras. And all this in a quality that need not shun comparison with any other city in the world.

Old farm houses, moated castles and palaces can be found in remote nooks, a living testimony to the fact that the Ruhr was once a romantic forest and agricultural region before the smoke stacks and winding towers took over. Come and see for yourself. You too will come to the conclusion that the supposed

The Lehmbruck Museum in Duisburg. Wilhelm Lehmbruck is one of the most important sculptors of the century.

210

"negative" reputation is quite unfounded. Quite the contrary ; it is - and will remain - a vital part of Germany, despite the decline of the coal and steel industry, which has naturally not left the area unscathed. The economic turbulence will result in a structural change, which will revitalise the area.

Perhaps the idea that was touted some years ago of fusing all the industrial cities of the Ruhr to form one gigantic megalopolis will be taken up again. Or perhaps - providing the German constitution allows this - a twelfth Federal State will develop. Currently this conurbation is the area with the greatest administrative expenditure in Europe. No fewer than 150 Lord Mayors, Mayors and regional councillors have their say in more than 60 City Halls and regional assemblies.

About 150 years ago approximately 28,000 people lived here, tilling the land, breeding cattle and trading. In 1965 the population had reached 5.5 Million - an increase that would seem to justify the initially mentioned superlatives. But clichés don't die easily and not even the rural and cultural charm still very much in evidence can change that. A survey revealed that while only ten per cent of German citizens would like to live here, ninety per cent of the people that do live here would like to continue to do so.

The industrial buildings dating from the last century were designed by architects who tried to overcome the dichotomy between what merely served its purpose and what was beautiful as well. That is why many of these buildings are now protected by the state and are deemed to be "palaces of labour". Another industry that has managed to survive all the turmoil of the past few years is the brewing industry. No matter whether it be the small breweries from Bochum and Bottrop or the big ones from Dortmund and Essen - they and their international distribution network are witness to the fact that the Ruhr is a notable beer producing region as well.

Duisburg's rowing regatta has an international reputation.

In 1793 Christian Friedrich Meyer returned from Düsseldorf to Prussia, where in Brockhausen he served in the royal court. During the trip he noted his impressions which he published in 1797 as a travelogue; "The mountains which give the region its name - Bergisches Land - start about one and a half hours from Düsseldorf on the road to Elberfeld and as they start to increase in height the fields grow less the forests more dense".

His account does leave a rather misleading impression of the nature of the countryside east of the Rhine between Düsseldorf and Cologne. The region isn't really mountainous at all. While Sauerland to the east has high peaks and Eifel opposite has rounded, sweeping summits affording distant views, the country in between is much more rolling than mountainous. There is little to take one's breath away, so gentle is the transition from hill to valley.

The highest point is less than 500 metres high and is actually a "Berg": **Unnenberg** rises above the dammed valley near **Marienheide**; and if its name is really derived from *unda*, the Latin word for wave, then this would be a far more apt description of the character of the region than the suffix "berg".

The Bergisches Land is dissected by rivers; The Wisser, Sieg, Bröhl, Agger, Leppe, Sülz, Dhünn, Wupper, Itter, Ruhr and many smaller streams and tributaries have all played their part in shaping the land, as has the more recent damming of the valleys to create the **Bergische Seenplatte** (lakes). Water comes from above as well. Indeed, with an annual rainfall of 1,300 millimetres, the Bergisches Land is about the wettest place in Germany.

In 1891 the **Eschbachtal Dam** near Remscheid was inaugurated to provide Germany with its first fresh water reservoir, with the first buttressed dam wall. Further similar projects followed as man

and masonry subdued the forces of nature, starting in the Wupper region and spreading to the Agger, the Wahnbach, the Dhünn. The **Dhünntal Dam** is the largest dam in the Federal Republic. It has a water surface area of 440 hectares, and a volume of 81 million cubic metres. The Eschbachtal Dam held back a mere 1.1 million cubic metres.

In the days before steam, the water was the source of the region's great prosperity. The water-wheels turned and the hammers rattled for the scythe and the clothmaker, the smith and the powdermaker. On the 18 streams around Remscheid there was soon no space for any more machinery. In Wuppertal it was the dyers and the bleachers who drew their wealth from the water.

The boundaries of the Bergisches Land are defined by the Rhine in the west, the Ruhr in the north and the Sieg in the

Preceding pages, lush landscapes in the outskirts of Düsseldorf. Left, the west window of Altenberg Cathedral is the largest church window in Europe. Right, Altenberg, the centre of spiritual life in the Bergisches Land.

south. At the bend in the River Wupper in the East, at the pretty border town of Beyenburg, the Bergisches Land meets the "Mark" (the marches) of the Middle Ages, where Franconia met Saxony and where the Rhineland met Westphalia.

When the region fell to Prussia after the downfall of Napoleon, the limits of the Bergisches land were increased to encompass an area including Gimborn Neustaadt and Homburg, once separate dominions of the Empire. They now form part of the "**Upper Bergisches**" - the region between the Wupper and the Sieg. The region between the Wupper and the Ruhr is known as the "**Lower Bergisches**", while the term "**Middle Bergisches**" refers to the area encompassed by the large bend in the river between the towns of Remscheid, Solingen and Wuppertal.

The whole region is therefore defined by rivers rather than mountains. And, contrary to what Meyer implies, the mountains didn't even give the region its name. Bernhard Schönneshöfer in his "History of Bergisches Land" published in 1895, explained quite categorically that the name derived from Burg, the German word for a castle, and not Berg meaning a mountain. "The Bergisches Land, also known as Bergische or Berg gets its name from the castle (Burg) Berg an der Dhünn, the seat of the local dukes. The only feature resembling a mountain in this vicinity is the outcrop of rock on which the castle is perched".

It was only through the names of the dukes who were called "De berge", officially "de monte" that the region first acquired any historical reference. Until their day, it lay off the beaten track, for it was a harsh and unfertile land. It was settled only very gradually, by the Saxons who came from the east and the Franks who came from the west. Finally in 870, the Bergisches Land was annexed as part of Franconia to the German Reich. Only with the arrival of feudalism, from the beginning of the 11th century, did the importance of the area begin to rise.

The famous "Bergisches" breakfast.

Meyer was right about one thing. In addition to the abundance of water, the only notable characteristic of the region was indeed its forests, which allowed only a small amount of grazing and agriculture. As was the case in his day, agriculture today becomes less and less feasible the further one travels from the west. Only in the "Garden of the Bergisches Land", to the west of the Wupper around Leichingen, is there any worthwhile cultivation of crops.

The story of the Knight Huhn of Windeck typifies the poor quality of the land. He travelled to the distant capital of Düsseldorf with specimens of the local bread in order that the Elector Johann Wilhelm could gauge the nature of the soil and thus set a suitable level of taxation. Presenting his loaves of rough oatmeal and bran, he swore that nothing better could be grown in his distant Sieg Valley. While this undoubtedly provided the court with a great source of amusement, taxes remained low. The land was indeed very poor. The populace

had always been dependant on crafts and trade. But then, with the arrival of ore mining and the development of the iron industry, there arose a clear division of labour. Manufacturing industry brought economic prosperity to the region, which was to last well into the 19th century.

There is mention of tools being produced in the region as early as 1125. Towns famous for certain products gradually developed, including **Remscheid** which became a producer of scythes from 1600 and **Solingen**, which became known as the "city of blades". The name of the town has been a trademark since 1938. In **Velbert** in the Lower Bergisches Land, the production of locks and keys was deeply rooted in the traditional way of life as early as the 15th century. And even today the pretty town is officially referred to by the pun "Velbert - an open city". Silk and velvet were produced in **Elberfeld** and **Barmen**. The region acquired its first machine-driven spinning mill in **Ratingen**,

Half-timbered buildings are a common sight in the Bergisches Land.

and in 1838 the steam locomotive made its first appearance in the Rhineland.

Today, **Wuppertal** is the main centre of the Bergisches Land. It lies on the "Bergisches Autobahn" and it is the home of the "Bergisches University". In front of the station at Eberfeld, two lions stand as a reminder that it was the "Bergisches Lion" which first appeared on local Coats of Arms, in the days before the "Lion of Limburg".

In the 19th century the population of Eberfeld grew from 21,000 to 126,000 within a space of 80 years. It took the same time for the numbers in Barmen to swell from 19,000 to 117,000. The conurbation on the Wupper was then colloquially known as "Little Manchester". By 1929, the towns and villages had so fused into one conglomerate mass that, much to the disapproval of the populace, a new name was found to describe it: Wuppertal.

To help hold the place together, a new form of transport was put into use along an artery where no roads were possible; a suspension railway running for 13.3 kilometres along the Wupper, mostly high above the water. Travelling at a height of 12 metres, today the whole trip takes 32 minutes. Any initial concern about the safety of this unique journey has been eliminated; to this very day there hasn't been a single accident, which isn't a bad record when one considers that over a billion people have used it.

"I love my town", writes Else Lasker-Schüler, who dedicated a little poem to the river: "And I am proud of the railway, a twisted mass of iron, a scaley serpent which clings to its lifeline as, with baleful eyes, it plies its way above the jet black river. Alarming creaks, as the gondola flies through the skies, along the water, with heavy ringed feet."

But another name already existed for Wuppertal: "Muckertal" - "The valley of the bigots" - on account of the numerous religious denominations which had established themselves in the region. The Bergisches Land had become Protestant very early on. A hundred years after Martin Luther, there were only 74 Catholic churches remaining, as against the 84 of the protestant faith. All the large Baroque churches in the Upper Bergisches Land were Evangelical, and out of a total of 16 new churches in to be built in the region between 1743 and 1789, only two were Catholic, four were Reformed and ten were Lutheran. Lutherism and Calvinism with their beliefs in predestination, interpreting economic success on earth as a reflection of favourable things to come in Heaven, were a fitting religion for the people of the Bergisches Land.

In the 7th century, from his island which later became known as Kaiserswerth, it was St Suidbert who first converted the populace to Christianity. Having denied the Vatican, further missionaries now followed in his footsteps. The most famous was Adolf Clarenbach, a Latin scholar from Lennep. He was also perhaps one of the most renowned martyrs of the Reformation. When he volunteered his moral support to a colleague at the ecclesiastical court in Cologne, he was himself arrested and later burned at the stake outside the gates of the city. His memorial lies in the entrance of the church in Lennep.

Many churches in the region look similar to this one. They are easy to recognise with their plain interiors. They are churches of the new order, where the liturgy is no longer at the centre, but the sermon, the Holy Communion, and the music. Whereas in the churches of the Catholic Baroque, the pulpit, the organ and the altar were all an integral part of the interior design, they now stand out from the plain background as individual, easily recognisable features.

Occasionally in the villages there are more richly decorated church interiors to be found. They are old churches from the Middle Ages, whose frescoes were whitewashed after the Reformation. Today they are exhibited again to show how, at one time, the story of the Bible was celebrated in pictures; almost sensual, even drastic, but never pious.

Apart from looking at churches, there are other ways of tracing the history of the Bergisches Land; through the preserved shacks along the banks of the Wupper to the elegant abodes of the upper classes, Bergisches Baroque houses, with with their grey slate facades and green shutters. Or through the lions which often appear on the local coats of arms.

But history is revealed more clearly when one visits the very first important settlements in the region, namely **Burg** on the River Wupper and **Altenberg**, situated above the River Dhünn. Altenberg was the original seat of the Dukes of Berg. With the extension of their domains to the east, they soon needed another castle, and chose a site close to a strategic crossing point on the River Wupper. A new name was found for the original castle of the Dukes, namely *mons vetus* - Altenberg.

Duke Adolf of Berg handed over this property to the Cistercians, who remained there for a short time before transferring the whole building down to the river! While on the Wupper, 10 kilometres to the north, the Dukes were putting the finishing touches to their new castle, the monks in their grey habits were busy dismantling the old one, transporting the stones down into the valley and using them to construct their very own, brand new monastery. It was founded in the year 1145 and is known by historians as Altenberg I.

Little remains of the original edifice today, for its walls were soon to provide the foundations for Altenberg II, built from 1259 to 1379. The length of time required for its construction reflects the problems of the age: there were earthquakes and floods; wars and plagues. But it still stands today, the so-called **Altenberg** "**Cathedral**". Although the building is very definitely Gothic, with its pointed arches and vaults and buttresses, it lacks the enormity and grandeur one normally associates with Gothic Cathedrals. There are no high towers and there is also very little superfluous

The unique suspension railway in Wuppertal.

decoration, for it was built as a plain and simple place of worship for the monks. But it is a masterpiece of architecture all the same, a jewel in its green valley, standing out against the hills like a highly polished stone.

The windows too are generally plain in design, though as building time progressed, the skills of the builders also developed to enable walls of stone to be replaced by glass. The magnificent West Window is the showpiece of the whole building. It is indeed the largest church window in Europe, 8 by 18 metres, a whole wall of glass which glows golden in the afternoon light.

The new castle of the Dukes of Berg gave that place its name: **Burg on the Wupper**. There are two monuments in the inner courtyard which testify to local history. One shows Adolf, the founder of the dynasty and the second Engelbert II, the martyr. It was he who had the original fortifications converted to give the building its present form: part of the walls were demolished to

make way for a palace with two floors. The separate ladies' apartments with their heated rooms were a luxury reflecting the wealth and status of the Dukes. Engelbert had been Imperial Administrator, guardian and tutor of the prince since 1222. Presumably his power had become too great, for he was killed by a distant relative in 1225.

After Engelbert's death, the Dukes' castle went the same way as their monastery on the Dhünn: in the middle of the last century, both lay in ruins, and it was only with a revival of historical awareness that the two buildings were duly restored to their former glory.

But the decline had set in well before that. In 1380 Berg became a duchy and in the same year Burg on the Wupper was converted to a hunting lodge. A small village on the Rhine had become more important; the capital of the Dukes of Berg was moved to Düsseldorf.

While the "Society for the Restoration of Burg on the Wupper" was busy rebuilding the castle, a few kilometres upstream a brand new edifice came into being: the **Müngstener Bridge**, a railway bridge connecting Solingen and Remscheid. Whereas most buildings up to that time had been designed by architects, this was purely the work of engineers. It was completed in 1897 and it still stands today, a miracle of 19th century engineering; its single cast-iron arch spans a full 170 metres, 107 metres above the river.

Since its completion it has been repainted twice. Today a new coat of paint would be more expensive than the original cost of its construction; 2,646,386 marks and 25 pfennigs. At the time the bridge was built it was looked upon as a major breakthrough in communications, a great symbol of industrial progress, of the new age. Today, it is a great tourist attraction.

And such is the development of the Bergisches Land; from a centre of Royalty to an important economic region to what it is today - a large area for recreation. Even at the turn of the century **Old traditions die hard.**

people came to visit the region. And as if there wasn't quite enough confidence to use local names, the hotels and inns that sprang up had names like "Zillertal" and "Bergisches Nizza". They still exist today and the area has meanwhile become a centre for hiking and even winter sports, in and around places like Eckenhagen, Morsbach and Marienheide. In the summer time the lakes are full of boats and bathers.

One of the most interesting destinations lies within a stone's throw of Düsseldorf, in the Düssel Valley between Hochdahl and Mettman: **Neandertal**. The beautiful valley is named after a composer of songs from Jan Wellem's day, Joachim Neander, the author of such famous hymns as "Praise to the Lord, the Almighty, the King of Creation..." Today, of course, the valley has much greater claim to fame, for it gave its name to Homo Neanderthalesis, the Neandertaler.

In the summer of 1859, quarry workers were busy chiselling away in one of the many deep caves hollowed out in this deeply indented valley by the waters of the River Düssel. They discovered bones, and according to the natural scientist Johann Carl Fuhlrott, they were the bones of early man.

For a long time Fuhlrott's hypothesis remained highly contentious. Virchow, the famous doctor from Berlin, could only confirm that the skeleton, while undoubtedly that of a human, showed signs of rickets, while Richard Wagner publicly declared that it was that of a Dutchman. There were many other theories; some claimed that the bones must have been those of a Cossack killed during the Napoleonic wars, seeing similarities in the bow-legs and the slanting forehead.

But Fuhlrott's theory was finally proven correct and early man became synonymous with the hymn writer, and the Bergisches Land, a region where, although one might have to do a bit of burrowing, one never has to dig too deep to discover the past.

Festivals always involve a brass band.

COLOGNE CATHEDRAL

As the train rolls slowly through Deutz on the right bank of the river, and then over the mighty steel bridge construction, the traveller has a chance to take in one of the finest urban panoramas in the world: the Rhine promenade with the colourful façades and gables of Cologne's historic centre, and rising above it all the mighty towers of the cathedral.

Downstream, supported by a single tower, the unmistakeable silhouette of the Severin bridge can be discerned through the steel lattice of the Deutz Bridge. Meanwhile the most important sacred Gothic edifice, the most ambitious construction project ever planned and executed within Germany, advances inexorably until the train finally comes to a halt scarcely 200 metres from the main portal. When Archbishop Konrad von Hochstaden put the church's seal of approval on the repeated wish to start

building, Cologne was the largest city in Germany. It was also the third-largest in Europe - after Paris and Constantinople - and was also one of the wealthiest. In 1164 the Shrine of the Magi had been transferred to the original cathedral. It was planned that Cologne should be given a more fitting repository for this unique treasure, to which pilgrims travelled from all over the world. The architects took the French cathedrals, in particular Amiens, as their model. They retained, however, the five-chambered nave of the 11th-century basilica. Cologne Cathedral was to become the most perfect example of "French" sacred architecture, the zenith of Gothic cathedral building. *Omnium ecclesiarum, quae sunt in Allemania, quasi mater et matrona* - the "Mother of all Churches in Germany" - thus the edifice was decribed by an English chronicler.

The chancel was completed in 1320, and dedicated in 1322. The transept and the nave, however, remained unfinished. Building work stopped in 1560; and

Preceding pages, main entrance of the Cologne Cathedral. Below, modern art meets Gothic architecture: the Ludwig Museum stoops before the Cathedral.

was only revived at the beginning of the 19th century, when historic consciousness was awakened and new enthusiasm for the Middle Ages resulted in a Gothic revival throughout Europe.

In 1843 King Friedrich Wilhelm laid the foundation stone marking the beginning of the resumption of construction work. The cathedral was finally finished in 1880, a masterpiece of Romantic conservation of a historic monument. In 1944 the bombing raids devastated the Old Town and the main station nearby. As if by a miracle, however, the cathedral remained intact.

The charm of Cologne Cathedral lies in the unmatched harmony of the individual elements, and the perfect unity of its external appearance. For this reason, any sightseeing tour of the cathedral should begin with a tour of its circumference. The interior is 144 metres long, 44.8 metres wide and 43.5 metres high. The towers, 157 metres high, were the tallest in the world in 1880; one can still climb to a height of 95 metres up the South Tower by means of a staircase with over 509 steps. The interior, with its circular columns and windows embellished with tracery, corresponds to the contemporary idea of weightlessness and the necessity of striving for perfection. The visitor's gaze is drawn automatically past the buttresses to the windows and the vaulting soaring above.

The Shrine of the Magi is situated in the middle of the chancel. The gold sarcophagus was started in 1184; it was the biggest of its kind in Western medieval Christendom, created by the renowned goldsmith Nicholas de Verdun. The Cross of Gero, a large-scale example of Othonian art, was produced in 969-76 in Cologne. It is the oldest larger-than-life-size wooden representation of the Crucifixion to be produced north of the Alps, and is thus the second treasure to find a permanent place within the chancel. The Baroque frame was added in the 17th century. The Treasury contains the most valuable items belonging to the Cathedral.

Cologne: Travelling upriver, just beyond the industrial metropolis of Leverkusen, where the chemical giant Bayer Leverkusen is based, and before the river valley narrows and the "Romantic Rhine", that continues right up to Mainz, begins to enchant the visitor, lies the old Roman capital, et hillije Kölle, "Holy Cologne". With a population of about one million, Cologne is not only the biggest city on the Rhine, it is also one of the most beautiful in Germany.

Few contest the fact that this is so; opinions differ, however, as to why this should be the case. Could it be because of the view? Or the magnificent cathedral? Because of the people, especially during the pre-Lenten Carnival? Because of the museums or the post-modern pavement architecture? Or because of the effect of all these elements together? If one considers the matter from a historical point of view, it is certainly surprising. In Spring 1945 there was so little left of the original city that the allied troops added insult to injury by suggesting that it would perhaps be easier to rebuild Cologne somewhere completely different. Only the Cathedral still stood proudly amongst the ruins; 157.38 metres high. Even that, too, had not entirely escaped damage. But the city had not been killed stone dead. Hanging outside a house which would normally have overlooked the Rose Monday Carnival procession was, as in previous years, the standard notice with which the local citizens let out their front room for this one day: "Room with a view". Underneath, a wit had scribbled three laconic words: "Bring your own floorboards".

It was not just a case of renewing the floorboards. Around the Gothic cathedral the city was completely built anew; which often meant in the style of the old. The Old City, for example, surrounding the **Church of St. Martin the Great**

and the Town Hall (15th-16th centuries), will offer the visitor no reminders of the nights the city was bombed during the war. This is the entertainment and tourist heart of the city; for some years now, the traffic has passed through this area underground. There is now nothing to hinder access to the Rhine through the lovely "**Rhinegarten**" park.

Only since 1888 has the Rhine actually flowed directly through Cologne; until that date, it flowed past the city. Cologne lay on the left bank; across the river was - even in Roman times - the "Land of the Barbarians" (thus it is written on a tombstone in the museum). Even Adenauer declared that Asia began on the right bank of the Rhine.

In 1888 Cologne's boundaries were redrawn to include **Deutz**, known since time immemorial as "the town opposite Cologne".

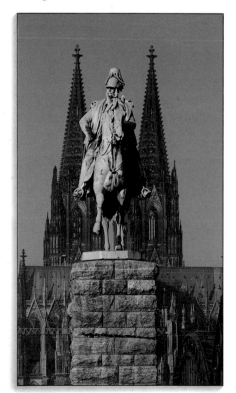

Left, in the mood at the Cologne carnival. *Right*, Cologne Cathedral alone is well-worth the short journey upriver.

Cologne could now expand on both the right and the left banks of the Rhine; the inner city, if measured according to its medieval boundaries, today occupies just one percent of the total area of the city. It is the part which visitors to the city will want to see because it contains most of the historical sights.

It was here that in olden times two Roman roads met and crossed. Their present-day names are **Hohe Strasse** and **Schildergasse**. There is the cathedral quarter, begun by one of the archbishops, Konrad von Hochstaden, in 1248 - and finished in 1880 by a Hohenzollern emperor. Directly next door stands the **Roman-Germanic Museum** containing the multiplicity of treasures still being unearthed from the ground in the area; all one has to do, it seems, is to dig. Next door again is the **Wallraf-Richartz Museum**, still the subject of controversy but undoubtedly one of the most significant buildings of the century. It contains two separate museums and is named after two benefactors; the second collection, the **Ludwig Museum**, bears the name of an honorary citizen of Cologne, a patron of the arts and chocolate manufacturer. Deep inside the building can be found a magnificent concert hall, the **Philharmonie**.

Cologne's Romanesque Churches are amongst her architectural jewels. Since their restoration (which was largely completed by 1985), they bear witness again to the city's vanished opulence; in the Middle Ages it was the wealthiest north of the Alps. Later on the Prince Bishops developed their love of Baroque pomp in Bonn and elsewhere, tearing down a number of old churches. Cologne, however, a secular city since the famous Battle of Wörringen in 1288, subsequently lapsed into poverty. Today it can only boast one large Baroque church: **Our Lady of the Assumption** in Marzellenstrasse, not far from the cathedral.

Cologne, famous as a city of art, is also a city renowned for its art of living. It was not long ago that a much-trav-

Interior of the Cologne Cathedral.

elled man, who was neither a native of the city nor even a German citizen, claimed that the gastronomy industry was better developed in the meeting places of the city than in New York. The latter is, after all, the capital of half the world. The favourite meeting place remains the **Kölsche Weetschaff**, a tavern which calls to mind the most extensive brewing tradition in the land (including Bavaria!) With a rough charm which takes some getting used to the *Köbesse*, as the waiters are called here, mostly deposit glasses of beer before guests unasked. So crucial is the role played by the foaming brew in the city's identity that it shares the name given to the local dialect: *Kölsch*.

Bonn: The post-war political situation has brought more change to Bonn and Godesberg than any previous reform. More than three years after the cessation of hostilities, on September 1st 1948, the Parliamentary Council came together between the stuffed mammals and preserved birds, next to the fish and amphibians of the still-intact museum of the research biologist Alexander König. On May 8th of the following year the constitution was agreed, and two days later Bonn was declared the temporary capital of the new Republic with a total of 200 votes to 176.

Bonn, which is now over 2,000 years old, had already savoured the taste of power and influence, as the residence of the electoral archbishops of Cologne. After that, the palace of **Clemensruhe**, the 18th-century **Poppelsdorf Castle** and the **Residence** in the Hofgarten became home to the sciences, for since 1816 they have housed the Friedrich Wilhelm University of the Rhineland, founded in 1786.

The political heart of Bonn developed farther to the south towards Godesberg and Plittersdorf between the Hofgarten and the main station (built in 1885 and immortalized over 25 years ago by Heinrich Böll's "Face of a Clown"). It still lives in a state of uneasy tension in relation to the town's image as a long-

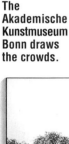

The Akademische Kunstmuseum Bonn draws the crowds.

established retirement centre as well as an the historical home of the aristocracy. Traces of this awkward equilibrium can be seen everywhere. Bonn, as an administrative town, has the highest percentage of civil service widows - and the highest percentage of dogs - per head of population.

The official residence of the Chancellor of the Federal republic is the **Villa Hammerschmidt on** the Adenauer Allee. Here, too, is the Schaumburg Palace, the **Federal Chancellery** (completed in 1977), and the Alexander König Zoological Museum. The **Bundeshaus** (at present undergoing rebuilding) and the Members' House (Langer Eugen), on Görrestrasse, have become the town's symbols.

Here, surrounded by busy commercial activity, the roots of Bonn's local history and the buildings dating from the town's Golden Age - the **Collegiate Church**, the palaces and the **Town Hall** - can be found packed together within a small area. Bonn became the base for a

Roman legion as long ago as 11 B.C.. About 50 years later the camp was fortified, and mentioned by Tacitus as the castra bonnensis. During the third century two Roman officers named Cassius and Florentius were condemned to death as martyrs because of their Christian faith. Their final resting place was on the spot where today the octagonal crossing tower of the Collegiate Church, 92 metres high, soars up to heaven. According to legend it was St. Helena, the mother of Constantine the Great, who financed the building of the first church here as a mausoleum for the two Christian marytrs. In approximately 1050 the **Collegiate Church of St. Cassius and St. Florentius** was constructed on the site of the Carolingian basilica. The church, originally built for a monastery, boasts a Romanesque cloister which - even in this stone jungle - encloses a little garden.

Not far away stands **Ludwig van Beethoven** (1770-1827), who, since 1845, has occupied a pedestal in front of

The grave of Heinrich Böil in the Eifel. The writer was a Nobel Laureate and campaigner for peace.

the Post Office, housed in a former nobleman's residence. Despite the image projection of political personalities, the genius of music is still the best-known native son of Bonn, and the visitor will encounter him several times on a journey across town: in the **Beethoven House** and the **Beethoven Hall**. His birthplace at Bonngasse 20 has been the town's house of remembrance for its great son for over a century now. It contains and archive and a museum, and - in the room in which he was born - a marble bust. Further on, you can see him again, larger than life in concrete. Here, too, is his famous determinedly grim, expression, which probably has less to do with the Tax Office opposite than with the futuristic concert hall behind: the Beethoven Hall , which was constructed between 1957 and 1959.

The town's focal point has always been the market place, with its baroque **Town Hall** built in 1737 after a design by Michael Leveilly. Its soft pastel-toned facade dominates the town centre. Charles de Gaulle and John F. Kennedy both spoke from its sweeping staircase to the citizens of the town, and hence to the citizens of the Republic. During the "Bonn Summer" festival, cultural events take place here. For the rest of the time, there is a daily market.

The town's heyday as an electoral city can also be experienced just outside its boundaries. On the **Kreuzberg** - with the Venusberg, one of the town's twin hills - there stands a little Pilgrimage Chapel dating from 1628. In 1746 it was transformed by the Elector Clemens August into an architectural jewel by the addition of a new wing and a staircase by the celebrated Balthasar Neumann. Behind the chapel lie the **Kottenforst** woods, once the royal hunting grounds and planted specifically for that purpose. The fashion of riding to hounds necessitated long open tracts of land, clearings as straight as a die through the forest. It has left its mark on the terrain to this day. Much else has disappeared, including the summer

hunting lodge "Herzogsfreude", built in 1854 and containing 100 rooms. It was pulled down on the orders of the occupying French army, and the materials used in the construction of the fortifications in Wesel.

Two other buildings also dating from the end of this feudal period have, however, remained: **Augustusburg Castle** and the **Falkenlust Hunting Lodge** in Brühl, which lies between Bonn and Cologne. For almost half a century, between 1725 and 1768, the most famous artists of the time were involved in the construction of a palace for Elector Clement Augustus. Then the most magnificent royal residence in the Rhineland was finished at last - and Clement Augustus was dead, having expired in 1761. From time to time the Federal government uses his legacy to invest state banquets with a little feudal pomp. Television audiences are all familiar with the staircase by Balthasar Neumann, said to be the most beautiful in the world.

Konrad Adenauer was the Federal Republic's first Chancellor.

TRAVEL TIPS

Getting There

BY AIR

The Rhein-Ruhr Airport in Düsseldorf-Lohausen is one of the largest and most modern airports in the German Federal Republic.

Annually over 10 million charter and regular passengers use the extensive airport facilities. 30 charter and 30 national airlines provide for regular and rapid connections between Düsseldorf and domestic and international destinations on four continents; 50 other airlines land in Düsseldorf from time to time. Singapore Airlines is the most recent airline to open up services to Düsseldorf. Passengers will arrive at Düsseldorf's Central Station in 13 minutes by taking the S–Bahn from the underground station at the airport. The trains leave every 20 minutes. From the station it takes only three minutes to get to the Altstadt by S-Bahn. Other cities in the North Rhine-Westphalia, the German Federal Republic and in neighbouring countries can also be reached by train from the station at the airport. Buses will take passengers to downtown Düsseldorf, Essen, Krefeld and Ratingen. During trade fairs a special shuttle bus service is available between the airport and the exhibition grounds. Many hotels offer shuttle services to and from Düsseldorf Airport.

Airport Information. Tel: (0221 Düsseldorf's area code) 42 12 23.
Airport Customs. Tel: 42 16 92.
Airport Police. Tel: 42 12 66.

A FEW AIRLINES

Aer Lingus. Tel: 4 21-64 76
Air Canada. Tel: 4 21-63 35
Air France. Tel: 4 21-62 72
Alitalia. Tel: 4 21-63 24
Austrian Airlines. Tel: 4 21-65 24
British Airways. Tel: 4 21-66 86

Condor Flight Service. Tel: 4 21-61 93
Hapag Lloyd Flight Service. Tel: 4 21-66 98
Iberia. Tel: 4 21-67 03
Japan Airlines. Tel: 4 21-63 60
KLM. Tel: 4 21-62 75
LTU Air Transport. Tel: 4 21-63 25
Lufthansa. Tel: 4 21-8 88-5
NUR Touristic. Tel: 4 21-67 31
Olympic Airways. Tel: 4 21-63 75
Sabena. Tel: 4 21-62 84
SAS Scandinavian Airlines. Tel: 4 21-62 88
Singapore Airlines. Tel: 13 20 02
Seissair. Tel: 4 21-62 91
Tjaereborg. Tel: 4 21-66 22
Touristic Union International. Tel: 4 21-67 24
Last Minute Service. Tel: 4 21-64 36.

BY RIVER

Düsseldorf is the landing point and overnight berth of cruises on the river Rhine with the cruise ships of the KD Köln-Düsseldorfer line.

For further information contact:
KD Köln-Düsseldorfer Deutsche Rheinschiffahrt AG, Frankenwerft 15, 5000 Köln 1. Tel: 0221-20 88-288, Telex 08 881 326, Telefax 0221-20 88-229. In Düsseldorf Tel: 32 60 72.

BY RAIL

Düsseldorf's Central Station at Konrad-Adenauer-Platz is one of the most modern railway stations in Europe. Good connections to places near and far guarantee punctual arrival and prompt departure. EC Euro City trains, IC Intercity trains, InterRegio trains, FD Express trains, D fast trains as well as buses in all directions, subway trains and trams are available to passengers.
Travel Information. Tel: 35 34 94.

BY CAR

Düsseldorf can be easily reached from all directions. Via motorway A 1 from the north when coming from Hamburg or Bremen, via motorway A 2 when coming from Hannover, motorway A 44 from the east when arriving from Kassel, motorway A 3 from the south when driving from Frankfurt. There are many different connections from the west: motorway A 44 and A 46 when coming from Belgium, Luxembourg and south of the Netherlands via Aachen; when driving from north of the Netherlands take motorway A 3 or A 44, A 52 or A 61.

In addition to parking lots in the city, there are 30 multi-storey and underground car parks in Düsseldorf. Parking on the city street is controlled by parking meters. A lot of hotels have car parks for their guests.

The international traffic laws prevail in Germany. Cars drive on the right side of the road and overtake on the left. In streets that have equal right of way and do not have any "give way" or "stop" signs, the person coming from the right has right of way. Cars circulating around the central island have the right of way in roundabouts.

ADDRESSES FOR MOTORISTS

Allgemeiner Deutscher Automobilclub e.V. (ADAC), Kaiserswerther Straße 207, Himmelgeister Straße 63, Oststraße 49. Tel: 3 10 93 33.

ADAC Roadside Assistance (round-the-clock). Tel: 1 92 11, Automobilclub von Deutschland e.V. (AvD), Heinrichstraße 153. Tel: 63 25 29.

Automobilclub ACE, Friedrich-Ebert-Straße 40. Tel: 35 37 41. ACE Roadside Assistance Stations. Tel: 3 5 40 00.

Police Emergency Number Tel: 110. Accident and Rescue Service, Fire Department Tel: 112, Emergency Doctor Service Tel: 192 92. Ambulance Service. Tel: 38 89 89.

TRAVEL ESSENTIALS

VISAS AND ENTRY REGULATIONS

This should not present any difficulties. Every travel agency should take care of all formalities for you. Members of the European Community need not attend to any formalities. They only need their identity cards or passports.

CUSTOMS

The usual amount of semi-luxuries (alcoholic beverages, tobacco products, tea) and perfumes can be imported and exported. The regulations are more generous to members of the European Community. Your travel agency will advise you before your departure.

In case of any doubts we recommend that you contact the Customs Authorities for further details. Tel: Düsseldorf 4 21 69 27.

MONEY AND CURRENCY

The currency in the German Federal Republic is DM = Deutsche Mark. There are 100 Pfennigs in one Mark. There are 1 Pfennig, 2 Pfennig, 5 Pfennig, 10 Pfennig (also called "Groschen" or "Zehner"), 50 Pfennig, 1 Mark, 2 Mark and 5 Mark coins. Bank notes consist of the 5 DM, 10 DM, 20 DM, 50 DM, 100 DM, 500 DM, 1000 DM notes; more bank notes are currently being issued. Some approximate exchange rates:

1 £ = 2.91 DM	1 US$ = 1.55 DM
100 Yen = 1.03 DM	1 c$ = 1.34 DM
1 A-$ = 1.20 DM	100 FF = 29 DM

WHERE TO CHANGE MONEY

You can change money from Monday to Friday during business hours at all Banks in Düsseldorf (see section: Shopping, Business Hours), at the exchange office of the Deutsche Verkehrs- und Kreditbank at the railway station, open daily from 7.30 a.m. to 8.00 p.m. and at the exchange office of the airport, open daily from 6.15 a.m. to 10.00 p.m. Checks and credit cards are basically accepted everywhere.

IMPORTANT PHONE NUMBERS

Düsseldorf's area code	0211
Telephone Information (domestic)	1188
Telephone Information (international)	00118
Operator (domestic)	010
Operator (international)	0010
Telegram Accepting Office	1131
Stock Exchange News	1168
Television Programs	11503
Poems and Short Prose	11510
Daily News	1165
Weather Report and Forecast for Holiday Areas	11600
Special Events, Exhibitions, Trade Fairs	11516
Road Report	1169
Weather Forecast	1164
Speaking Clock Announcement	1191

NATIONAL TOURIST OFFICES

Contact these offices before your departure to obtain detailed information about Düsseldorf:

Amsterdam: Duits Reis-Informatiebureau, Hoogoorddreef 76, NL-1101 BG Amsterdam Z.O.. Tel: (020) 97 80 66. Telex: 15408 dzt am nl.

Brussels: Office Allemand du Tourisme, Duitse Dienst voor Toerisme, 23, Rue du Luxembourg, B-1040 Bruxelles. Tel: (02) 51277 66/51277 44, and 512 36 62, Telegram Address: Tourallem Bruxelles.

Copenhagen: Tysk Turist-Central, Vesterbrogade 6 D III, DK-1620 Kobenhavn 1. Tel: (01) 127 095.

London: German National Tourist Office, 61, Conduit Street, GB-London W1R OEN. Tel: (071) 734 26 00/734 58 53, Telegram Address: Germantour London.

Los Angeles: German National Tourist Office, 444 South Flower Street, Suite 2230, Los Angeles CA 90071. Tel: (213) 688 73 32.

Madrid: Oficina Nacional Alemana, San Augustin 2, Plaza de las, Cortes, E-Madrid 14. Tel: (91) 429 35 51/429 58 77.

Milan:.Ente Nazionale Germanico per il Turismo, Via Soperga 36, I-20127 Milano. Tel: (02) 28 20 807. Telex: 312 271 dz tita i.

Montreal: Office National Allemand du, Tourisme, General National Tourist Office, 2 Fundy, P.O. Box 417, Place Bonaventure, Montreal, P.Q.H5A 1B8. Tel: (514) 878 98 85.

New York: German National Tourist Office, 747 Third Avenue, 33rd floor, New York, Ny 10017. Tel: (212) 308 33 00. Telex: 49572363 gerrto.

Paris: Office National Allemand , du Tourisme, 9, Boulevard de la Madeleine, F-75001 Paris. Tel: (1) 40 20 01 88.

Stockholm: Tyska Turistbyran, Birger Jarlsgatan 11, Box 7520, S-103 92 Stockholm. Tel: (08) 14 50 95.

Tokyo: German National Tourist Office, Deutsches Kultur-Zentrum, (OAG-Haus), 7-5 56 Akasáka, Minato-ku, Tokyo 107. Tel: (03) 586 03 80.

Vienna: Deutsche Zentrale für Tourismus e.V. (DZT), Vertretung in Österreich, Schubertring 12, A-1010 Wien. Tel: (0222) 513 27 92.

Zurich: Deutsches Verkehrsbüro, Talstraße 62, CH-8001 Zürich. Tel: (01) 221 13 87.

Representatives of the German National Tourist Office

Hong Kong: German National Tourist Office, c/o Lufthansa German Airlines, Landmark East, 5th floor, 12 Ice House Street, Hong Kong. Tel: 5 21 42 75.

Johannesburg: German National Tourist Office, c/o Lufthansa German Airlines, 22, Girton Road, Parktown, Johannesburg 2193. Tel: (011) 643 16 15.

Ljubljana: Predstavnistvo DZT, TTG Turisticna poslovalnica, Titova cesta 40, YU-61000 Ljubljana. Tel: (061) 314 242. Telex: 313 -70 yu fertur.

Mexico City: Oficina Nacional Alemana, de Turismo, c/o Lufthansa Lineas Aéreas Alemanas, Paseo de la Reforma 76, Mexico 6, D.F.. Tel: 5 66 03 11.

Moscow: German National Tourist Office, c/o Lufthansa German Airlines, Kusnetzky Most, 3, Moscow. Tel: 2 23 04 88/2 23 05 76.

New Dehli: German National Tourist Office, c/o Lufthansa German Airlines, 56 Janpath, New Dehli. Tel: 32 11 33.

Oslo: Tysk Turistbra, Klingenberggt. 7, Postboks 1761, Vika, N-0122 OSLO 1. Tel: (02) 42 23 80.

Sao Paulo: Centro de Turismo Alemao, c/o Lufthansa Linhas Aéreas, Alemas, Av. Sao Luis, 71-1 andar, 01046 Sao Paulo, SP. Tel: (011) 256 10 54.

Sydney: German National Tourist Office, Lufthansa House, 12th floor, 143 Macquarie Street, Sydney 2000. Tel: (02) 221 1008.

Tel Aviv: German National Tourist Office, c/o Lufthansa German Airlines, 1 Ben Yehuda Street, Tel Aviv. Tel: (03) 65 80 35.

Toronto: German National Tourist Office, 1290 Bay Street, Toronto, Ontario M5R 2C3. Tel: 968 1570. Telex: 06-217 578.

GETTING ACQUAINTED

GOVERNMENT AND ECONOMY

Düsseldorf is the capital city of the Federal State of North Rhine Westphalia which along with other federal states forms the Federal Republic of Germany. The city lies on the River Rhine, 77 Kilometres to the north of the country's capital, Bonn.

Two separate German states were created in 1949 after World War II when Germany was liberated from fascism by the allied powers: in the east the German Democratic Republic, a socialist country, and in the west the Federal Republic. Since the spectacular developments in east-west relations which began in the autumn of 1989 and led to the election of a democratic government in East Germany, preparations for the reunification of East and West Germany are now running at full tilt. This historic event took place in October 1990, and a single German general election will follow in December. The reunification will add a further five federal states to the united Germany, which will continue its close links to the west and remain part of NATO and the EC.

Düsseldorf is a modern metropolis with a rich history and a versatile cultural tradition. Railway lines and roads from all directions lead to Düsseldorf; the airport links the city to the entire world. As a State capital, Düsseldorf is far more significant than just another industrial area in North Rhine Westphalia. The stock exchange, banks, the Chamber of Industry and Commerce, industrial associations and the Federation of Trade as well as many international companies have a seat or perhaps even their headquarters here. Apart from heavy manufacturing industry (for example, Thyssen and Mannesmann in the steel and tube industry), the service and trading sectors are of great importance. Düsseldorf, as a political and economic centre, is host to many congresses and international trade fairs and exhibitions.

Düsseldorf is an international city. It maintains a close relationship with its twin towns: Karl Marx City (now reverted to Chemnitz) in the German Democratic Republic, Reading in England, Haifa in Israel and Warsaw in Poland.

GEOGRAPHY AND POPULATION

Düsseldorf is spread out on the right and left side of the Rhine. Each side is linked with the other by a number of bridges. But of a total area of 217 square metres, 204 are situated on the right bank. The city extends over 25 Kilometres from the north to the south and 18 Kilometres from the east to the west. In Düsseldorf the Bay of Cologne broadens to the lowlands of the Lower Rhine. The river winds its way through the city whose highest hill is the Sandberg in Hubelrath at 165 metres above sea level; the average height in Düsseldorf is 38 metres. The exact position of the city, with Johanneskirche at Martin- Luther-Platz being the centre, is 51° 13' 32" northern latitude and 6° 46' 58" eastern longitude.

Düsseldorf has approximately 600,000 inhabitants and thus it is in the lower third category among the top ten largest cities in the Federal Republic of Germany. Almost 80,000 "foreigners" reside in the cosmopolitan city of Düsseldorf, two thirds of whom are labourers and clerks. Over 100,000 people from the outlying towns commute to work in Düsseldorf every day. Almost half of the population is Roman Catholic, 1/3 is evangelical. All inhabitants of Düsseldorf live tolerantly side by side with unbelievers and believers of many other religions.

TIME ZONES

All of Central Europe is in one time zone, Central European Time (CET): Greenwich Meantime plus 1 hour. From the last Sunday in March to the last Sunday in September all watches are set an hour ahead of standard time.

CLIMATE

The temperate climate typical of Central Europe is moderated by the Gulf Stream. The winters, only occasionally very snowy, are not unbearably cold. The average temperature in January is 2.5°C; that does not mean, however, that it cannot get colder. The average temperature in July is 18°C; on some days it may get a good deal hotter. It can rain in all seasons.

WEIGHTS AND MEASURES

In common with most other European countries, the metric system is used in Germany.

1. Linear Measures
The unit is the metre (m).
1 metre = 100 centimetres (cm) = 1000 millimetres (mm)
1000 metres = 1 Kilometre (km).
1 inch = 2.54 cm
1 foot = 0.305 m
1 yard = 0.914 m
1 statute mile = 1760 yards = 1609.34 m.

2. Square Measurement
The units are hectares and square metres.
1 square Kilometre (sqkm) = 100 hectares (ha) = 1,000,000 square metres
1 hectare (ha) = 10,000 square metres.
1 square inch = 6.4516 square centimetres
1 square yard = 9 square feet = 0.836 square metres
1 acre = 4046.7 square metres = 0.40467 hectares
1 square mile = 640 acres = 2.59 square kilometres.

3. Body Measurements
The unit is the cubic metre.
1 cubic metre = 1,000,000 cubic centimetres.
1 cubic yard = 27 cubic feet = 0.765 cubic metres.

4. Measures of Capacity
The unit is litre (l).
1 cubic metre = 1000 litres.
1 imperial pint = 0.57 litres.

5. Weights
The unit is the kilogramme (kg).
1 ton (t) =1000 kg
1 kilogramme = 1000 grammes (g).
1 ounce = 28.35 g
1 lb = 453.6 g

ELECTRICITY

The supply voltage is 220 volts A.C.

BUSINESS HOURS

Basically, shopping hours are 8.30 or 9.00 a.m. to 6.30 p.m. Monday to Friday. Smaller shops, especially in suburbs or in the country are closed between 12.30 and 3.00 p.m. Shops can stay open longer on Thursdays; the larger ones in the centre of the city remain open until 8.30 every Thursday night giving their clients the chance to go late night shopping. Shops may stay open till 2.00 p.m. on Saturdays. They may also remain open until 6.00 p.m. on the first Saturday of every month. The last four Saturdays before the Christmas Holiday are long Saturdays meaning that shops are open all day.

Banks are open from Monday to Friday from 8.30 a.m. to 12.30 p.m., and from 1.30 to 3.30 p.m.. On Thursdays they are often open until 6.00 p.m. The post office on Charlottenstraße 61 is open from Monday to Saturday from 8.00 a.m. to 9.00 p.m. and on Sundays from 10.00 a.m. to 6.00 p.m..

Public offices (also consulates) are open in the morning from Monday to Friday. The shops, banks and post offices at the Central Station and the airport give travellers the opportunity to shop or take care of urgent matters on Sundays. They are also open after regular shops have closed on working days.

PUBLIC HOLIDAYS

The following days are observed as official public holidays in the German Federal Republic:
New Year's Day, 1st January
Twelfth Night
Good Friday, **Easter Sunday and Easter Monday**
May Day, 1st May
Ascension
Whit Sunday, **Whit Monday** (Pentecost)
National Holiday (German Unity Day), 17th June
Day of Prayer and Repentance
Christmas Day and Boxing Day, 25th and 26th December.

There are two more public holidays in Düsseldorf and in the entire state of North Rhine Westphalia:

Corpus Christi Day
All Saints' Day, 1st November.

Monday before Lent is not a public holiday but it is a festive day in the truest sense of the word; it is the culmination of the carnival season which begins on 11th November.

FESTIVALS

47 Markmen's Associations and 68 Carnival Associations help preserve the traditions in Düsseldorf. Hoppeditz is Prince Carnival's fool and the carnival season begins with his awakening and ends on Ash Wednesday - with his burial. The carnival is celebrated in over 200 festivals and balls in halls and on the streets and in public places. The procession on Monday before Lent is one of the highlights.

The marksmen celebrate their traditional festivals in different parts of the town from May to August. The major marksmen's festival is at the same time the largest country fair on the Rhine and is celebrated in mid-July on the fairgrounds of Oberkassel's river bank.

There are many festivals throughout the year: the Kö-Festival, the Ehrenhof Festival and many others in different parts of the town and in the Altstadt. The summer occasions a competition for children that involves cartwheeling in the Altstadt. The Hofgarten Concerts are held from May to October.

To honour Saint Martin's memory all children of Düsseldorf march through the streets of the city on the night of the 10th November carrying self-made lanterns. The saint mounted on a horse leads the way. The Christmas Market and the Santa Claus Market are held at Schadowplatz beginning at the end of November.

RELIGIOUS SERVICES

Adventists' Community, Stockkampstraße 32. Tel: 46 42 53.

Altkatholishe Kirche (Catholic Church), Neubrandenburger Straße 15. Tel: 70 85 75.

Anglican Church, Rotterdamer Straße 135. Tel: 45 27 59.

Apostolic Community, Cantadorstraße 11. Tel: 35 03 99.

Bahà'i Community. Tel: 700 91 90.

The Christian Community, Teerstegstraße 58. Tel: 4 3 42 20.

Protestant Community, General Union, Hohe Straße 16. Tel: 1 39 09 0.

Protestant Community Services, Langerstraße 20a. Tel: 73 53-0.

Protestant Church in the Rhineland, Church Administration and District Church Office, Hans-Böckler-Str. 7. Tel: 45 62-0, Other facilities:, Rochusstraße 44. Tel: 36 10-1.

Student Community, Witzelstraße 76. Tel: 34 62 68.

Travellers' Aid Society, Hauptbahnhof. Tel: 36 28 28.

Protestant Free-church Community (baptists), Luisenstraße 51. Tel: 37 26 70.

Protestant Methodist Church, Hohenzollernstraße 32 . Tel: 35 77 95.

Free Protestant Community, Bendemannstraße 16. Tel: 35 84 08.

Bohemian Brethren, Remscheider Straße 6. Tel: 37 52 95.

Islamic Community, Erasmusstraße 14. Tel: 31 69 77.

Islamic Centre, Worringer Platz 18. Tel: 16 11 85.

Jewish Community, Zietenstraße 50. Tel: 48 03 12.

Catholic Municipal Deanery, Hubertusstraße 5. Tel: 39 50 61.

Association of Municipalities of the Catholic Parish, Hubertusstraße 5 . Tel: 39 50 64.

Catholic University Community, Brinckmannstraße 15. Tel: 33 43 41.

Catholic Youth Welfare Office, Hubertusstraße 5. Tel: 39 50 65.

Union of Catholic Welfare Work for Young Girls, Schloßallee 2. Tel: 21 30 31.

Church of Jesus Christ, Mörsenbroicher Weg 184. Tel: 62 67 45.

New-Apostolic Church. Tel: 27 92 60, 15 28 38.

Dutch Ecumenical Community. Tel: 50 22 91.

Greek Orthodox Community, Am Schönenkamp 1. Tel: 74 10 51.

Orthodox Community Centre (Russian, Rumanian and Ukranian, Orthodox Community), Werstener Feld 65. Tel: 76 22 36.

Orthodox Community of the Holy Archangel, Pattscheider Straße 30 . Tel: 76 22 36.

Serbian Orthodox Community. Tel: 63 89 60, 42 25 03.

Independent Protestant-Lutheran Church, Eichendorffstraße 7. Tel: 43 30 32.

COMMUNICATIONS

NEWSPAPERS AND PERIODICALS

Düsseldorfer Express (tabloid) daily, Königsallee 27. Tel: 13 30 10.

Düsseldorfer Anzeiger, advertising paper, weekly, Blumenstraße 22. Tel: 13 80 90.

Düsseldorfer Rhein-Bote (advertising paper), weekly, Münsterstraße 94 . Tel: 48 30 21.

NRZ Neue Rhein Zeitung, Rhenish-Westphalian newspaper, for Düsseldorf (independent, open to new opinions), daily (supplement every Tuesday: AKKU, magazine for young, people), Schadowstraße 80. Tel: 16 70 80.

Rheinische Post; Newspaper for politics and the Christian culture, (Düsseldorf's largest newspaper), daily, Zülpicher Straße 10. Tel: 50 50.

WZ Westdeutsche Zeitung, News about Düsseldorf (supraparisan), daily, Königsallee 27. Tel: 83 82 0.

Handelsblatt, economic and financial newspaper, Industriekurier, daily Mo-Fr, Kasernenstraße 67. Tel: 8 38 80.

Biograph, reports on the cultural scene in Düsseldorf, monthly, Citadellstraße 14. Tel: 32 96 30.

Düsseldorf à la Carte, a culinary guide to interesting hotels and restaurants, annually, (in Bielefeld).

Düsseldorf Magazin, the magazine for the friends of, the city of Düsseldorf around the world, quarterly, Presseamt, Marktplatz 2. Tel: 899 31 03.

Düsseldorfs Überblick, cultural magazine with an extensive calendar of events, monthly, Zollhof 15. Tel: 39 10 01-3.

Prinz, the illustrated magazine of the city of Düsseldorf; 4 weeks of music, theater, sports and art, Oststraße 115. Tel: 13 37 55-59.

International newspapers and magazines are on sale at the airport, the railway station and at many other points in the city.

RADIO AND TELEVISION

You not only listen to radio programmes of the Westdeutscher Rundfunk and the neighbouring Radio Luxembourg RTL but strong transistor radios can receive broadcasts from the entire world. And there is also Radio Düsselwelle, a private radio station.

WDR broadcasts a third, regional programme in addition to the national German television stations ARD (*Arbeitsgemeinschaft der öffentlich-rechtlichen Rundfunkanstalten der Bundesrepublik Deutschland*) and ZDF (*Zweites Deutsches Fernsehen*). Other channels can be received via cable or satellite. You can watch up to 19 television channels in hotels - not only in German.

POSTAL SERVICES

The post office 1 on Charlottenstraße 61 (Tel: 16 30) is open from Monday to Saturday from 8.00 a.m. to 9.00 p.m., on Sundays from 10.00 a.m. to 6.00 p.m.. The other post offices close at 5.30 p.m. on working days and at noon on Saturdays. The post office at the airport has the following phone number: 41 55 276/7. Other important phone numbers of the German Federal Post after office hours: outgoing mail 1 63 19 80, incoming mail 1 63 19 51, express delivery 163 24 33. You can make international phone calls from all post-offices; you also have the possibility to send and receive faxes or telexes; a lot of hotels offer these services to their clients and you can also place international calls from your hotel.

EMERGENCIES

ACE Breakdown Service Station. Tel: 35 40 00.

ADAC Emergency Service. Tel: 1 92 11.

Aids Assistance. Tel: 35 37 95.

Medical Emergency Service. Tel: 1 92 92.

Chemist's Emergency Supply. Tel: 11 41.

DRK German Red Cross. Tel: 6 21 11.

DRK Ambulance Service. Tel: 6 21 13 27

Fire-Brigade, Rescue Service, First Aid. Tel: 1 12, 3 88 91, 38 89 89.

Lost-Property Office, Heinrich-Erhardt-Straße 61, Monday to Friday 8.00 a.m. to 12.30 p.m., 2.00 p.m. to 3.00 p.m. Tel: 8 99 32 85.

Maltese Emergency Service. Tel: 37 02 12.

Maltese Emergency Service. Ambulance Service. Tel: 37 33 88.

Medical and Meteorological Information. Tel: 1 16 01.

Police, Emergency Number. Tel: 110.

Police Headquarters. Jürgenplatz 5. Tel: 8 70 -0.

Society for the Prevention of Cruelty to Animals. Animal Home, Rüdigerstraße 1. Tel: 65 18 50.

Dental Emergency Service. Tel: 66 6291/2.

Lost-Property Office of the Rheinbahn, Graf-Adolf-Platz 5, Monday to Friday 8.00 a.m. to noon, 1.00 p.m. to 4.00 p.m.. Tel: 5 82 14 69.

Lost-Property Office of the Federal Railways, Central Station, Monday to Friday 8.00 a.m. to 1.00 p.m.. Tel: 3 68 04 54.

WHERE TO STAY

ACCOMMODATION BUREAU

Enquiries concerning accommodation, including private accommodation, can be made at:

Verkehrsverein der Stadt Düsseldorf (Tourist Office of the City of Düsseldorf), Konrad-Adenauer-Platz, opposite main-station, P.O. Box 8203, D-4000 Düsseldorf 1. Tel: (0211)35 05 05. Telex: 8 587 785, Telefax: (0221) 16 10 71. Open daily, from 8.00 a.m. to 10.00 p.m., Sundays and Public Holidays, from 4.00 to 10.00 p.m.

Further information can be obtained from:

Compass Tours Incoming GmbH, Barbarossawall 11-23, D-4000 Düsseldorf 31. Tel: (0211) 40 70 21. Telex: 8585 518.

Etrav, Worringer Platz 11, D-4000 Düsseldorf 1. Tel: (0211) 35 80 61.

Hagen GmbH Destination Service Germany, Grafenberger Allee 100, D-4000 Düsseldorf 1. Tel: (0211) 67 93 50.

Reisebüro Hartmann Incoming Division, Airport Terminal, D-4000 Düsseldorf 30. Tel: (0211) 421 65 20. Telex: 858 45 15.

Reisebüro Jonen KG, Konrad-Adenauer-Platz 11, D-4000 Düsseldorf 1. Tel: (0211) 160 66 30. Telex: 8 588 427.

HOTELS

* First Class Hotels.

Downtown

Alt Graz, Klosterstraße 132, D-4000 Düsseldorf 1. Tel: 35 77 91, 35 rooms, bed and breakfast.

Amsterdam, Stresemannstraße 20, D-4000 Düsseldorf 1. Tel: 8 40 58 9, 24 rooms, bed and breakfast.

Anton, Prinz, Karl-Anton-Straße 11, D-4000 Düsseldorf 1. Tel: 3 5 20 00. Telex: 8 588 925, 60 rooms, bed and breakfast.

Astor, Kurfürstenstraße 23, D-4000 Düsseldorf 1. Tel: 3 60 66 1-2. Telex: 858 62 01, 30 rooms, bed and breakfast.

Bahn-Hotel, Karlstraße 74, D-4000 Düsseldorf 1. Tel: 3 60 471-3. Telex: 85 88 709, 66 rooms, bed and breakfast.

Benkwitz, **Guesthouse**, Kölner Straße 26, D-4000 Düsseldorf 1. Tel: 3 5 00 31-2, 23 rooms, bed and breakfast.

Bismarck, Bismarckstraße 97, D-4000 Düsseldorf 1. Tel: 3 6 09 25. Telex: 85 82 482, 65 rooms, bed and breakfast.

Bratmann, Grupellostraße 4, D-4000 Düsseldorf 1. Tel: 3 62 615, 26 rooms, pension.

* Breidenbacher Hof, Heinrich-Heine-Allee 36, D-4000 Düsseldorf 1. Tel: 130 30. Telex: 858 26 30, 230 rooms, hotel.

Concorde, Graf-Adolf-Straße 60, D-4000 Düsseldorf 1. Tel: 3 6 98 25, Telex 8 588 008, 120 rooms, bed and breakfast.

CVJM-Hotel, Graf-Adolf-Straße 102, D-4000 Düsseldorf 1. Tel: 3 60 76 45, 36 rooms, bed and breakfast.

Graf Adolf, Stresemannplatz 1, D-4000 Düsseldorf 1. Tel: 3 6 05 91. Telex: 8 58 7844, 128 rooms, bed and breakfast.

Großer Kurfürst, Kurfürstenstraße 18, D-4000 Düsseldorf 1. Tel: 3 5 08 91-3. Telex: 858 18 38, 40 rooms, bed and breakfast.

Hintz, Bahnstraße 70, D-4000 Düsseldorf 1. Tel: 3 5 08 91-3. Telex: 8 581 838, 30 rooms, bed and breakfast.

* Holiday Inn Königsallee, Graf-Adolf-Platz 10, D-4000 Düsseldorf 1. Tel: 3 87 30, Telex 8 586 359, 275 rooms, hotel.

Ibis, Konrad-Adenauer-Platz 14, D-4000 Düsseldorf 1. Tel: 167 20. Telex: 8 581 838, 249 rooms, bed and breakfast.

Komet, Bismarckstraße 93, D-4000 Düsseldorf 1. Tel: 3 5 79 17, 31 rooms, bed and breakfast.

Lancaster, Oststraße 166, D-4000 Düsseldorf 1. Tel: 3 5 10 66, 60 rooms, bed and breakfast.

Lindenhof, Oststraße 124, D-4000 Düsseldorf 1. Tel: 3 60 963. Telex: 8 587 012, 59 rooms, bed and breakfast.

Madison I, Graf-Adolf-Straße 94, D-4000 Düsseldorf 1. Tel: 168 50, 143 rooms, hotel.

Majestic, Cantadorstraße 4, D-4000 Düsseldorf 1. Tel: 3 67 030. Telex: 8 584 640, 88 rooms, hotel.

Minerva, Cantadorstraße 13a, D-4000 Düsseldorf 1. Tel: 3 5 09 61-2, 26 rooms, bed and breakfast.

Mondial, Graf-Adolf-Straße 82, D-4000 Düsseldorf 1. Tel: 3 6 05 91. Telex: 8 587 844, 58 rooms, bed and breakfast.

* Nikko, Immermannstraße 41, D-4000 Düsseldorf 1. Tel: 83 40. Telex: 8 582 080, 600 rooms, hotel.

Nizza, Ackerstraße 8, D-4000 Düsseldorf 1. Tel: 3 6 08 23-4. Telex: 858 64 17, 35 rooms, bed and breakfast.

* Parkhotel, **Steigenberger**, Corneliusplatz 1, D-4000 Düsseldorf 1. Tel: 86 51. Telex: 8 582 231, 230 rooms, hotel.

Plaza, Karlstraße 4, D-4000 Düsseldorf 1. Tel: 3 6 50 57. Telex: 8 584 947, 60 rooms, bed and breakfast.

* Savoy, Oststraße 128, D-4000 Düsseldorf 1. Tel: 3 60 336. Telex: 8 584 215, 160 rooms, hotel.

Schumacher, Worringer Straße 55, D-4000 Düsseldorf 1. Tel: 3 60 434. Telex: 8 586 610, 49 rooms, bed and breakfast.

Terminus, Am Wehrhahn 81-83, D-4000 Düsseldorf 1. Tel: 3 5 05 91, Telex: 8 586 576, 70 rooms, bed and breakfast.

Uebachs, Leopoldstraße 3-5, D-4000 Düsseldorf 1. Tel: 3 6 05 66, Telex: 8 587 620, 110 rooms, hotel.

Weidenhof, Oststraße 87, D-4000 Düsseldorf 1. Tel: 3 2 54 54. Telex: 8 586 271, 56 rooms, hotel.

Altstadt - Karlstadt

Am Füchschen, Ratinger Straße 32, D-4000 Düsseldorf 1. Tel: 3 2 05 43-4, 14 rooms, bed and breakfast.

Am Rathaus, Rheinstraße 3, D-4000 Düsseldorf 1. Tel: 3 2 65 56, 40 rooms, bed and breakfast.

An der Oper, Heinrich-Heine-Allee 15, D-4000 Düsseldorf 1. Tel: 806 21-5. Telex: 8 581 970, 70 rooms, bed and breakfast.

Barcelona, Hunsrückenstraße 5, D-4000 Düsseldorf 1. Tel: 133 952, 21 rooms, bed and breakfast.

El Rancho, Burgplatz 7, D-4000 Düsseldorf 1. Tel: 3 2 77 53, 17 rooms, bed and breakfast.

Esser, Mertengasse 1, D-4000 Düsseldorf 1. Tel: 3 2 74 67, 16 rooms, bed and breakfast.

Rheinblick, Haus, Mühlenstraße 15, D-4000 Düsseldorf 1. Tel: 3 25 316, 31 rooms, bed and breakfast.

Zum St. Maximilian, Citadellstraße 8, D-4000 Düsseldorf 1. Tel: 848 55, 12 rooms.

Friedrichstadt

Acon, Mintropstraße 23, D-4000 Düsseldorf 1. Tel: 3 7 70 20, 48 rooms, bed and breakfast.

Ambassador, Harkortstraße 7-9, D-4000 Düsseldorf 1. Tel: 3 7 00 03. Telex: 8 586 286, 115 rooms, bed and breakfast.

Astoria, Jahnstraße 72, D-4000 Düsseldorf 1. Tel: 3 8 20 88. Telex: 858 18 34, 40 rooms, bed and breakfast.

Bellevue, Luisenstraße 98, D-4000 Düsseldorf 1. Tel: 3 7 70 71. Telex: 858 47 71, 65 rooms, bed and breakfast.

Beyer, Scheurenstraße 57, D-4000 Düsseldorf 1. Tel: 3 7 09 91-3, 35 rooms, bed and breakfast.

Central, Luisenstraße 42, D-4000 Düsseldorf 1. Tel: 3 7 90 01. Telex: 858 21 45, 123 rooms, bed and breakfast.

Christina, Gustav-Poensgen-Straße 79, D-4000 Düsseldorf 1. Tel: 3 4 40 91-2. Telex: 182 11 46 53, 58 rooms, bed and breakfast.

Cornelius, Corneliusstraße 82, D-4000 Düsseldorf 1. Tel: 3 8 20 55-9. Telex: 8 587 385, 70 rooms, hotel.

Dani, Corneliusstraße 118, D-4000 Düsseldorf 1. Tel: 3 3 22 71-2. Telex: 858 74 99, 59 rooms, bed and breakfast.

Diana, Jahnstraße 31, D-4000 Düsseldorf 1. Tel: 3 7 50 71. Telex: 8 588 709, 38 rooms, bed and breakfast.

Domo, Scherenstraße 4, D-4000 Düsseldorf 1. Tel: 3 7 40 01, 26 rooms, bed and breakfast.

Eden, Adersstraße 29-31, D-4000 Düsseldorf 1. Tel: 3 8 970. Telex: 8 582 530, 200 rooms, hotel.

* Esplande, Fürstenplatz 17, D-4000 Düsseldorf 1. Tel: 3 7 50 10. Telex: 8 582 970, 110 rooms, hotel.

Fürstenhof, Fürstenplatz 3, D-4000 Düsseldorf 1. Tel: 3 7 05 45. Telex: 8 586 540, 75 rooms, bed and breakfast.

Herzog, Herzogstraße 23, D-4000 Düsseldorf 1. Tel: 3 7 20 47, 38 rooms, bed and breakfast.

* Holiday Inn, Graf-Adolf-Platz 10, D-4000 Düsseldorf 1. Tel: 3 87 30. Telex: 8 586 359, 275 rooms, hotel.

Kürten, Friedrichstraße 93, D-4000 Düsseldorf 1. Tel: 3 3 40 19, 26 rooms, bed and breakfast.

Madison II, Graf-Adolf-Straße 47, D-4000 Düsseldorf 1. Tel: 3 7 02 96, 42 rooms, bed and breakfast.

Manhattan, Graf-Adolf-Straße 39, D-4000 Düsseldorf 1. Tel: 3 7 02 44.

Schaum, Gustav-Poensgen-Straße 63, D-4000 Düsseldorf 1. Tel: 3 1 30 68. Telex: 8 586 326, 40 rooms, bed and breakfast.

Stadt München, Pionierstraße 6, D-4000 Düsseldorf 1. Tel: 3 7 50 80. Telex: 8 587 787, 80 rooms, bed and breakfast.

Tal, Talstraße 36, D-4000 Düsseldorf 1. Tel: 3 7 00 51-2, 40 rooms, bed and breakfast.

Wurms, Scheurenstraße 23, D-4000 Düsseldorf 1. Tel: 3 7 50 01. Telex: 8 584 290, 40 rooms, bed and breakfast.

Derendorf, Düsseltal, Golzheim, Mörsenbroich, Pempelfort

Am Ehrenhof, Fischerstraße 25, D-4000 Düsseldorf 30. Tel: 4 43243, 16 rooms, bed and breakfast.

Am Hofgarten, Guest House, Arnoldstraße 5, D-4000 Düsseldorf 30. Tel: 4 4 63 82, Telex: 858 14 26, 43 rooms, bed and breakfast.

Am Spichernplatz, Ulmenstraße 68, D-4000 Düsseldorf 30. Tel: 4 4 50 05, 48 rooms, hotel.

Am Vogelsanger Weg, Vogelsanger Weg 36, D-4000 Düsseldorf 30. Tel: 6 2 67 51-3, 100 rooms, bed and breakfast.

Am Zoo, Sybelstraße 21, D-4000 Düsseldorf 1. Tel: 6 2 63 33, 30 rooms, bed and breakfast.

Consul, Kaiserswerther Straße 59, D-4000 Düsseldorf 30. Tel: 4 9 20 78. Telex: 858 46 24, 60 rooms, bed and breakfast.

Diplomat, Collenbachstraße 58, D-4000 Düsseldorf 30. Tel: 4 8 20 24-6, 50 rooms, bed and breakfast.

Doria, Duisburger Straße 1a, D-4000 Düsseldorf 30. Tel: 4 8 03 01, 39 rooms, bed and breakfast.

Excelsior, Kaiserstraße 20, D-4000 Düsseldorf 30. Tel: 4 8 60 06. Telex: 858 47 37, 100 rooms, bed and breakfast.

Germania, Freiligrathstraße 21, D-4000 Düsseldorf 30. Tel: 4 9 40 78. Telex: 858 79 54, 36 rooms, bed and breakfast.

Geuer, Haus, Schäferstraße 4, D-4000 Düsseldorf 30. Tel: 4 9 90 39, 18 rooms, bed and breakfast.

* Gildors, Collenbachstraße 51, D-4000 Düsseldorf 30. Tel: 4 8 80 05. Telex: 858 44 18, 70 rooms, bed and breakfast.

Gneisenau, Guest House, Gneisenaustraße 37, D-4000 Düsseldorf 30. Tel: 4 8 57 72, 17 rooms, bed and breakfast.

* Hilton International, Georg-Glock-Straße 20, D-4000 Düsseldorf 30. Tel: 4 37 70. Telex: 858 43 76, 556 rooms, hotel.

Imperial, Venloer Straße 9, D-4000 Düsseldorf 30. Tel: 4 8 30 08. Telex: 858 71 87, 58 rooms, bed and breakfast.

* Inter-Continental, Karl-Arnold-Platz 5, D-4000 Düsseldorf 30. Tel: 4 55 30. Telex: 858 46 01, 580 beds, hotel.

Leonhard, Kaiserwerther Straße 265, D-4000 Düsseldorf 30. Tel: 4 34 498-9, 40 rooms, bed and breakfast.

Merkur, Mörsenbroicher Weg 49, D-4000 Düsseldorf 30. Tel: 6 3 40 31, 42 rooms, bed and breakfast.

Michelangelo, Roßstraße 61, D-4000 Düsseldorf 30. Tel: 4 8 01 01. Telex: 858 86 49, 110 rooms, bed and breakfast.

National, Schwerinstraße 16, D-4000 Düsseldorf 30. Tel: 4 9 90 62-5. Telex: 858 65 97, 67 rooms, bed and breakfast.

* Ramada Renaissance, Nördlicher Zubringer 6, D-4000 Düsseldorf 30. Tel: 6 21 60. Telex: 858 64 35, 387 rooms, hotel.

Rhein Residence, Kaiserswerther Straße 20, D-4000 Düsseldorf 30. Tel: 4 99 90, 126 rooms, hotel.

Rheinpark, Bankstraße 13-17, D-4000 Düsseldorf 30. Tel: 4 9 91 86, 41 rooms, bed and breakfast.

Rheinperle, Kaiserswerther Straße 214, D-4000 Düsseldorf 30. Tel: 4 5 06 55, 23 rooms, bed and breakfast.

Royal, Gartenstraße 30, D-4000 Düsseldorf 30, Phone:49 00 49, 50 rooms, bed and breakfast.

Stern, Sternstraße 53, D-4000 Düsseldorf 30. Tel: 4 9 41 46-7. Telex: 858 84 52, 27 rooms, bed and breakfast.

Ufer, Gartenstraße 50, D-4000 Düsseldorf 30. Tel: 4 9 90 31, 36 rooms, bed and breakfast.

Wieland, Wielandstraße 8, D-4000 Düsseldorf 1. Tel: 3 5 01 71-3. Telex: 858 89 23, 52 rooms, bed and breakfast.

Windsor, Grafenberger Allee 36, D-4000 Düsseldorf 1. Tel: 6 7 10 91, 30 rooms, bed and breakfast.

Bilk, Flehe, Oberbilk, Unterbilk, Volmerswerth

Aida, Ubierstraße 36, D-4000 Düsseldorf 1. Tel: 159 90. Telex: 172114029, 140 rooms, bed and breakfast.

Am Deich, Haus, Abteihofstraße 50, D-4000 Düsseldorf 1. Tel: 15 47 57, 16 rooms, bed and breakfast.

Arcade, Ludwig-Erhard-Allee 2, D-4000 Düsseldorf 1. Tel: 7 70 10. Telex: 172114084, 310 rooms, bed and breakfast.

Berliner Hof, Ellerstraße 110, D-4000 Düsseldorf 1. Tel: 7 84 744-5, 28 rooms, bed and breakfast.

Berna, Guest House, Eifeler Straße 6, D-4000 Düsseldorf 1. Tel: 7 2 61 76, 27 rooms, bed and breakfast.

Blättler, Fleher Straße 242, D-4000 Düsseldorf 1. Tel: 1518 67, 10 rooms, bed and breakfast.

Fährhaus, Volmerswerther Deich 151, D-4000 Düsseldorf 1. Tel: 15 58 28, 35 rooms, hotel.

Flora, Auf'm Hennekamp 37, D-4000 Düsseldorf 1. Tel: 3 4 70 66, 45 rooms, bed and breakfast.

Iffland, Querstraße 4, D-4000 Düsseldorf 1. Tel: 7 7 50 88-9, 30 rooms, bed and breakfast.

Karolinger, Haus, Karolinger Straße 104, D-4000 Düsseldorf 1. Tel: 3 3 00 17, 20 rooms, bed and breakfast.

Kastens, Jürgenplatz 52, D-4000 Düsseldorf 1. Tel: 3 0 82 05. Telex: 858 69 34, 60 rooms, bed and breakfast.

Kirschniok, Haus, Merowingerstraße 37, D-4000 Düsseldorf 1. Tel: 3 4 30 21, 8 rooms, bed and breakfast.

Lessing, Volksgartenstraße 6, D-4000 Düsseldorf 1. Tel: 7 2 30 53. Telex: 858 72 19, 60 rooms, bed and breakfast.

Metropol, Brunnenstraße 20, D-4000 Düsseldorf 1. Tel: 3 4 40 07. Telex: 858 72 19, 80 rooms, bed and breakfast.

Philipshalle, Siegburger Straße 15, D-4000 Düsseldorf 1. Tel: 7 2 10 45, 22 rooms, bed and breakfast.

Gerresheim, Grafenberg, Hubbelrath, Ludenberg, Rath

Am Rather Kreuzweg, Rather Kreuzweg 76, D-4000 Düsseldorf 30. Tel: 6 5 13 22, 11 rooms, bed and breakfast.

Am Weinberg, Bergische Landstraße 618, D-4000 Düsseldorf 12. Tel: 2 8 93 33, 14 rooms, bed and breakfast.

Gerricus, Schönaustraße 15, D-4000 Düsseldorf 12. Tel: 2 8 20 21-2, 36 rooms, bed and breakfast.

Gut Moschenhof, Am Gartenkamp 20, D-4000 Düsseldorf 12. Tel: 2 8 10 21-2, 26 rooms, bed and breakfast.

Nord, Rather Broich 30, D-4000 Düsseldorf 30. Tel: 6 2 34 92, 11 rooms, pension.

Rheinischer Hof, Am Poth 2a, D-4000 Düsseldorf 12. Tel: 2 8 30 81-2, 40 rooms, hotel.

Rolandsburg, Rennbahnstraße 2, D-4000 Düsseldorf 12. Tel: 6 1 00 90, 80 rooms, hotel.

Eller, Flingern, Lierenfeld, Unterbach, Vennhausen

Am Zault, Gerresheimer Landstraße 40, D-4000 Düsseldorf 1. Tel: 2 5 10 81. Telex: 858 18 72, 72 rooms, hotel.

Engelbert, Engelbertstraße 15, D-4000 Düsseldorf 1. Tel: 7 33 41 69, 37 rooms, bed and breakfast.

Enger Hof, Grafenberger Allee 257, D-4000 Düsseldorf 1. Tel: 6 6 00 01, 24 rooms, hotel.

Gumbert, Haus, Gumbertstraße 178, D-4000 Düsseldorf 1. Tel: 2 1 38 09, 25 rooms, hotel.

Heidelberger Hof, Grafenberger Allee 103, D-4000 Düsseldorf 1. Tel: 6 6 62 65-7, 51 rooms, bed and breakfast.

Im Tönnchen, Wetterstraße 4, D-4000 Düsseldorf 1. Tel: 6 8 44 04, 44 rooms, bed and breakfast.

Stemmer Stübchen, Bunzlauer Weg 47, D-4000 Düsseldorf 12. Tel: 2 7 58 37, 10 rooms, pension.

Lörick, Oberkassel

Arosa, Sonderburgstraße 48, D-4000 Düsseldorf 11. Tel: 5 5 40 11-3. Telex: 858 22 2, 44 rooms, bed and breakfast.

Fischerhaus, Bonifatiusstraße 35, D-4000 Düsseldorf 11. Tel: 5 9 20 07. Telex: 858 44 49, 58 rooms, hotel.

Modern, Leostraße 15, D-4000 Düsseldorf 11. Tel: 5 8 90 13 , 8 rooms, bed and breakfast.

Oberkassel, Haus, Düsseldorferstraße 93, D-4000 Düsseldorf 11. Tel: 5 7 04 46, 14 rooms, bed and breakfast.

Ramada, Am Seestern 16, D-4000 Düsseldorf 11. Tel: 5 9 10 47. Telex: 858 55 75, 321 rooms, hotel.

Rheinstern Penta, Emauel-Leutze-Straße 17, D-4000 Düsseldorf 11. Tel: 5 99 70. Telex: 858 42 42, 436 rooms, hotel.

Wilke, Haus, Adalbert Straße 11, D-4000 Düsseldorf 11. Tel: 5 7 31 89, 14 rooms, bed and breakfast.

Benrath, Garath, Hassels, Holthausen, Reisholz, Urdenbach, Wersten

Am Hoxbach, Reisholzer Bahnstraße 56, D-4000 Düsseldorf 13. Tel: 7 48 90 01-2, 14 rooms, bed and breakfast.

Apparte, In der Donk 6, D-4000 Düsseldorf 13 . Tel: 7 4 84 80. Telex: 172 11 4332, 250 rooms, bed and breakfast.

Dase, Bonner Straße 7, D-4000 Düsseldorf 13. Tel: 7 9 90 71, 54 rooms, bed and breakfast.

Novotel, Am Schönenkamp 9, D-4000 Düsseldorf 13. Tel: 7 4 10 92. Telex: 858 43 74, 240 rooms, hotel .

Rheinterrasse Benrath, Bernrather Schloßufer 39, D-4000 Düsseldorf 13. Tel: 7 1 10 70. Telex: 858 24 59, 80 rooms, hotel.

Waldesruh, Am Wald 6, D-4000 Düsseldorf 13. Tel: 7 1 60 08-9, 43 rooms, hotel.

Angermund, Kaiserswerth, Lohhausen, Stockum, Wittlaer

Air-Hotel Wartburg, Niederrheinstraße 59, D-4000 Düsseldorf 30. Tel: 4 5 59 10. Telex: 858 48 30, 220 rooms, hotel.

Barbarossa, Niederrheinstraße 365, D-4000 Düsseldorf 31. Tel: 4 0 27 19, 39 rooms, bed and breakfast.

Bletgen, Haus, Bockumer Straße 26, D-4000 Düsseldorf 31. Tel: 4 0 16 97, 20 rooms.

Eiden, Haus, Carl-Sonnenschein-Straße 34, D-4000 Düsseldorf 30. Tel: 4 36 02 57, 10 rooms, bed and breakfast.

Falkenberg, Guest House, Arnheimer Str. 36-40, D-4000 Düsseldorf 31. Tel: 4 0 72 12, 8 rooms, bed and breakfast.

Fashion-Hotel, Am Hain 44, D-4000 Düsseldorf 30. Tel: 4 3 41 82-9. Telex: 858 44 52, 43 rooms, hotel.

Hein, Niederrheinstraße 34, D-4000 Düssel-dorf 30. Tel: 4 5 06 75-6, 19 rooms, bed and breakfast.

Ikarus, Airport, Hall 4, D-4000 Düsseldorf 30. Tel: 4 2 45 87-9, 30 rooms, pension.

Im kühlen Grund, Lohauser Dorfstraße 41, D-4000 Düsseldorf 30. Tel: 4 3 29 64, 21 rooms, hotel.

Litzbrück, Haus, Bahnhofstraße 33, D-4000 Düsseldorf 31. Tel: 0203/744 81, 36 rooms, hotel.

Rittendorf, Haus, Fr.-von-Spee-Straße 44, D-4000 Düsseldorf 31. Tel: 4 0 40 41-2, 20 rooms, bed and breakfast.

Rosenhof, Bahnhofstraße 2, D-4000 Düsseldorf 31. Tel: 0203/ 744 11, 30 rooms, hotel.

Roth, Guest House, Nagelsweg 24, D-4000 Düsseldorf 30. Tel: 4 3 33 42. Telex: 858 69 29, 8 rooms, pension.

Schnellenburg, Rotterdamer Straße 120, D-4000 Düsseldorf 30. Tel: 4 3 41 33. Telex: 858 18 28, 90 rooms, hotel.

Sonnen, Guest House, Bockumer Straße 4, D-4000 Düsseldorf 31. Tel: 4 0 22 74, 8 rooms, bed and breakfast.

CAMPING

Camping Lörick, Düsseldorf-Lörick, (15th April to 15th October). Tel: 5 9 14 01.

Camping Rheinblick, Düsseldorf-Baumberg, (1st April to 30th September). Tel: 02173/636 23.

Camping Unterbacher See, Düsseldorf-Erkrath-Unterbach, (Easter to 15th September). Tel: 899 20 38.

YOUTH HOSTELS

Düsseldorf-Oberkassel, Düsseldorfer Straße 1. Tel: 5 7 40 41.

GETTING AROUND

IMPORTANT SIGHTS

Come to Düsseldorf and you will be coming to a host of sights worth seeing.

The Thyssen High-Rise Building at Jan-Wellem-Platz, constructed in three "plates", has had an epoch-making effect on high-rise construction in the Federal Republic. Other landmarks of this kind have been created in the shape of the Mannesmann and State Insurance (LVA) Buildings respectively.

The Rheinturm (Rhine Tower), Düsseldorf's highest building, is conspicuous also for its revolving restaurant and unusual time-display: the building itself is the biggest decimal clock in the world. In its shadow stands the newly completed **State Government Building**. Its low, circular plan affords a charming contrast.

One of the most significant architectural creations of the years following the First World War is the **Ehrenhof** quadrangle, which includes the recently refurbished Museum of Art (Kunstmuseum). The Ehrenhof ("Court of Honour") was built in 1926 for the "Gesolei" Fitness and Health Exhibition. This complex of buildings sets off the Hofgarten, designed by the landscape gardener, Maximilian Friedrich Weyhe at the beginning of the last century, from the Rhine embankment.

The **Altstadt** has made Düsseldorf world famous. Its trademark is more than the rich array of food and drinks that is certainly to be had there; the Altstadt is also its churches,

St. Lambert's, a thirteenth-century building, being one of the oldest parish churches. The most significant testimony of the Rhenish Jesuit style may be said to be embodied in the **St Andrew's Church** (Andreaskirche, first half of seventeenth century). Do not miss the opportunity, either, of taking a look inside the former Franciscan monastery church of St Maximilian of the eighteenth century.

The pièce de résistance of the city is an avenue - some say, a fashion promenade - the **Königsallee**, affectionately dubbed the "Kö". Not only do Düsseldorfers believe it to be one of the most splendid boulevards of the Old World. It is only one kilometre long, but nobody dashes through the "Kö" in 12-15 minutes!.

There are many sights beyond the city centre, too. The best-known must be the Late Baroque **Château Benrath**, built 1753-75. Its architect was Nicolas de Pigage, the patron the Elector Palatine Jan Wellem. The numerous visitors marvel again and again at the architectonic harmony of park and castle.

Parks and gardens are another feature Düsseldorf enjoys in plenty. Apart from the Castle Gardens at Benrath and the equally renowned Hofgarten or, again, Nordpark with its Japanese Garden, Südpark is one of the city's most important areas of green. Recently laid out, its realisation involved an entire six-lane motorway disappearing underground - contributing space to what is now seventy hectares (almost 173 acres) of land for regeneration.

Several of the outlying communities are older than the inner city and are well worth a visit. This includes **Gerresheim** and the Quadenhof and former Collegiate Church of St. Margaret. In the North lies **Kaiserswerth**, its history eventful and documented right back to the eigth century. The little community, which still preserves its idyllic atmosphere today, obtained its city charter in 1181 and was for centuries the powerful base of German kings and emperors. Today the imperial palace erected by Barbarossa is a lovingly tended ruin; but the ancient face of the township is essentially intact. The square (Stiftsplatz) round the eleventh-century collegiate church, now the Parish Church of St Suitbert (Swidbert), is one of the most beautiful and evocative along the Lower Rhine.

Brisk walkers can explore Düsseldorf's Altstadt and downtown on foot. For example, walking along the Kö from the south to the north, through the Hofgarten and along the Rhine to the Ehrenhof and on to the Altstadt.

To reach your destination quickly you can take a cab; Tel: 3 33 33, 7 77 60.

PUBLIC TRANSPORT

The **Rheinbahn** (*Rheinische Bahngesellschaft AG*) is practical and inexpensive. The Düsseldorf public transport system consists of 6 light-railways, 12 tramlines and 71 bus routes. Weekly it conveys more than 525,000 passengers - making it the biggest of the 21 carriers in the Rhine-Ruhr Transport Association (VRR). A curiosity unique in Europe is the **tram with the dining-car**: this is the speciality on the Rheinbahn's light-railway number 79 connecting the central railway stations of Duisburg and Düsseldorf. It is worth interrupting the journey (at Klemensplatz) for a detour to Kaiserswerth with its distinctly medieval flavour and the ruins of Barbarossa's imperial palace.

In Düsseldorf, the **Central Station** (**Hauptbahnhof**), **Jan-Wellem-Platz** and **Heinrich-Heine-Allee/Wilhelm-Marx-Haus** are important junctions from which almost any destination in and around the town can be reached.

You buy your ticket in the usual way from the driver of trams and buses. If you begin your journey on the Light Railways (trams U 76, U 78 or U 79), on the German Railways or on the Wuppertal Schwebebahn (suspension railway), then you must get your ticket from the automatic machines at the stations. These machines also sell discounted multi-ride tickets. It is important that tickets bought from machines be validated (machine-stamped) on beginning the FIRST section of each journey. You will find these orange machines near the doors of all trams and buses, and at the entrances to the stations of tram subways or railways.

In summer the Rheinbahn's "White Fleet" of four passenger ships invites you to cruises on the Rhine between Landtag (State Government Building)/Rheinturm (Rhine Tower), Rathausufer (Town Hall Embankment) and Kaiserswerth. At week-ends (Fridays to Saturdays from the end of April to the end of September) the ships cast off for an evening's Dance on the Rhine. Then there are boat trips to the historic little town of Zons or the dockland of Duisburg-Ruhrort. For that all-out celebration on the Rhine with family, friends or colleagues, the Rheinbahn ships can be chartered, too. Tel: 3 7 50 20.

Being a member of the **Verkehrsverbund Rhein-Ruhr (VRR)** means that the Rheinbahn is part of an efficient mass transport system. Through the VRR, passengers can now use the S-Bahn (commuter train) with its 25 stops in Düsseldorf, the non-surcharge trains of the German Railways (DB) and buses and trams and in addition the well-known Schwebebahn in Wuppertal - all on the same ticket.

The "visitors ticket" for Düsseldorf is the "Tageskarte".

For short trips of about 2 kilometres we would suggest the Short Hop-Ticket (Kurzstrecken-Fahrausweis) of the VRR. It is sold in buses, trams, sales offices and automats. At each stop you can read how far the Short Hop-Ticket reaches.

At the VRR there are also single tickets, economy multiple-journey tickets, and passes for set periods (per week or month) that work out even cheaper.

Further information, including fares and timetables, may be requested from the Rheinische Bahngesellschaft at 58 228.

For hotel bookings, city tours, tourist guides and interpreters, transfer and excursions, car and bus rentals, theatre and concert tickets, daily arrangements, fashion shows, congresses and conferences, tours for a weekend and special programmes contact: **Verkehrsverein der Stadt Düsseldorf** (Tourist Office of the City of Düsseldorf), Konrad-Adenauer-Platz opposite the Central Railway Station. Tel: 3 5 05 05, Telefax: 16 10 71.

GUIDED TOURS

The **tourist office** also organizes **city tours** in Düsseldorf. City tours including a boat trip on the Rhine and a visit to the Rhine Tower are arranged daily from April to mid-October (from mid-October to the end of March only on Saturdays). The buses depart at 2.30 p.m. in Friedrich-Ebert-Straße, bus stop 14, opposite the Central Railway Station. The city tour lasts 150 minutes.

You can also book a three hour ride on the "**Merry Tramcar**" at the Tourist Office.

Groups can arrange to have a guide who is familiar with the city and speaks foreign languages; tourists are given the choice between 14 different languages.

A special arrangement offered by the Tourist Office is the tour "**Sightseeing in Düsseldorf's Altstadt**". It begins at 11.00 a.m. with a bus tour of the city accompanied by a guide. Tourists are welcomed at 12.30 p.m. - and are, of course, offered a pint of Düsseldorf's famous "Altbier". Lunch is eaten at one of Düsseldorf's good restaurants at 1.00 p.m. and a game of skittles is arranged for 2.00 p.m. The group takes a short walk to the Rhine at about 3.30 p.m. and then boards ship. Coffee is served whilst on board. After docking the group walks through the alleys and streets of Düsseldorf's Altstadt. A "Schneider-Wibbel-Platte" (a local speciality) is served for dinner at one of the typical restaurants in the Altstadt at 6.30 p.m.

Another tour is arranged between 7.00 to 9.00 p.m. and is called the "**Hospitable Altstadt**". The group meets in front of the Jan-Wellem-Monument at the Market Square and is accompanied by a guide familiar with the city. Tourists are taken to a historical restaurant where a typical dinner is served. A stroll through the Altstadt is arranged for later on with five stops at different pubs. Of course, you can order Altbier everywhere. And last but not least a midnight snack of cheese and bread is served before going home.

Düsseldorf's Town Hall is open to all visitors every Wednesday from 3.00 p.m. There is a special arrangement for the working population: they can visit the Town Hall on the first Wednesday of every month at 6.00 p.m. This guided tour through the Town Hall is organized by Düsseldorf's Press and Information Office, Marktplatz 2 (Town Hall). Tel: 899 -31 31. The tour is an hour and a half long and consists of 12 different sections including the old city wall dating back to the 15th century - 8 metres below ground - and the city model of present-day Düsseldorf, the 380 stove plates in the vicinity of the Town Hall's portal, the Assembly Hall, the Heinrich Heine Chamber, the Baroque Gallery and the Jan Wellem Hall. Tourists are even allowed to look around the Mayor's office if he is out. However, Düsseldorf's Mayor, Klaus Bungert, does not mind the tourists looking over his shoulder and will answer their questions himself. Guided tours for groups can also be arranged. (Tel: 8 99-31 11).

From hotel reservations to boat excursions - incoming services can take care of everything for you:

CTI compass tours incoming, Barbarossawall 11-23. Tel: 4 0 70 21.

Etrav, Worringer Platz 11. Tel: 3 5 80 61/62.

Hartmann Incoming Service, Rhein-Ruhr-Airport, Arrival Terminal. Tel: 4 21 63 20, 4 21 65 20.

Jonen Reisebüro (Travel Agency), Konrad-Adenauer-Platz 11. Tel: 1 60 66 30/56/27.

CAR HIRE SERVICE

Avis Rent-a-Car, Berliner Allee 32. Tel: 3 2 90 50, Airport. Tel: 4 21 67 48, Erkrather Straße 158. Tel: 7 33 54 21.

Buchbinder Car Hire Service, Erkrather Straße 256. Tel: 7 33 43 44.

ES Europa Service, Klosterstraße 140. Tel: 3 5 35 48.

Claus Fassbender Car Hire Service, Volmerswerther Straße 30. Tel: 15 42 42, 15 28 88.

Hertz, Airport. Tel: 4 1 10 83, Immermannstraße 65. Tel: 3 5 70 25.

interRent, Airport. Tel: 4 2 70 33, 42 37 65, Charlottenstraße 50 (near Central Station). Tel: 3 5 00 33.

Raule Car Hire Service, Ronsdorfer Straße 71a.. Tel: 7 33 78 88.

No matter how you explore Düsseldorf, you must be careful not to throw anything away. For even minor environmental sins are punished in West-Germany. An "Admonitory Booklet" lays down the **fines to be paid**: 10 Marks must be paid for throwing away a cigarette-packet, there is a 30 Mark fine for throwing away glass or plastic bottles, cans of beer or waste paper on the streets, at public places and in park.

THINGS TO DO

EXCURSIONS FROM DUSSELDORF

Düsseldorf, itself a city full of sights, is surrounded by remarkable towns and sites which can be easily reached by car or by means of public transport. Arrangements and excursions are also offered by:

Verkehrsverein der Stadt Düsseldorf (Tourist Information Office), Konrad-Adenauer-Platz (opposite Central Railway Station). Tel: 3 5 05 05.

CTI compass tours incoming, Barbarossawall 11-23. Tel: 4 0 70 21.

ETRAV, Worringer Platz 11. Tel: 3 5 80 61/62.

Hartmann Incoming Service, Airport. Tel: 4 21 63 20, 421 65 20.

Jonen Reisebüro, Konrad-Adenauer-Platz 11. Tel: 1 60 66 30/56/27.

Excursions do not necessarily have to be on land. Düsseldorf is a berth to the "KD Köln-Düsseldorfer" which organizes major cruises on the Rhine. The "Rhein-Tourist" not only offers excursions but also congresses and celebrations can be held on board its ships.

KD Köln Düsseldorfer, Deutsche Rheinschiffahrt AG, Frankenwerft 15, 5000 Köln 1. Tel: 0221-20 88-288.

Rhein-Tourist, Generalagent für die Fahrgastschiffahrt, der Rheinischen Bahngesellschaft AG, Graf-Adolf-Platz 5. Tel: 3 7 50 20.

SUGGESTIONS FOR EXCURSIONS

Dormagen with its quarter "Zons", also known as "Rothenburg on the Lower Rhine", lies to the south of Düsseldorf. The historic city wall enclosing the town is 1100 metres long. The Zons District Museum in Schloß Friedestrom, where you can admire Art Nouveau pewter ware, is just as famous as the windmill. Historic tournaments take place from June to September with the citadel being in the background. The educational institution for nature "Tannenbusch" in Dormagen's quarter Delhoven is surrounded by an open-air enclosure for deers and a geological park.

Fremdenverkehrsamt (Tourist Information Office), Schloßstr. 37, 4047 Dormagen. Tel: 02106/535 18.

Heimat- und Verkehrsverein der Feste Zons (Tourist Information Office Zons). Tel: 02106/ 535 19.

The town of **Monheim** lies on the other side of the Rhine and can be reached by a car ferry from Dormagen. The motto inscribed on the town's coat of arms warns: "idle talk is harmful". Paths dating back to 12th century lead through town past remarkable old and modern buildings, fountains and sculptures.

Stadt Monheim, Der Stadtdirektor (Monheim, Town Manager), Rathaus, Rathausplatz 2, 4019 Monheim. Tel: 02173/ 5970.

Only a stone's throw from Monheim to the South, brinking on the Bergisches Land, lies **Leverkusen**. The town came into being in 1930 after several villages merged and was later joined by Opladen. Carl Leverkus transferred his ultramarine factory from Wermelskirchen to the Rhine in 1860. The Elberfelder Colour Factory (the one-time Friedrich Bayer & Cie) took over Leverkus' factory in 1891. Bayer, a major trade-mark of the town, also determines the fate of local football.

Not only industry and sports are important features of Leverkusen. This modern town is marked by the great variety of its cultural life. The Städtische Museum (Municipal Museum) is located in Schloß Morsbroich.

Presse- und Verkehrsamt (Press and Tourist Information Office), Rathaus, Friedrich-Ebert-Platz 1, 5090 Leverkusen. Tel: 0214/352 83 10.

Leverkusen borders on **Cologne** in the south which is only 47 Kilometres away from Düsseldorf. Like Leverkusen, the quarter Deutz lies on the right side of the Rhine. That is where Cologne's trade fairs are held. Many bridges lead to the left side, to the "holy" Cologne, the one-time Roman Colonia Agrippina; many objects dating back to this period are on display at Roman-Germanic Museum and other museums.

A visit to Cologne is not only worthwhile during the carnival. The majestic gothic cathedral that towers above every other building in Cologne houses among other things the Shrine of the Three Wise Men. A whole world of painting, from classical to contemporary works of art, can be admired at the double museums Wallraf-Richartz-Museum/Museum Ludwig, situated in the vicinity of the cathedral.

Cologne is a city of arts, nine municipal museums and many private one welcome visitors. But culture is not always painting; there are museums for handicraft articles and for technology; even the first Beatles Museum in the world is situated in Cologne (on Heinsbergstraße 13). Go for a stroll in Cologne and many aspects of this city will be revealed to you, the many churches from the Romanesque Period, the tempting shopping streets.

Verkehrsamt der Stadt Köln (Tourist Information Office of the City of Cologne), Unter Fettenhennen 19, 5000 Köln. Tel: 0221/221 33 40.

Brühl lies only a few Kilometres to the south-west. Brühl is a destination for excursions during which the interest for art and culture can be combined with adventure and show. The Max-Ernst-Kabinett is located in Brühl and is dedicated to works of art by famous surrealists. The castle museums "Augustusburg" and "Falkenlust" are also in Brühl. Phantasieland with super magic shows, star parade, space centre, western saloon and many other attractions is on Berggeiststraße.

Bonn, the capital city of the Federal Republic of Germany, is 27 Kilometres away from Cologne and 78 Kilometres from Düsseldorf. Political trademarks are the "Bundestag" (German parliament), the "Abgeordnetenhaus" (chamber of deputies), also called "Langer Eugen", Office of the Federal Chancellor and Villa Hammerschmidt, the official residence of Germany's president. The city's image is not only characterized by the ministries, administrative offices and embassies but it has managed to preserve its one-time character as a residential and university city. Although the German chancellors, from Adenauer to his self-appointed grandson Kohl may be famous, they are not always loved by all their subjects. The most famous citizen of Bonn, popular in the entire world, is undoubtedly Ludwig van Beethoven who was born in this city in 1770 and who still charms the world with his music.

The first city on the right side of the river is **Moers**. Its remarkable "Altstadt" reaches from the old Town Hall to the Castle (once the residence of Count of Moers, today the local museum and Castle Theatre) and is encircled by the moat. The water mill on Venloer Straße, mentioned as early as in 1600, or the Motorrad-Museum (motorbike museum) are also worth a visit. The festival of the colourful kites is held on the Patterberg in September.

Moers borders on **Duisburg** in the north. It is only 27 Kilometres away from Düsseldorf. Duisburg used to be called "Montan" before the mining crisis and is a centre of today's steel industry. The world's largest inland port is located in Duisburg, at the mouth of the Rhine. The Rhine-Ruhr-Port of Duisburg with its 19 docks encompasses a water area of 213 hectares.

However, Duisburg is not only a city of industry and trade but also a modern city. The city is immersed in green areas and surrounded by the charms of the Lower Rhenish countryside. There are windmills and village churches in Duisburg as well as the leisure and adventure park "Revierpark Mattlerbusch", the Botanical gardens and the zoo. There are theatres, concert halls and the German Opera House on the Rhine. The Wilhelm Lehmbruck Museum is dedicated to contemporary art and the works of Lehmbruck, one of the most famous sculptors in the 20th century. The Niederrheinische Museum houses the works of the great geographer Mercator. The Museum of German Inland Navigation and the Navigation Museum Oscar Huber are in Ruhrort.

The Ruhrgebiet with the towns, Mühlheim, Oberhausen, Gladbeck, Bottrop, Essen, Gelsenkirchen, Bochum, Herne, Recklinghausen, Castrop-Rauxel and Dortmund is spread out to the east of Duisburg.

Only separated from Düsseldorf by the Rhine and on the left side of the river lies the city of **Neuss**. It is an ancient city where you visit Roman ruins. It is also a modern city where many sights from the past can be admired. Concerts are held in the "Zeughaus". The "Obertor" is connected to the Clemens Sels Museum where art collections from the Roman Period to contemporary works are on display. The "Haus Rottels" with its collection is in the vicinity. Nixhütter Weg is worth the visit for old and for young; you can pet animals and see what life is like on a farm.

The estate agent and art collector Karl-Heinrich Müller has set up his Museum Insel Hombroich on an island in the meadows of the Erft (river flowing into the Rhine), lying before the city of Neuss. Five sculptural buildings designed by Erwin Heerich are spread throughout the park and meadowland. The house was constructed according to the plans of Anatol Herzfeld, two historical buildings. Art treasures from ancient times to contemporary works from China, Iran, Cambodia, Africa, Australia and New Zealand, paintings and sculptures are exhibited here in natural surroundings. Music and poetry contribute to the harmonious interplay of nature and culture in Hombroich. The museum is open everyday (also on Mondays); April-September 10.00 a.m. - 7.00 p.m., October-November and February-March 10.00 a.m. - 5.00 p.m., December, January 10.00 a.m. - 4.00 p.m. There is an entrance fee of 15 Marks from Monday to Friday, 20 Marks on weekends and public holidays; students and the handicapped are granted 50% reduction, children to the age of 12 are admitted free of charge, but the drinks and food from the buffet is a complimentary service of the museum.

Museum Insel Hombroich, 4040 Neuss-Holzheim. Tel: 02182/2094.

Mönchengladbach, the largest city on the left side of the Lower Rhine, is only 15 Kilometres away from Neuss. Today, the one-time centre of the textile industry is a modern city of trade and manufacturing industry. Sports are taken as seriously as art and culture. The local football team Borussia Mönchengladbach plays in the Federal League, trotting races are held on the Niersbrücke and Steffi Graf plays tennis here.

In addition to historical buildings in and around the city, the Zoological Gardens in Odenkirchen, the numerous half-timbered buildings and farms and last but not least the museums are worth a visit: Municipal Museum Schloß Rheydt, the Karnevalsmuseum (Carnival Museum) in the old Zeugenhaus, the Municipal Museum Abteiberg. The museum, itself a work of art by the architect Hans Hollein, exhibits works of art from the 20th century from expressionism to Andy Warhol and Joseph Beuys.

Verkehrsverein (Tourist Information Office), Bismarckstr. 23.27. Tel: 02161/220 01.

Presse- und Informationsamt (Press and Information Office), Rathaus Abtei, 4050 Mönchengladbach. Tel: 02161/25 24 53.

Krefeld is over 10 Kilometres to the north-east of Mönchengladbach. Although other branches of industry have become more important today, Krefeld is still a centre of silk and velvet production. The German Textile Museum in Krefeld is dedicated to velvet, silk and other textiles. Works of art and handicrafts are on display at Kaiser Wilhelm Museum - the exhibits range from the Middle Ages to contemporary works.

The two buildings, Museum Haus Lange and Haus Esters are architectural feats that were constructed by Ludwig Mies van der Rohe and house exhibitions. Castle Linn is one of the original moated castles of the Lower Rhine and is now a museum. The Niederrhein Museum is only a few minutes away. It houses collections from prehistorical and ancient times, from the Roman and Franconian Periods. Krefeld's new meeting point for culture and communications is the historical factory Heeder. Everything from exhibitions to magic shows is held here. Apart from velvet and silk, art and culture Krefeld's zoo and Botanical Gardens, the sports facilities, the recreation Park at Elfrather Lake, the Rheinlandhalle (ice-hockey), the Grotenburg Stadium (football), the race track and the historical Krefelder Railway should be on every visitor's agenda.

Informationshaus Seidenweberhaus Ver-kehrsverein (Tourist Information Office), Theaterplatz 1, 4150 Krefeld. Tel: 02151/29 290, 29 293

The town of **Erkrath**, the gate to the Neander Valley, is situated in the east of Düsseldorf. The city's sights range from old churches and chapels to the two moated castles Haus Brück and Haus Unterbach and the Stinder Mill. The composer of church songs, Joachim Neander, went to the Valley of Düssel to sing as loud as his heart desired. The area was named after him; the skeleton of the Neandertal Man was found in this area and was given the name of the valley. The

Neandertal Man lived between 200,000 and 400,000 years B.C. The Neanderthal Museum is dedicated to him.

Amt für Presse und Öffentlichkeitsarbeit (Press and Information Office), Bahnstr. 16, 4006 Erkrath. Tel: 0211/24 07 0.

Zweckverband Erholungsgebiet Neandertal (Local Administration Union Neandertal), Diepensiepen 2, Haus Winkelsmühle, 4020 Mettmann. Tel: 02104/64 91 2.

The town of **Hilden** is separated from Düsseldorf's quarter Benrath only by the Autobahn. The town was a settlement area even in ancient times. The embankment Holterhöfchen dates back to the ninth century. In addition to historical half-timbered buildings, there is also the Reformation Church from the 12th century.

Stadtverwaltung (Town Administration), Am Rathaus, 4010 Hilden. Tel: 02103/72 204.

Solingen is only a few minutes away by car in the south-east of Düsseldorf, in the Bergisches Land. Blades for thrust and cutting weapons used to be manufactured here and today the skills of the past have been adapted for the production of cutlery and scissors. Thus, it is not surprising that there is a German Blade Museum in Solingen.

The Schloß Burg dates from the 12th century, was home to Dukes and houses the Bergische Museum. It is on the river Wupper. The historical mills Balkhauser Kotten and Wipperkotten are also on the river Wupper. The Rhenish Industriemuseum is in the drop-forging shop of Hendrich. The Müngstener Bridge, Germany's highest railway bridge made of steel, is also worth a visit. The bridge was built in 1897. And last but not least the Sengbach Dam and the historical Market-Place Gräfrath.

Verkehrsverein/Presse- und Informationsamt (Tourist/Press and Information Office), Rathaus, Potsdamerstr. 41, 5650 Solingen.

The Müngstener Bridge or the Solinger Straße lead past the river Wupper to **Remscheid**, the centre of German tool industry. The German Tool Museum (Werkzeugmuseum) is in Remscheid. It is in the same building as the Museum of Local History and Culture. The industrial monument Steffenshammer in Clemenshammer bears witness to the industrial past of the town. The German X-Ray Museum (Röntgen-Museum) in Lennep is dedicated to the discoverer of x-rays, Wilhelm Conrad Röntgen. Lennep is the oldest town in Bergisches Land that has managed to preserve its impressive historical centre.

Stadt Remscheid, Rathaus, 5630 Remscheid. Tel: 021 91/44 22 52.

"I am in love with my city," the famous poet Else Laske-Schüler said about her home town **Wuppertal**. Wuppertal lies in the valley of Wupper, north of Remscheid. It is also famous for its suspension railway which passes through the city over the river.

Friedrich Engels, co-founder of socialism, was also a native of Wuppertal; the Engelshaus, where exhibtions about his life and work are held, is in the historical centre of city. The Museum for Early Industrialization (Museum fur Fruhindustrialisierung) is situated behind Engel's house. Other important museums: the Wuppertaler Uhrenmuseum (Wuppertal's Watch and Clock Museum), the Von der Heydt-Museum with a collection of paintings from the 19th and 20th century. The monument KZ Kemna (concentration camp Kemna) awakens memories of atrocities in recent history. In addition to the city's monuments, a visit to Luisenstraße in the Altstadt and excursions to the Zoo and the Botanical Gardens are worthwhile.

Informationszentrum Pavillon am Döppersberg, Nähe Bahnhof Elberfeld, 5600 Wuppertal. Tel: 0202/563 22 70.

Münsterland with its moated castles is one of the interesting places for excursions that can be reached from Düsseldorf. The city of Münster is 135 Kilometres away.

The ancient imperial city of **Aachen** is 80 Kilometres away from Düsseldorf. The wildlife park "Nordeifel" is on the way to Aachen. Charlemagne's Cathedral Aix La Chapelle and its treasure-vault are worth a visit. Of the great number of historical buildings only the Town Hall and the Burg Frankenberg with the Museum for Municipal History are worth mentioning. Other museums: Neue Galerie Sammlung Ludwig, Suermondt-Ludwig-Museum - both exhibit art collections, Couven-Museum (art of living and Adler Pharmacy), Internationales Zeitungsmuseum (International Newspaper Museum). Aachen has a casino and is also known as Bad Aachen, a health and bathing resort.

Verkehrsverein Bad Aachen, Informationsbüro (Tourist Information Office), Haus Löwenstein, Markt 39, 5100 Aachen. Tel: 0241/180 29 60/61.

Büro Bahnhofplatz, Bahnhofplatz 4, 5100 Aachen. Tel: 0241/60 19 27.

You will find other suggestions and ideas for excursions from Düsseldorf to places near and far in the *Insight Guide* "The Rhine" and *Insight Guide* "Germany" both available in leading bookshops.

FOOD DIGEST

RESTAURANTS

Düsseldorf offers a great variety of local specialities, such as the Rhenish stewed **pickled beef** (*Sauerbraten*), black pudding or pea soup. You can have **Altbier** to go with these specialities. Altbier is a full-flavoured, dark beer that is brewed in the old way. It is a top-fermented beer where the yeast rises to the top during fermentation, as against most beers in Germany, where the yeast sinks to the bottom. Altbier isn't only available in

the Altstadt; it can be drunk all over the city, and like Mostert, Düsseldorf's famous mustard, it is popular even beyond the city's borders. Mustard may not be the right choice for every kind of food but Altbier seems to go well with everything. Often you see two people standing in a bar eating oysters, she drinking a glass of French Champagne, he a pint of Altbier.

Düsseldorf has a variety of original, cosy pubs and restaurants that will satisfy every gourmet and every palate; some of them are even among the best in Germany.The list below will give you an idea of the great variety of speciality restaurants in Düsseldorf, no matter if you are looking to eat "German", "Italian" or "international" food, Düsseldorf has a great deal to offer.

But before going out to a restaurant, call and book a table. If your stomach starts rumbling while you are strolling through the streets of downtown drop in at **Carsch Haus'** gourmet department at Heinrich-Heine-Paltz 1. In the gourmet department you can enjoy all kinds of culinary delights. Have a glass of French Champagne or Altbier to go with your food. Or buy some goodies to eat back at your hotel. You can also quench your thirst or satisfy your hunger at the Kö-Galerie. The choice ranges from all kinds of pastries to the very finest caviar.

RHENISH RESTAURANTS

Een de Canon, Zollstraße 7. Tel: 3 2 97 98.

The Düsseldorfer at Holiday Inn (local and international cuisine, specialities served with mustard), Graf-Adolf-Platz 10. Tel: 3 8 73 -0.

Haus Krevet, Himmelgeist, Steinkaul 3. Tel: 7 5 49 29.

Im Füchschen, Ratinger Straße 28-30. Tel: 8 40 62.

Im goldenen Ring, Burgplatz 21-22. Tel: 13 31 61.

Pfannkuchenhaus am Rheinstadion, Lohausen, Europaplatz 2. Tel: 4 3 41 76.

Rheinbiergarten, Rheinterrassen, Hofgartenufer 7. Tel: 4 8 40 43.

Schumacher Bräu, Oststraße 123. Tel: 3 2 60 04.

Weinhaus Tante Anna, Andreasstraße 2. Tel: 13 11 63.

Gaststätte Tonhalle, Clemensplatz 7. Tel: 4 0 13 00.

Zum St. Maximilian, Citadellstraße 8. Tel: 8 48 55.

Zum Schiffchen (oldest restaurant in Düsseldorf, not to be, mistaken with "Im Schiffchen" in Kaiserswerth), Hafenstraße 5. Tel: 13 24 21.

Zum Schlüssel, Bolkerstraße 45-47. Tel: 3 2 61 55.

Zum Trompeter, Fürstenwall 66b. Tel: 3 9 36 98.

Zum Uerige, Obergärige Hausbrauerei, Berger Straße 1. Tel: 844 55.

GERMAN NOUVELLE CUISINE

Aalschokker, Kaiserswerth, Kaiserswerther Markt 9. Tel: 4 0 39 48.

Bit am Schloßturm, Burgplatz 28. Tel: 3 2 41 96.

Das kleine Restaurant, Düsselthaler Straße 22. Tel: 3 5 19 44.

INTERNATIONAL CUISINE

Am Zault, Unterbach, Gerresheimer Landstraße 40.. Tel: 2 5 1081-85.

An'ne Bell, D 30, Rotterdamer Straße 11.. Tel: 4 37 08 88.

Beranek, Höher Weg 61. Tel: 7 33 66 23.

Café des Artistes (Mövenpick), Königsallee 60. Tel: 3 2 03 14.

Calvados, Hohe Straße 33. Tel: 3 2 84 96.

Les Continents at Interconti, Golzheim, Karl-Arnold-Platz 5. Tel: 4 5 53 11 36.

La Crème, Oberkassel, Oberkasseler Straße 100. Tel: 5 7 56 72.

Grill Royal at Breidenbacher Hof, Heinrich-Heine-Allee 36. Tel: 1 30 38 76.

Gut Höhne, Mettmann, Düsseldorfer Straße 253. Tel: 02104/750 06.

Haus Litzbrück, Angermund, Bahnhofstraße 33. Tel: 0203/7 44 81.

Landhaus Werth, Kaiserswerth, St.-Göres-Straße 11.. Tel: 4 0 12 27.

Monte Christo, Gustaf-Gründgens-Platz 1. Tel: 3 5 78 33.

Naschkörbchen, Königsallee 27. Tel: 3 2 95 50.

Orangerie, Bilder Straße 30. Tel: 13 18 28.

La Residence at Residence Hotel, Derendorf, Kaiserswerther Straße 20.. Tel: 4 9 99 9 22.

Rheinturm Top 180, Stromstraße 30. Tel: 8 48 58.

San Francisco at Hilton, Golzheim, Georg-Glock-Straße 20. Tel: 4 3 77 - 741.

Schneider-Wibbel-Stuben, Schneider-Wibbel-Gasse 7. Tel: 8 00 00.

Schwarzes Schaf (Lamb Specialities), Frankenstraße 1. Tel: 4 3 21 07.

Vasco da Gama at Hotel Ramada, Oberkassel, Am Seestern 16. Tel: 5 9 10 47.

Vier Jahreszeiten, Airport. Tel: 421 60 88 - 97.

ARGENTINE CUISINE

(apart from a number of Steak Restaurants).

La Candela, Schneider-Wibbel-Gasse 10. Tel: 3 2 87 59.

CHINESE CUISINE

China-Sichuan, Graf-Adolf-Platz 7-8. Tel: 3 7 96 41.

Chün Chü Deh, **Peking-Enten-Haus**, Neustraße 41. Tel: 13 25 83.

Dragon City, Berliner Allee 56/I.. Tel: 3 7 99 99.

Dschunke, Charlottenstraße 59. Tel: 16 19 77.

Ho King, Liesengangstraße 15. Tel: 3 5 25 87.

Hung Wan, Oststraße 156. Tel: 16 18 83.

King Long, Immermannstraße 19. Tel: 3 5 71 58.

Lee Garden, Grafenberger Allee 67. Tel: 6 6 04 04.

Me Lai Wah, Roßstraße 32. Tel: 4 4 17 17.

Nan King, Schadowstrße 84. Tel: 3 5 18 64.

Perle, Oberkassel, Belsenstraße 11. Tel: 5 5 53 51.

San Boo, Bahnstraße 65. Tel: 3 6 34 17.

Shing-Kee, Mintropstraße 5. Tel: 3 7 57 26.

Wah Nam, Mertensgasse 19. Tel: 3 2 84 86.

FRENCH CUISINE

La Camrgue, Markstraße 12-14. Tel: 32 56 76.

Heinrich-Heine-Stuben, Bolkerstraße 50/I. Tel: 13 23 14.

Holzenthal, Kaiserswerther Straße 402. Tel: 4 5 32 23.

Hummer-Stübchen, Lörick, Bonifatiusstraße 35. Tel: 5 9 44 0.

Im Schiffchen, Kaiserswerth, Kaiserswerther Markt 9. Tel: 4 0 10 50.

Recha's im Nest, Dürkheimer Weg 37. Tel: 7 8 73 22.

Rôtisserie at Steigenberger Parkhotel, Corneliusplatz 1. Tel: 86 51.

Victorian, Königstraße 3a. Tel: 3 2 02 22.

Zum alten Exerzierplatz, Kaiserswerther Straße 408. Tel: 4 36 06 11.

GREEK CUISINE

Hermes, Adersstraße 8. Tel: , 3 7 45 01.

Kavela, Bilk, Brunnenstraße 37. Tel: 3 1 31 32.

Orpheus, Rath, Westfalenstraße 24-26. Tel: 6 58 12 35.

INDIAN CUISINE

Maharadja, Immermannstraße 32. Tel: 3 5 64 01.

Tandoori, Hohe Straße 39-41. Tel: 3 2 34 50.

ITALIAN CUISINE

Amalfi, Ulmenstraße 22, Derendorf. Tel: 4 3 38 09.

Arlecchino, Andreasstraße 3. Tel: 3 2 43 50.

Da Bruno, Graf-Adolf-Straße 73. Tel: 3 8 23 00.

La Capannina, Hansaallee 30. Tel: 5 5 26 72, Frankenstraße 27. Tel: 4 4 16 52.

Colopic bei Aldo, Mertensgasse 5-9. Tel: 3 7 73 18.

12 Apostoli, Tannenstraße 31. Tel: 4 3 55 19.

La Galleria, Kaiserstraße 27. Tel: 4 9 31 24.

Gatto Verde, Rheinbahnstraße 5. Tel: 4 6 18 17.

La Grappa, Cantadorstraße 4. Tel: 3 5 72 92.

De' Medici, Oberkassel, Amboßstraße. Tel: 5 94 51.

Pigage, Benrath, Benrather Schloßallee 28. Tel: 7 1 40 66.

Rosati, Felix-Klein-Straße 1. Tel: 4 36 05 03.
Sanscone, Schloßstraße 62. Tel: 4 8 22 56.

Savini, Strommstraße 47. Tel: 3 9 39 31.

La Terrazza, Königsallee 30. Tel: 3 2 75 40.

Verona, Benrath, Urdenbacher Allee 3. Tel: 7 18 75 87.

JAPANESE CUISINE

Benkey at Nikko Hotel, Immermannstraße 41. Tel: 86 61.

Daitokai, Mutter-Ey-Straße 1. Tel: 3 2 50 54.

Edo, Oberkassel, Am Seestern 33. Tel: 5 9 10 82/83, Kö-Galerie, Königsallee 60 E. Tel: 13 28 38, Carsch-Haus, Heinrich-Heine-Platz 1. Tel: 3 2 66 18.

Kikaku, Immermannstraße 55. Tel: 3 5 31 35, Oststraße 63. Tel: 3 5 02 13.

Ohno-Jo, Klosterstraße 30. Tel: 16 17 00.

KOREAN CUISINE

Arirang, Mühlenstraße 9. Tel: 3 2 51 10.

Han Il, Kirchfeldstraße 61. Tel: 3 1 57 05.

Han Kook Kwan, Bismarckstraße 66. Tel: 3 61 31 38.

Mi Rak, Klosterstraße 45. Tel: 3 5 27 68.

Seoul, Friedrichstraße 5/I. Tel: 37 87 44.

CROATIAN CUISINE

Kroatia Grill, Burgplatz 13. Tel: 13 33 69.

LEBANESE CUISINE

Libanon Express, Berger Straße 21. Tel: 3 2 95 93.

Zedern Restaurant, Nordstraße 13. Tel: 4 9 08 08.

MEXICAN CUISINE

Cancun, Ellerstraße 123. Tel: 7 2 49 36.

SWISS CUISINE

Walliser Stube, Citadellstraße 8. Tel: 8 48 55.

SPANISH AND ARGENTINE CUISINE

El Amigo, Schneider-Wibbel-Gasse 9. Tel: 3 2 32 03.

Casa España, Berger Straße 27. Tel: 13 41 80.

Casa Kiki, Scheurenstraße 27. Tel: 3 7 31 91.

El Lazo, Bolkerstaße 11. Tel: 3 2 54 23.

La Paella, Neustraße 33. Tel: 3 2 51 04.

Las Palomas, Kirchfeldstraße 169. Tel: 3 3 50 08.

THAI CUISINE

Baan Thai, Berger Straße 28. Tel: 3 2 63 63.

Napalai, Königsallee 60/c Grünstraße. Tel: 3 2 50 81.

Krung Thep, Berliner Allee 30. Tel: 13 28 51.

TURKISH CUISINE

Ak Demiz, Friedrichstraße 132. Tel: 3 1 82 29.

Istanbul, Brunnenstraße 2a. Tel: 3 3 14 13.

Kösk, Friedrichstraße 138. Tel: 3 4 03 33.

Tadim, Roßstraße 21. Tel: 4 6 37 97.

HUNGARIAN CUISINE

Zum Csikos, Andreasstraße 9. Tel: 3 2 97 71.

SEAFOOD RESTAURANTS

Fischerstuben Mulfinger, Rotterdamer Straße 15. Tel: 4 3 26 12.

Carl Maassen, Hallenrestaurant Kaistraße 4. Tel: 3 9 61 25, Hafenrestaurant Kaistraße 4. Tel: 3 0 45 47, Fischrestaurant Berger Straße 7. Tel: 3 2 88 94.

La mer, Schneider-Wibbel-Gasse 6. Tel: 13 28 91.

Muschelhaus Reusch, Burgplatz/Kurze Straße. Tel: 3 2 64 66.

VEGETARIAN RESTAURANTS

Das vegetarische Restaurant, Glockenstraße 20. Tel: 4 6 37 22.

CAFES

Café Bistor Léger, Klosterstraße 53. Tel: 3 6 57 68.

Café Otto Bittner, Königsallee 44. Tel: 3 1 09 80.

Café de la Paix at Interconti, Karl-Arnold-Platz 5. Tel: 4 98 13 61.

Café extra dry, Friedrichstraße 125. Tel: 3 4 47 01.

Café Heinemann, Berliner Allee 47. Tel: 13 13 50, Kö-Center. Tel: 3 2 79 33.

Café Nouvelle, Kasernenstraße 1. Tel: 3 2 06 86.

Chaplen, Nachtcafé, Hüttenstraße 25. Tel: 3 7 65 38.

Cream, Königsallee 18. Tel: 3 2 44 14.

fab. Bar, Musik, Café, Birkenstraße 66. Tel: 6 8 41 88.

König, Königsallee 36. Tel: 3 2 60 60.

Lord Nelson, Bolkerstraße 18. Tel: 3 2 57 57.

NT Nachrichtentreff, Königsalee 27. Tel: 13 23 11-12.

Rheinpark, Kaiserwerther Straße 228. Tel: 4 3 12 13.

Tiffany, Stresemannstraße 31. Tel: 3 6 91 38.

NIGHTLIFE

Düsseldorf is not only a major German city but also the capital of the state of North Rhine Westphalia and a centre for international trade fairs. Therefore, its night-life provides a variety for every taste and every budget ranging from harmless rock-and-rolling to sublime erotic. Every hotel receptionist can give you inside information about where to go.

BARS

Etoile at Hotel Park, Corneliusplatz 1. Tel: 86 51.

Front-Page (Sinatra style live music), Manesmannufer 9. Tel: 3 2 32 64.

Kurrassier Lounge, Piano Bar at Interconti, Karl-Arnold-Platz 5. Tel: 4 55 30.

Maltal, Caribbean Cocktails, Hunsrückenstraße 14-16. Tel: 3 2 95 42.

Terii-Bar at Nikko Hotel, Immermannstraße 41. Tel: 86 61.

Bei Tino, Königsallee 21. Tel: 3 2 64 63.

JAZZ PUBS

Jazz im Knoten, Kurze Straße 1a. Tel: 13 32 20.

NIGHT CLUBS AND DISCOS

Big Ben, Aderstraße 17. Tel: 3 8 17 14.

Checker's Club, Königsallee 28. Tel: 3 2 75 21.

Club 1001 at Hilton. Tel: 4 3 77-0.

Flash Disco-Club, Berger Straße 8. Tel: 3 2 44 48.

Paradise, Burgplatz 11. Tel: 3 2 57 55.

Pferdestall, Schneider-Wibbel-Gasse 8. Tel: 3 2 69 16.

Pierre's, Breite Straße 3. Tel: 13 19 35.

Sam's West Club, Königsallee 27. Tel: 3 2 81 71.

Weindorf, Düsseldorfs größtes Tanzlokal, Aderstraße 17. Tel: 38 17 14.

Werner's Musikladen, Hansaallee 28.

Wintergarten, Adersstraße 26. Tel: 3 7 28 88.

CLUBS AND CABARETS

Clubhaus Lotus, Auf der Geisten 12. Tel: 4 1 47 40.

Femina (with Japanese Film Club), Graf-Adolf-Straße 45. Tel: 3 7 95 47.

Globus (Film and Peep), Graf-Adolf-Straße 39 and 100.

Gretna Green, Kontakt-Café, Bahnstraße 52. Tel: 3 7 59 43.

Salome, Friedrich-Ebert-Straße 13. Tel: 3 5 95 63.

Saunaclub, Rethelstraße 77. Tel: 6 7 37 69.

Roberta's (transvestite), Liefergasse 3. Tel: 3 2 36 70.

Violetta, Karl-Rudolf-Straße 176a. Tel: 3 7 38 18.

ESCORT SERVICE

Baccara.	Tel: 3 5 69 05.
Escort Service.	Tel: 59 35 87.
Exclusive.	Tel: 4 4 52 71.
Nobelle.	Tel: 4 54 25 88.
Penthouse.	Tel: 4 9 97 84.
Venus in furs.	Tel: 4 9 97 84.

CASINOS

Those who are not afraid of taking risks should also not mind long distances, either. The next casinos from Düsseldorf are:

Spielbank Bad Neuenahr, Felix-Rütten-Straße 1. Tel: 026 41/22 41.

Internationales Spielcasino Aachen, Kurpark, Monheimallee 44. Tel: 0241/15 30 11.

Westdeutsche Spielbank, Dortmund 2, Hohensyburg. Tel: 0231/7 74 00.

Spielcasino Haus Schwarzbachtal, Ratingen, Mettmanner Straße 113. Tel: 021 02/8 33 32.

CULTURE PLUS

MUSEUMS

The Museum of Fine Art, the State Academy of Art, the State Art Collection of North Rhine-Westphalia, the City Exhibition Hall and Art Society are situated on the "Kunstachse Düsseldorf" encompassing an area starting in Ehrenhof between Hofgarten and Rhine to Grabbeplatz in the Altstadt. The cultural diversity is complemented by galleries on the Kunstachse, of which no small number are lined up along the tiny Mutter-Ey-Straße.

There are also a large number of old and contemporary sculptures and memorials dotted around the city, particularly in the parks.

Dumont-Lindemann-Archiv (Dumont-Lindemann Archives), Museum of the Theatre, Jägerhofstrasse 1. Tel: 899 61 15/6. Contains documents from Düsseldorf theatre history; archives for research in theatrical history.

Forum Bilker Straße, Municipal Gallery and Art-Loan, Bilder Straße 12. Tel: 899 61 40.

Goethe Museum, The Kippenberg Foundation, Schloss Jägerhof, Jacobistraße 2. Tel: 899 62 62. Permanent Exhibition on Goethe in his time. Original manuscripts on the life and work of Germany's most famous writer.

Heinrich-Heine-Institut (Heinrich Heine Institue), Bilkerstraße 14, Heine-Haus. Tel: 899 53 71/53 75. Permanent Exhibition: H. Heine and his times - Manuscripts, 1st editions, letters, contemporary portraits, the death-mask.

Hetjens Museum - The German Museum of Ceramics, Palais Nesselrode, Schulstraße 4. Tel: 899 42 10. 8,000 years of ceramics - Near East, E. Asia, Greek and Roman, Medieval Europe, German Stoneware, European Faience, European Porcelain, 20th-Century Ceramics. Temporary Exhibitions.

Kunstmuseum/Kunstpalast Düsseldorf (Museum of Fine Art), Ehrenhof 5. Tel: 899 24 60. European art from the medieval to the present-day; emphasis on German art of 19th and 20th centuries. Glass from classical antiquity to the present, Hentrich Collection of Art Nouveau Glass; Collection of Prints and Drawings, Library; Temporary exhibitions of Old Masters, modern and contemporary art, exhibitions for children and young people in the "Museum for Young Visitors".

State Art Collection of North Rhine-Westphalia, Grabbeplatz. Tel: 13 39 61. 20th century paintings; Klee Collection.

Art Society of the Rhineland and Westphalia (Kunstverein), Grabbeplatz 4 (in the Kunsthalle). Tel: 3 2 70 23. Temporary Exhibitions.

Landesmuseum Volk & Wirtschaft (State Museum of Society and Economy), Ehrenhof 2. Tel: 4 4 61 08. Graphics, diagrams, dioramas, light-up maps and models, for interesting demonstrations of processes and connections in society and the economy. Guided tours for groups at any time (advance notice please) and for individuals Weds at 6.00 p.m., Sundays 11.00 a.m.

Löbbecke Museum and Aquazoo, Kaiserswerther Straße 380, Nordpark. Tel: 899 61 50. Natural History Exhibitions, Aquarium (fresh and salt-water), Terrarium and Insectarium. Permanent Exhibition: The Löbbecke Collection - Molluscs, Octopuses.

Restaurierungszenturm der Landeshauptstadt Düsseldorf (Restoration Centre of the City of Düsseldorf) - Henkel Donation, Ehrenhof 3 a. Tel: 899 24 66/24 36. Restoration of old and contemporary painting, art objects and glass. Viewing in groups by appointment only.

Schiffahrt-Museum, -Navigation Museum in the Castle Tower, Burgplatz, the Castle Tower. Tel: 899 41 95. 2000 years of navigation on the Rhine (models, many pictures and original documents).

Schloß Benrath (Benrath Château), Benrather Schlossallee 104. Tel: 899 61 72, 899 72 71. Important Late-Baroque pleasure palace and park, unaltered original environment uniquely preserved. It was planned and built from 1755 to 1770 by Nicolas de Pigage for Elector Palatine Carl Theodor. The château holds collections on the architecture and its patron, including precious maquetry furniture, Frankenthal porcelain. Basement: Lapidarium (original statuary) and models of former buildings. Architectural history of the Castle.

Naturkundliches Heimatmuseum Benrath (Local Natural History Museum, Benrath), Benrather Schlossallee 102 (West Wing of the Castle). Tel: 899 72 19. Exhibitions on the natural history of the Lower Rhenish Bight and Lower Bergisches Land.

Stiftung Ernst Schneider (The Ernst Schneider Foundation), Schloss Jägerhof, Jacobi-Straße 2. Tel: 899 62 62. Meissen and other porcelains, 18th century silverware.

The Kunsthalle/City Exhibition Hall, Grabbeplatz 4. Tel: 13 14 69. Temporary Exhibitions.

Stadtmuseum/Municipal History Museum, Bäckerstraße 7-9. Tel: 899 61 70. Founded in 1874; the one-time palace of the Counts of Spee. Collections on the history and culture of Düsseldorf and its geographical and historical context.

THEATRES

Deutsche Oper am Rhein (Opera House), Heinrich-Heine-Allee 16a. Tel: 13 39 49/40.

Düsseldorfer Schauspielhaus (Theatre), Gustaf-Gründgens-Platz. Tel: 3 6 30 11, Ticket Reservation: 36 99 11.

Kammerspiele Düsseldorf, Jahnstraße 3. Tel: 37 83 53.

Das Kommödchen, **Cabaret**, Hunsrückenstraße, Entrance City Exhibition Hall. Tel: 3 2 54 28.

Komödie, Boulevardtheater Düsseldorf, Steinstraße 23. Tel: 3 2 51 51.

Düsseldorfer Marionettentheater (Puppet Theatre), Bilker Straße 7. Tel: 3 2 84 32.

Puppentheater am Fürstenplatz, Helmholtzstraße 38. Tel: 3 7 13 68.

Theater an der Luegallee, Luegallee 4. Tel: 5 7 22 22.

Junges Theater in der Altstadt (Youth Theatre), "Brücke", Kasernenstraße 6. Tel: 3 2 72 10 and 32 72 37.

(For more theatres see Cultural Centres)

EDUCATIONAL INSTITUTIONS

Hauptstaatsarchiv (Central State Archives), Mauerstraße 55. Tel: 4 49 71.

Stadtarchiv (Municipal Archives), Heinrich-Ehrhardt-Straße 61. Tel: 899 57 37.

Mahn- und Gedenkstätte für die Opfer der nationalsozialistischen Gewaltherrschaft in Düsseldorf (Memorial for the Victims of National Socialism in Düsseldorf), Mühlenstraße 29. Tel: 899 62 06.

WBZ - Weiterbildungszentrum Stadtbüchereien Düsseldorf, **Zentralbibliothek**, **Musikbibliothek** (Centre for Further Education, Municipal Library, Central, Library, Music Library), Bertha-von-Suttner-Platz 1 (Central Railway Station East). Tel: 8 99 43 99. There are branches of Municipal Library in the centre of the city and in Benrath, Bilk, Derendorf, Eller, Flingern, Garath, Gerresheim, Hassels, Kaiserswerth, Oberkassel, Rath, Schulzentrum Hennkamp, University Clinics, Unterrath and Wersten. Mobile Libraries with stations in many parts of the city.

Bibliotheksstelle der Kulturinstitute der Landeshauptstadt Düsseldorf (Library of the Cultural Institutes of Düsseldorf), Heinrich-Heine-Allee 23. Tel: 899 55 73/55 69.

Universitätsbibliothek (University Library), Universitätsstraße 1. Tel: 3 1 11.

Institut Français, in Palais Wittgenstein, Bilker Straße 7-9.

Goethe-Institut, Willi-Becker-Allee 10. Tel: 7 7 10 81.

Lernort Studio, Killegschule Kikweg, Schloßallee 14. Tel: 2 1 02 - 317/3 26.

Literaturbüro NRW e.V., Bilker Straße 6. Tel: 3 2 44 70.

Städtische Clara-Schuhmann-Musikschule, Bilkerstraße 11. Tel: 899 29 28/24 91.

Robert-Schuhmann-Hochschule für Musik, Fischerstraße 110. Tel: 4 8 40 38.

Staatliche Kunstakademie, Eiskellerstraße 1. Tel: 3 2 93 34.

Volkshochschule, Studienhaus, Fürstenwall 5. Tel: 899 41 50.

Universität Düsseldorf (University of Düsseldorf), Rector and Administration, Universitätsstraße, Building 23.31/32. Tel: 3 1 11.

Fachhochschule Düsseldorf (Technical College of Düsseldorf), Universitätsstraße, Building 23.31/32. Tel: 3 11 - 35 55 - 35 58/ 51 42.

Filminstitut der Landeshauptstadt Düsseldorf - Black Box (Film Institute of Düsseldorf), Kasernenstraße 6. Tel: 8 99 24 90.

CULTURAL CENTRES

Die Brücke, Kasernenstraße 6, in the out-building of Wilhelm-Marx-Haus.

Palais Wittgenstein, Bilker Straße 6. Tel: 8 99 61 04.

Die Werkstatt e.V., Börnestraße 10. Tel: 3 6 03 91.

ZAKK - Zentrum für Aktion, Kultur and Kommunikation (Centre for Projects, Culture and Communications), Fichtenstraße 36-38. Tel: 7 33 66 44.

CONCERT HALLS

Tonhalle (2 halls, 300 or 1,900 seats), Ehrenhof 1. Tel: 8 99 55 40.

Kammermusik-Saal (Chamber Music Hall), in Palais Wittgenstein (234 seats), Bilker Straße 7-9. Tel: 8 99 61 04.

Philipshalle (up to 5,600 seats), Seigburger Straße 15. Tel: 8 99 38 06.

Stadthalle (up to 3,478 seats), Fischerstraße. Tel: 8 99 38 06.

Radschläger Saal (Cartwheeler Hall, up to 1,900 seats), Sittarder Straße/Corner of Fischerstraße. Tel: 4 9 90 16-17.

Messe-Kongress-Center (Fair and Congress Centre, MKC) der Düsseldorfer Messegesellschaft mbH (NOWEA, up to 1,200 seats), Stockummer Kirchstraße 61. Tel: 4 5 601.

Robert-Schumann-Saal (Robert Schumann Hall, up to 1,089 seats), Ehrenhof 4a. Tel: 899 38 29.

Malkasten (Paint Box, up to 600 seats), Jacobistraße 6. Tel: 3 5 04 01.

Orangerie Benrath (173 seats), Urdenbacher Allee 4-6. Tel: 8 99 61 75.

Studiengebäude (up to 496 seats), Fürstenwall 5. Tel: 899 30 06/30 07.

CINEMAS

Telephone Announcements of Movie Programmes, city centre. Tel: 1 15 11, Düsseldorf - North: 1 15 12, Düsseldorf - South: 1 15 13.

Bambi-Filmstudio, Klosterstraße 78. Tel: 35 36 35.

Apollo 69, Graf-Adolf-Straße 47. Tel: 37 60 00.

Atelier, Graf-Adolf-Straße 47. Tel: 37 60 66.

Cinema, Schneider-Wibbel-Gasse 5. Tel: 13 13 74.

Europa-Theater, Graf-Adolf-Straße 108. Tel: 3 5 41 61.

Filminstitut der Landeshauptstadt Düsseldorf, Kasernenstraße 6. Tel: 89 91.

Lichtburg and Lichtburg-Studio, Königsallee 40. Tel: 3 2 57 07.

Lux am Bahnhof, Graf-Adolf-Straße 96. Tel: 3 5 99 40.

Metropol, Brunnenstraße 20. Tel: 3 4 97 09.

Neues Rex, Sunset, Oscar, Movie, Friedrich-Ebert-Straße 59-61. Tel: 3 5 00 00.

Residenz, Graf-Adolf-Straße 20. Tel: 3 7 12 07.

Savoy und Linse 1 und 2, Graf-Adolf-Straße 47. Tel: 3 7 70 00.

Theater im Filmforum, Prinz-Georg-Straße 80. Tel: 4 6 32 12.

Ufa-Berolina, Berliner Allee 46. Tel: 3 7 12 07.

Ufa-Universum, Berliner Allee 59. Tel: 3 2 66 55.

SHOPPING

You can buy everything in Düsseldorf. From candy to works of art, from antiques to sable coats, from full-flavoured Altbier to flashy necklaces. Shopping in Düsseldorf is always an adventure. Some people fly in with their private jets, take a cab to Kö, go shopping, drive back to the airport and fly home. No matter which means of transport you use to come to Düsseldorf, you shouldn't miss a shopping spree on the Kö. A whole chapter in our guide has been dedicated to shopping on the Kö. And don't forget to drop in at Kö-Galerie, the Kö-Center, the Trinkhaus-Center and the WZ-Center. The Schadow- and the Graf-Adolf-Straße, too, are tempting shopping streets. The traditional Carsch-Haus and the Art Nouveau department store Kaufhof are also worth a visit. You will find art dealers and antique shops in Karlstadt.

The stalls at Market Square and the closeby Karlplatz offer local and international culinary delights and delicacies. The Radschlägermarkt (cartwheelers' market) is a completely different kind of a market. It is a flea market which is held every second Saturday from May to October at the lower Rhine dockyard between the Schloßturm (Castle Tower) and the Tonhalle.

But Düsseldorf is not only a city of fashion and glamour, of food and drinks but also a city of sciences and art; here are some useful addresses:

BOOKSHOPS

Akzent-Buchhandlung Heinrich Heine, Ackerstraße 3.

Bahnhofsbuchhandlung Grauert, Konrad-Adenauer-Platz 14.

C.G. Boerner, Kasernenstraße 13.

Esoterische Buchhandlung Bornemann, Flinger Straße 10.

Buch + Bazar Wilhelm Ebbing, Konrad-Adenauer-Platz 11.

Buchhandlung Bibabuze, Aachener Straße 1.

Buchladen Lutz Lewejohann, Friedrichstraße 6, Hohe Straße 7.

Büchergilde Gutenberg, Bismarckstraße 104.

Cockpit Yacht & Motorbuchhandlung, Hohe Straße 48.

Buchhandlung Walter Dietsch, Görresstraße 3.

Buchhandlung Droste, Martin-Luther-Platz 23.

Fergana Buchhandlung, Münsterstraße 96.

Gerresheimer Bücherstube, Benderstr. 58.

Goethe-Buchhandlung Teubig, Duisburger Straße 11.

Hin Chung Got, Ming Fan, Stresemannstraße 3.

Buchhandlung Heinz Holte, Duisburger Straße 57.

Buch- und Landkartenhandlung, Michael Horst, Steinstraße 32.

Kaufhaus Horten, Buchhandlung im Carsch-Haus, Heinrich-Heine-Platz (in other department, stores in Horten).

Jugendhaus Düsseldorf, Carl-Mosters-Platz 1.

Kaufhof, Buchhandlung im Kaufhaus Kö (and in other Kaufhof stores).

Buch- und Kunsthandlung Kinet, Heinrich-Heine-Allee 53.

Buchhandlung Walther König, Heinrich-Heine-Allee 15.

Buchhandlung Claus Lincke, Königsallee 96.

Antiquariat Hans Marcus, Ritterstraße 10.

Montanus, Glinger Straße 43, Graf-Adolf-Straße 22.

Hans-Jürgen Niepel, Orangeriestraße 6.

Antiquariat Franz Roberg, Friedrichstraße 17.

Buchhandlung C. Schaffnit Nachf., Berliner Allee 8.

Schrobsdorff'sche Buchhandlung, Königsallee 22.

Stern-Verlag, Buchhandlung und Antiquariat, Friedrichstraße 24, Universitätsstraße 1.

Verlag Stahleisen, Buchhandlung, Sohnstraße 65.

Antiquariat Horst Wehrens, Oststraße 13.

Japanische Buchhandlung T. Takagi, Immermannstraße 31.

ANTIQUES

Antik Siegried Blau, Hohe Straße 16.

Antike Uhren Winkel (clocks), Bilker Straße 23a.

Antikes Spielzeug (toys), Bilker Straße 16.

Antik-Markt P & L's, Worringer Straße 72.

Antiquitäten am Benrather Schloß, Urdenbacher Allee 5.

Art Deco Ruthmann, Bilkerstraße 8.

Antiquitäten Aufreiter, Hohe Straße 27.

Antiquitäten Fassbender, Steinstraße 4.

Antiquitäten Heintzen + Adams, Hohe Straße 2.

Antiquitäten M. & M. Heyduck, Bastionstraße 12.

Antiquitäten Päpke & Janowitz, Hohe Straße 28.

Antiquitäten Schulenburg, Rethelstraße 123.
Antiquitäten Eva Schulte, Königsallee 56.

Antiquitäten Gabriele Vierzig, Königsallee 21-23.

Antiquitäten Vogelsang, Bastionstraße 8.

Antiquitäten von Borcke, Bastionstraße 8.

Galerie Art 204, Contemporary Art, Rethelstraße 139.

Galerie Avantgard Gestern, Beethovenstraße 16.

Galerie Norbert Blaeser, Bilkenstraße 5.

Galerie Citadellehen, Citadellstraße 10.

Galerie Heike Curtze, Citadellstraße 11.

Galerie des Arts, Graf-Adolf-Straße 41.

Galerie Dünnebacke, Graf-Adolf-Straße 18.

Galerie Ehlenbeck, Dreherstraße 22.

Galerie EP, Blumenstraße 12.

Galerie Konrad Fischer, Mutter-Ey-Straße 5.

Galerie Förster, Poststraße 3.

Galerie Gmyrek, Mutter-Ey-Straße 5.

Galerie Hans Mayer, Grabbeplatz 2.

Galerie Hartmann, Brehmstraße 86.

Galerie Hete Hühnermann, Ratinger Tor 2.

Galerie C. Hölzl, Mutter-Ey-Straße 5.

Galerie Keppel, Rethelstraße 91.

Galerie Jülich, Herderstraße 92.

Galerie Kunst und Leben, Oberkasseler Straße 52.

Galerie Ludorff, Königsallee 22.

Galerie Mode und Art, Hohe Straße 6.

Galerie Paffrath, Königsallee 46.

Galerie Remmert & Barth, Bilkerstraße 20.

Galerie Schmela, Mutter-Ey-Straße 3.

Galerie Ursus-Presse, Kaiserswerther Straße 272.

Galerie Vömel, Königsallee 30

CUSTOMS

The usual amounts of semi-luxury goods (alcoholic beverages, tabacco, tea) and perfumes can be imported and exported. The regulations are friendlier towards members of the European Community. Contact the customs authorities for detailed information when in doubt: Tel: 4 21 69 27.

SPORTS

SPECTATOR

The ice hockey, soccer, basketball, table tennis, indoor handball and football matches of the Federal League are the most attractive events which turn into public feasts. Horse racing is in Grafenberg. The Tennis World Team Cup is held in the Rochus club.

DEG Düsseldorfer Eislaufgemeinschaft 1935 e.V., Brehmstraße 27a. Tel: 6 2 21 93.

Ice Stadium, Brehmstraße 27. Tel: 6 2 71 01.

Fortuna 1895 e.V. Düsseldorfer Turn- und Sportverein (Düsseldorf's Gymnastics and Sports Club), Flinger Broich 87. Tel: 2 3 30 50/59, Youth Department. Tel: 2 3 32 22.

Sportverein Agon 08 e.V., St.-Franziskus-Str. 139. Tel: 6 3 21 77.

Turu Rasensportunion 1880 e.V., Feuerbachstraße 82. Tel: 3 3 43 22, Youth Department. Tel: 3 3 00 80.

American Football club Panther e.V., Adersstraße 48. Tel: 3 7 30 83.

Düsseldorfer Reiter- und Rennverein e.V. (Düsseldorf's Riding Club), Rennplatz Grafenberg, Rennbahnstraße 24.

Rochusclub, Düsseldorfer Tennisclub e.V., Rolander Weg 15. Tel: 6 2 69 63, 62 61 18.

PARTICIPANT

Everyone can do sports at the Rheinstadion, Europaplatz. Tel: 899 52 04, 899 52 16. Plastic track, lawn and ash playing fields, smaller grounds out of synthetics and plastic lawn for football, handball, volleyball, hockey, basketball, in addition to facilities for discus, javelin, shot putting, high and long jump; tennis courts and special wall for practising tennis, room for heavy athletics in the sports hall; locker room and shower facilities.

The Recreation Centre Unterbacher See, Kleiner Torfbruch 31. Tel: 8 99 2094, Boat Pier Tel: 899 20 42, Surf Centre Tel: 8 99 23 59, opens its outdoor swimming pool from May to September. Boats can be rented from April to October. There are open-air swimming pools north and south with sauna facilties and nudists' area, a sailing and surfing school, sailing and pedal boats and surf boards for rent, hiking trails, playground for children and barbecue facilities at the Recreation Centre.

FISHING

You can go fishing at Unterbacher Lake, in the Rhine or in Hafenbecken, at Habes and Josef Lake. Shops selling fishing tackle will help you get a permission for fishing in these areas. Contact the Fishing Authorities for more information: Auf'm Hanekamp 45. Tel: 899 27 79.

BILLIARDS

You can play a game of billiards at Europa-Bowling, Stockumer Kirchstraße 55, and at Rheinland-Bowling, Erkrather Straße 372.

BOCCIA

Can be played at Kürtenhof, Bruchstraße and at the outdoor swimming pool Lörick.

ICE SKATING

You can go ice skating at the Eissporthalle Benrath, Paulsmühlenstraße 6 and at Eisstadion, Brehmstraße 27.

GOLF

Is played at Golf Clubs such as the Düsseldorfer Golf Club in Ratingen and at Land and Golf Club Düsseldorf in Hubbelrath or at the public golf course at Lausward.

RIDING

You can go riding at riding schools: Am Dammsteg. Tel: 2 1 46 21, Am Galberg. Tel: 2 8 56 67, Gut Wolfsaap. Tel: 6 3 38 33, Rumstich. Tel: 2 89 738, Talihoh. Tel: 6 6 17 03, Wirtz. Tel: 6 6 17 03.

SWIMMING

Apart from the facilities at Unterbacher Lake, you can go swimming at the outdoor swimming pools of Rheinstadion, Lörick, Flinger Broich, Benrath and Kaiserswerth and at the indoor swimming pools in the centre of the city and in other quarters.

TENNIS

You can try your hand at a game of tennis like Steffi Graf and Boris Becker either at the Rochus club, Rolander .Weg 15 or at the Rheinstadion or in the Sportpark Niederheid.

SQUASH

Go for a game of squash at Squash City on Brachtstraße 1, and at King's Squash Club on Bruchstraße 111.

AQUATIC SPORTS

You can hire motor, sailing and rowing boats at Unterbacher Lake.

For further information contact the Sports Office on 899 52 04 or the Municipal Sports Office on 34 64 55.

Parks & Reserves

The Hofgarten (Court Garden) encompasses an area of 26 hectares. This historical garden north of the Kö extends in the east to the Schloß Jägerhof (Jägerhof Château) and in the west to the Tonhalle and the Ehrenhof on the Rhine.

The Rheinpark begins to the north of the Rhine terraces and extends over 2 Kilometres along the river.

The Nordpark with its Japanese Garden on the Rhine lies further north.

The Floragarten is situated between Bilker Allee and Bachstraße.

You can go hiking or on an excursion at Düsseldorf's Stadtwald (City Forest), that encompasses an area of approximately 1800 hectares. The Aaper Forest, a branch of the Bergisches Land, is situated in its northern part. The Grafenberger Wald (Grafenberger Forest) extends over Rennbahnstraße to the Grafenberg Game Park where red deer, fallow deer, roe and wild boar live. In the south lies an extension of the Stadtwald, Die Hardt; the Ostpark with its pond is located in the south-west of the Hardt.

The Speesche Graben with its public gardens is between Berger Allee and Poststraße. Extending over Haroldstraße and to the south of the Schwanenmarkt lie Schwanenspiegel and Kaiserteich in green surroundings.

Volksgarten is located in the south of the city and verges on the Südpark. The Botanical Garden outstretches Werstener Straße and is in the vicinity of the university. It is open daily from 8.00 a.m. and closes depending on the season at 5.00 p.m. (November to February), 7.00 p.m. (March, April, September, October), 8.00 p.m. (May to August).

Schloß Benrath and its Castle Gardens are situated in the south-east. Doesn't Düsseldorf have a zoological park? The Zoo Park is located behind the Ice Stadium on Brehmstraße. But the only animals you will find here are kept on the lead. Apart from the occasional dog you might even come across a squirrel. Düsseldorf's zoo was closed down in 1945. But a lot of Düsseldorfers are pressing for a new zoo. Lore Lorentz once said: "A Düsseldorfer is someone who wants his Zoo back."

Special Information

BUSINESS INFORMATION

The majority of visitors do not come to Düsseldorf because of art and culture or its sights (although anyone coming here should take his time to visit the sights) but because Düsseldorf is a business centre. 3,000 foreign enterprises, manufacturing companies and trading concerns have set up business here. Half of all European multinational concerns have opened a branch in Düsseldorf. This metropolis on the Rhine is a centre of production, trade, finance, advertising, fairs and congresses. Many unions have either a seat or their headquarters here. And there is no end in sight. The cornerstone for a new centre, the industrial estate "An der Düssel" was laid in Derendorf by the Swedish loyal couple, King Karl XVI Gustaf and Queen Silvia on 6th October, 1989.

To acquire business information in Düsseldorf contact:

Landeshauptstadt Düsseldorf, Werbe-und Wirtshafftsförderungsamt (Advertising and Business Promotion Agency), Mühlenstraße 29. Tel: 8 99 55 00.

Industrie- und Handelskammer zu Düsseldorf (Chamber Of Industry and Commerce in Düsseldorf), Ernst-Schneider-Platz 1. Tel: 3 5 57 1.

Wirtschaftsvereinigung Ziehereien und Kaltwalzwerke (Trade Union of Cold-Rolling Mills), Kaiserswerther Str. 137. Tel: 4 56 41. Telex: 8584945.

Deutscher Gießereiverband e.V. (German Association of Foundries), Sohnstraße 70. Tel: 6 8 711.

Wirtschaftsverband Eisen, Blech und Metallverarbeitende Industrie e.V. (Trade Association of Iron, Tin and Metal Industry), Kaiserswerther Str. 135. Tel: 4 5 49 30. Telex: 8584985.

Bundesverband Glasindustrie und Mineralfaserindustrie e.V. (Federal Association of Glass and Mineral Fibre Industry), Stresemannstr. 26. Tel: 16 89 40. Telex: 8587686.

Verein Deutscher Eisenhüttenleute (German Union of the Employees in Metallurgical Plants), Sohnstraße 65. Tel: 6 70 70. Telex: 8582512.

Handwerkskammer Düsseldorf (Chamber of Handicrafts Düsseldorf), Breite Straße 7-11. Tel: 87 950.

Außenhandelsstelle für die Mittelständische Wirtschaft Nordrhein-Westfalen e.V. (Foreign Trade Office for medium-sized Business Enterprises, in North Rhine-Westphalia), Schneider-Platz 1. Tel: 3 55 72 28. Telex: 8582815.

Verein Deutscher Gießereifachleute (Union of German Foundrymen), Sohnstr. 70. Tel: 6 87 11. Telex: 8586885.

Deutscher Verband für Schweißtechnik e.V. (German Association of Welding Engineering), Aachener Str. 172. Tel: 15 40 40. Telex: 8582523.

Wirtschaftsvereinigung Metalle e.V. (Trade Union of the Metal Industry), Tersteegenstr. 28. Tel: 4 5 47 10. Telex: 8584721.

Verein Deutscher Ingenieure (Union of German Engineers), Graf-Recke-Str. 84. Tel: 6 2 140. Telex: 8586525.

Bundesverband Deutscher Stahlhandel e.V. (Federal Association of the German Steel Trade), Adolf-Platz 12. Tel: 3 7 00 94. Telex: 8587760.

Wirtschaftsvereinigung Bauindustrie e.V. NW. (Trade Union of the Building Industry), Hauptgeschäftsstelle Düsseldorf, Uhlandstr. 56. Tel: 6 70 31.

Einzelhandelsverband Nordrhein e.V. (Association of Retail Industry), Kaiserstraße 42a. Tel: 4 9 80 60.

Landesverband Gaststätten- und Hotelgewerbe Nordrhein-Westfalen (Regional Association of Catering and Hotel Trade), Liesegangstr. 22. Tel: 3 5 60 46.

Unternehmensverband des Großhandels Düsseldorf-Niederrhein e.V. (Association of Entrepreneurs in the Whole-Sale Business, Düsseldorf-Lower Rhine), Achenbachstr. 28. Tel: 6 7 20 76.

Wirtschaftsverband der Handelsvertreter und Handelsmakler Rhein-Ruhr (Trade Association of Commercial Agents and Merchant Brokers), Lindemannstr. 90. Tel: 6 8 50 02.

Verband des Verkehrsgewerbe Nordrhein e.V. (Association of Transport Services), Engelbertstr. 11. Tel: 7 33 54 95.

Verein rheinisch-westfälischer Zeitungs-Verleger e.V. (Union of Rhenish-Westphalian Newspaper Publishers), Schadowstr. 39. Tel: 3 6 33 33.

Landesvereinigung der Arbeitgeberverbände NRW e.V. (Regional Union of Employer's Association), Uerdinger Str. 58.60. Tel: 4 57 31.

Verband der Chemischen Industrie e.V. (Association of the Chemical Industry), Steinstr. 4. Tel: 8 38 90. Telex: 8389136.

Unternehmerschaft Düsseldorf und Umgebung e.V. (Employers in Düsseldorf and surrounding Areas), Achenbachstr. 28. Tel: 6 8 10 20.

CLUBS/UNIONS

Industrie Club e.V., Elberfelder Str.6/8. Tel: 3 2 93 07.

Rotary-Club, Königsallee 4. Tel: 13 17 97.

Lions Club, Breite Str. 27. Tel: 889 43 44. Telex: 8587086.

OTHER IMPORTANT ADDRESSES

Arbeitamt Düsseldorf (Labour Office), Fritz-Roeber-Str. 2. Tel: 822 61.

Deutsche Bundesbahn (German Federal Railways), Konrad-Adenauer-Platz. Tel: 3 6 801.

Flughafen Düsseldorf (Düsseldorf Airport), P.O. Box 30 03 63. Tel: 4 2 11.

Düsseldorfer Messegesellschaft mbH (Düsseldorf's Fair Association), - NOWEA - P.O. Box 32 02 03. Tel: 4 5 60 01.

Messe- und Kongreßcenter der NOWEA (Fair and Congress Centre), Stockumer Kirchstr. Tel: 4 5 601.

IGEDO - International Modemesse Kronen AG (International Fashion Show), Danzingerstr. 101. Tel: 4 5 07 71.

Ministerium für Wirtschaft, Mittelstand und Technologie (Ministry for Economy and Technology), Haroldstr. 4. Tel: 837 02.

Verkehrsverein der Stadt Düsseldorf (Transport Executive of the City of Düsseldorf), Adenauer-Platz. Tel: 3 5 05 05. Telex: 858 77 85.

Being an important city in Germany, the trade unions have also set up their headquarters in Düsseldorf:.
DGB Deutscher Gewerkschaftsbund (German Federation of Trade Unions), Bundesvorstand, Hans-Böckler-Str. 39. Tel: 4 3 01 0.

CHAMBERS OF COMMERCE

Trade and Investment Promotion Organizations:

CHINA

Minmetals German GmbH, Kaiserswerther Str. 22. Tel: 4 96 80. Telex: 8584662.

China Sichuan Corporation for International Techno-, Economic Cooperation, Graf-Adolf-Platz 7.8. Tel: 3 7 96 41.

China National Nonferrous Metals Import, and Export Corporation (CNIEC), Grafenberger Allee 140. Tel: 6 6 10 85.

China Metallurgical Improt and Export, Corporation (CMIEC), Emanuel-Leutze-Str. 1. Tel: 5 9 68 35/36.

Deutsch-Chinesische Wirtschaftsvereinigung e.V., Königsallee 37. Tel: 886 29 05 or 57 80 04.

Tianjin Handelsgesellschaft, c/o Olympia-Reisen, Kappelerstr. 3a. Tel: 7 15 075.

Repräsentanz der Stadt Shenyang, Mr. Chen, Kaiserswerther Str. 22. Tel: 4 9 68 29.

DENMARK

Marktinformationsstelle der dänischen Molkereiwirtschaft (Information Centre of the Danish Dairy Farming), Sternwartstr. 54. Tel: 3 9 20 35. Telex: 8587534.

GERMAN DEMOCRATIC REPUBLIC

Ständige Vertretung der Deutschen Demokratischen Republik (Permanent Representation of the German Democratic Republic), Handelspolitische Abteilung, Sternwartstr. 27-29. Tel: 3 9 10 31.

Leipziger Messeamt (Leipzig's Exhibition Office), Sternwartstr. 31. Tel: 3 9 65 40.

FRANCE

Französische Industrie- und Handelskammer in Deutschland (French Chamber of Industry and Commerce), Orangeriestr. 6. Tel: 13 99 20. Telex: 8583476.

Sopexa - Förderungsgemeinschaft für französische Landwirtschaftserzeugnisse (Association of French Agricultural Products), Sternstr. 58. Tel: 4 9 80 80. Telex: 8587744.

INDIAN

Deutsch-Indische Handelskammer (German-Indian Chamber of Commerce), Oststr. 84. Tel: 3 6 05 98. Telex: 8581496.

Indische Technische Handelsberatung (Indian Technical Trade Counsel), Immermannstr. 59. Tel: 3 5 90 11.

INDONESIA

Repräsentanz der Deutsch-Indonesischen, Industrie- und Handelskammer EKONID (Representation of the German-Indonesian, Chamber of Industry and Commerce), Stockumer Kirchstr. 41. Tel: 4 5 29 08. Telex: 8587260.

IRAN

DIO Contact Office, Kaiserswerther Str. 142. Tel: 4 5 10 18/9.

Pouschineh Baft/NIIO, Berliner Allee 40. Tel: 3 2 43 95.

IRELAND

Irische Außenhandelsstelle (Irish Foreign Trade Office), Jacobistr. 3. Tel: 3 2 52 72.

ITALY

Italienisches Institut für Außenhandel I.C.E. (Italian Institute for Foreign Trade), Italienisches Handelszentrum, Jahnstr. 3. Tel: 3 8 79 90. Telex: 8581967.

JAPAN

Deutsch-Japanisches Wirtschaftsförderungsbüro (German-Japanese Business Promotion Office), Oststr. 110. Tel: 3 5 80 48/49.

Japanische Industrie- und Handelskammer zu Düsseldorf e.V. (Japanese Chamber of Industry and Commerce), Immermannstr, 45. Tel: 3 6 90 01.

Jetro Japan Trade Centre, Königsallee 58. Tel: 13 60 20. Telex: 8587449.

Electronic Industries Association of Japan, Schadowstr. 41. Tel: 3 6 98 16. Telex: 8587986.

CANADA

Regierung von Quebec (Government of Quebec), Königsallee 30. Tel: 3 2 08 16. Telex: 8587659.

Regierung von British Columbia (Government of British Columbia), c/o Canadia Consulate General, Immermannstr. 65d. Tel: 3 5 34 71.

KOREA

Korean Foreign Trade Association, Düsseldorf Branch, Immermannstr. 65a. Tel: 3 6 20 44. Telex: 8584754.

German-Korean Business Association, Immermannstr. 65a. Tel: 3 6 56 73. Telex: 8584754.

NETHERLANDS

German-Dutch Chamber of Commerce, Freiligrathstr. 29. Tel: 4 98 72 01. Telex: 8584980.

NORWAY

Handelsabteilung des Norw. Generalkonsulats (Trade Department of the Norwegian Consulate General), Uerdinger Str. 5. Tel: 4 5 890. Telex: 8586456.

AUSTRIA

Österreichische Handelsdelegation (Austrian Trade Delegation), Bahnstr. 9. Tel: 3 2 40 36. Telex: 8582401.

PORTUGAL

Portugiesisches Handelsbüro (Portugese Trade Office), Kreuzstr. 34.

SWEDEN

Schwedischer Handelsbeauftragter in der Bundesrepublik Deutschland (Swedish Trade Commissioner in the German Federal Republic), Berliner Allee 32. Tel: 13 23 03.

Schwedische Handelskammer in der Bundesrepublik Deutschland (Swedish Chamber of Commerce in the German Federal Republic), Uerdinger Str. 106. Tel: 4 5 20 74. Telex: 8584218.

SWITZERLAND

Deutsch-Schweizerische Wirtschaftsvereinigung e.V. (German-Swiss Business Association), Kaiserswertherstr. 287. Tel: 4 3 44 88.

SINGAPORE

Trade Development Board Singapore, c/o Intern. Schiffskontor ISKON GmbH, Kaiserstr. 42. Tel: 4 9 92 69.

SPAIN

Spanische Handelsabteilung I.N.F.E. (Spanish Trade Department), Jögerhofstr. 30. Tel: 4 806 21. Telex: 8582765.

SRI LANKA

Sri Lanka Trade and Investment Centre, Emanuel-Leutze-Str. 1a. Tel: 5 9 30 53. Telex: 8581302.

TAIWAN

Taiwan Trade Service, Berliner Allee 61. Tel: 848 11. Telex: 8582232.

USA

State of Missouri, International Business Office, Emanuel-Leutze-str. 1. Tel: 5 9 20 25/26.

State of North Carolina, European Office, Wasserstr. 2. Tel: 3 2 05 53.

U.S. Department of Commerce, Foreign Commercial Service (U.S. FCS Handelsdienst), Emanuel-Leutze-str. 1b. Tel: 5 9 67 98/99. Telex: 8584246.

GREAT BRITAIN AND NORTH IRELAND

Handelsabteilung des Brit. Generalkonsulats (Trade Department), Georg-Glock-Str. 14. Tel: 4 3 740.

Industrieförderungsorganisation von Nordirland (Industrial Promotion Organization of Northern Ireland), Schloßparkstr. 3. Tel: 7 1 90 11. Telex: 172114082

DÜSSELDORF'S FAIR

Düsseldorfer Messegesellschaft mbH (Düsseldorf's Fair Corporation), NOWEA, P.O. Box 32 02 03. Tel: 4 5 60 1.

Official Incoming Partner of NOWEA: ETRAV, Worringer Platz 11. Tel: 3 5 80 61/62.
In Düsseldorf the Ideal Situation has many Names:

From DRUPA through METAV to BOOT

International market leaders for capital goods include, for example, DRUPA - International Fair for Printing and Paper, INTERPACK - International Fair for Packaging Machinery, Packaging Materials, Confectionery Machinery, "K" - International Fair for Plastics + Rubber, or ENVITEC - Technology for Environmental Protection. Along with numerous other events, they are for the international professional world as inseparably linked to the name Düsseldorf as BOOT, the International Watersports Show, or IGEDO, which has done much to establish Düsseldorf's reputation as an international fashion centre.

From MEDICA to WIRE

With fairs such as MEDICA, A + A - Industrial Safety and Occupational Health, REHA - Help for the Handicapped and INTERHOSPITAL - Düsseldorf offers the most comprehensive programme of medical fairs, tailor-made for every target group, a programme which was ideally complemented off by AKTIV - for Fitness, Leisure and Healthy Living. TUBE - International Tube and Pipe Trade Fair and PACPRO - International Fair for Packaging Production: Machines, Materials, Processes, were successfully introduced to the market in 1988.

The Düsseldorf Exhibition Centre: The International Standard

The quality of the location, grounds and service are important factors on which the exhibiting industry bases its decision. Düsseldorf possesses an exhibtion centre which, in terms of location, architecture, technology and infrastructure, sets the trend and which acts as a model for international trade fair architecture. Many of its competitors from abroad - Birmingham, Paris, Milan, Chicago and Osaka - have either copied or adapted the characteristic "Düsseldorf Model" exhibition centre.

Apart from the International Fashion Show in Düsseldorf, there is a permanent fashion show at **Düsseldorf Fashion House**, Danziger Straße 101. Tel: 4 5 07 77.

There is a variety of possibilities for planning congresses and conferences in Düsseldorf. The offices, authorities and associations already mentioned in the last pages would be pleased to help; in addition, you can contact:

Messe-Kongreß-Center der NOWEA, Stockumer Kirchstraße 61. Tel: 4 5 60 1.

Verkehrsverein der Stadt Düsseldorf, Konrad-Adenauer-Platz. Tel: 3 5 05 05,

and the incoming services already listed for further information.

USEFUL ADDRESSES

CONSULATES

Argentina, Consulate, Graf-Adolf-Str. 16, II. Tel: 3 2 42 05, Mon-Fri 9.30 a.m. - 1.00 p.m.

Belgium, Consulate General, Jägerhofstr. 31. Tel: 4 9 89 87-89, Mon-Fri. 8.00 a.m. - 1.00 p.m.

Benin, Honorary Consulate, Ubierstr. 20. Tel: 15 50 95.

Bolivia, Honorary Consulate, Kasernenstr. 21. Tel: 3 2 09 90, Tues, Thurs 10.00 a.m. - 1.00 p.m.

Botswana, Honorary Consulate, Berliner Str. 1, 4030 Ratingen. Tel: 02102/47 32 11, Mon., Wed., Fri. 8.00 a.m. - 1.00 p.m., 2.00 - 4.00 p.m.

Denmark, Honorary Consulate, Königsallee 4. Tel: 13 14 00, Mon.-Fri. 10.00 a.m. - 1.00 p.m.

Finland, Honorary Consulate, Tonhallenstr. 14/15. Tel: 3 6 72 04, Mon.-Fri. 9.00 a.m. - noon, 2.00 - 4.00 p.m.

France, Consulate General, Cecilienallee 10. Tel: 4 9 90 77, Mon.-Fri. 9.00 a.m. - 12.30 p.m.

Gabun, Honorary Consulate General, Roseggerstr. 5a. Tel: 6 2 73 71, Mon.-Fri. 8.30 a.m. - 12.30 p.m., 1.00 - 5.00 p.m.

Gambia, Honorary Consulate, Königstr. 9. Tel: 3 2 65 37, 10.00 a.m. - 1.00 p.m.

Ghana, Honorary Consulate, Lindemannstr. 43. Tel: 6 8 28 58, Tue, Fri 3.00 - 5.00 p.m.

Greece, Consulate General, Kaiserstr. 30a. Tel: 4 9 92 46, Mon.-Fri. 9.00 a.m. - 1.00 p.m., Tue, Thurs. 5.00 - 7.00 p.m.

Great Britain, Consulate General, Georg-Glock-Str. 14, Nordsternhaus. Tel: 4 3 74 0, Mon.-Fri. 9.00 a.m. - noon.

Guatemala, Honorary Consulate, Lindemannstr. 18. Tel: 6 6 74 94, Mon.-Fri. 2.00 - 4.00 p.m.

Iceland, Honorary Consulate, Otto-Hahn-Str. 2, 4006 Erkrath 1. Tel: 0211/250 94 41, Mon.-Fri. 9.30 a.m. - noon, 2.00 - 4.00 p.m.

Japan, Consulate General, Immermannstr. 45. Tel: 3 5 33 11, Mon.-Fri. 9.00 - 11.30 a.m., 1.30 - 4.00 p.m.

Jordan, Honorary Consulate, Poststr. 7. Tel: 800 75, Mon.-Fri. 10.30 a.m. 12.30 p.m.

Yugoslavia, Consulate, Lindemannstr. 5. Tel: 6 7 30 67/69, Mon.-Sat. 9.00 a.m. - 1.00 p.m.

Cameroon, Honorary Consulate, Marienstr. 10. Tel: 3 5 69 16, Mon, Thurs. 9.00 a.m. - noon.

Canada, Consulate General, Immermannstr. 65d. Tel: 3 5 34 71, Mon.-Fri. 9.00 a.m. - 5.30 p.m.

Korea, Honorary Consulate, Immermannstr. 65a. Tel: 3 6 59 39, Mon.-Fri. 10.00 a.m. - noon.

Lebanon, Honorary Consulate, Kaiserswertherstr. 166. Tel: 4 3 15 12.

Liberia, Honorary Consulate, Golzheimer Platz 3. Tel: 4 54 17 70, Tue, Thurs. 10.00 a.m. - noon.

Luxembourg, Honorary Consulate, Jägerhofstr. 10. Tel: 4 9 81 366, Mon.-Fri. 9.00 a.m. - noon.

Madagaskar, Honorary Consulate, Schadowplatz 14. Tel: 13 00 30, Mon.-Fri. 9.00 a.m. - noon, 3.00 - 4.00 p.m.

Malawi, Honorary Consulate, Angermunder Str. 64. Tel: 0203/74 12 24.

Malta, Honorary Consulate General, Schadowstr. 59. Tel: 3 5 82 66, Tue, Wed. 10.00 a.m. - noon, Fri. 2.00 - 6.00 p.m.

Morocco, Consulate General, Cecilienallee 14. Tel: 4 5 10 41, Mon.-Fri. 9.00 a.m. - 15.00 p.m.

Mauritius, Honorary Consulate General, Jacobistr. 7. Tel: 3 5 67 54, Mon.-Fri. 9.00 a.m. - 1.00 p.m.

Monaco, Honorary Consulate, Freiligrathstr. 1. Tel: 4 97 91 41, Mon.-Fri. 10.00 a.m. - noon.

Netherlands, Consulate General, Oststr. 10. Tel: 3 61 30 55, Mon.-Fri. 9.00 a.m. - noon.

Norway, Consulate General, Uerdinger Str. 5. Tel: 4 58 90, Mon.-Fri. 9.00 a.m. - noon, 3.00 - 4.00 p.m. (except on Wed. afternoon).

Austria, Consulate General, Cecilienallee 43a. Tel: 4 3 41 41, Mon.-Fri. 9.00 a.m. - noon.

Pakistan, Honorary Consulate General, Königsallee 30. Tel: 3 2 92 66, Wed. Thurs. 10.00 a.m. - noon, 2.00 - 4.00 p.m.

Panama, Honorary Consulate, Hebbelstr. 20. Tel: 6 8 44 86, Mon.-Fri. 10.00 a.m. - noon.

Paraguay, Honorary Consulate, Waldseestr. 31, 4030 Ratingen 4. Tel: 02102/184 40.

Peru, Honorary Consulate, Grafenberger Allee 100. Tel: 6 6 78 39, Mon.-Fri. 8.00 a.m. - 1.00 p.m.

Philippines, Honorary Consulate, Elisabethstr. 52a. Tel: 3 7 03 66, Mon.-Thurs. 9.00 a.m. - noon.

Portugal, Consulate General, Graf-Adolf-Str. 16/IV. Tel: 80 633, Mon.-Fri. 8.00 a.m. - 2.00 p.m.

Sweden, Honorary Consulate General, Königsallee 46. Tel: 3 2 46 32, Mon.-Fri. 8.00 a.m. - noon.

Spain, Consulate General, Homberger Str. 16. Tel: 4 3 47 77, Mon.-Fri. 8.00 a.m. - 1.00 p.m.

South Africa, Honorary Consulate, Cecilienallee 59. Tel: 4 5 26 27, Mon.-Fri. 9.00 a.m. - noon.

Swasiland, Honorary Consulate, Worringer Str. 59. Tel: 3 5 08 66, Mon.-Fri. 10.00 a.m. - 1.00 p.m.

Thailand, Honorary Consulate, Königsallee 27. Tel: 838 22 47, Mon.-Fri. 9.00 a.m. - noon.

Togo, Honorary Consulate, Lindemannstr. 35. Tel: 6 8 10 14, Mon.-Fri. 9.00 - noon.

Tonga, Honorary Consulate, Angermunderstr. 64. Tel: 0203/74 12 11, Mon., Wed., Fri. 9.30 a.m. - 12.30 p.m.

Tunesia, Consulate, Graf-Adolf-Platz 7/8. Tel: 3 7 10 07.

Turkey, Consulate General, Cecilienstr. 41. Tel: 4 5 09 99, Tue.-Sat. 8.30 a.m. - 12.30 p.m.

Uruguay, Honorary Consulate, Wagnerstr. 26. Tel: 3 5 34 35, Mon.- Fri. 10.00 a.m. - noon, 2.00 - 4.00 p.m.

Zaire, Honorary Consulate General, Marienstr. 10. Tel: 3 5 36 43, Mon.-Fri. 9.00 a.m. - 4.00 p.m.

INTERNATIONAL SOCIETIES

Deutsch-Japanische Gesellschaft am Niederrhein e.V. (German-Japanese Society on the Lower Rhine), P.O. Box 20 02 62. Tel: 3 2 69 89.

Deutsch-Mexikanische Gesellschaft e.V. (German-Mexican Society), Breite Str. 13. Tel: 85 52 20.

Deutsch-Englische Gesellschaft e.V. (German-English Society), Lindemannstr. 64. Tel: 6 7 64 11.

Deutsch-Amerikanischer Freundeskreis Niederrhein e.V. (German-American Society of Friends), In den Blamüsen 44, 4000 Düsseldorf 31. Tel: 0203/740 770.

Deutsch-Italienische Gesellschaft - Dante Alighieri (German-Italian Society), Am Hackenbruch 88. Tel: 2 2 34 14.

Deutsch-Niederländische Gesellschaft Düsseldorf e.V. (German-Dutch Society), Ostrerather Str. 51, 4005 Meerbusch. Tel: 02159/62 56.

Deutsch-Spanischer Kulturkreis e.V. (German-Spanish Culture Group), Schliemannstr. 47, 4006 Erkrath 2. Tel: 02104/45 887 (from 7.00 p.m.).

Deutsch-Französischer Kreis e.V. (German-French Society), Friedrich-Ebert-Str. 40. Tel: 3 5 47 66.

ADDRESSES FOR WOMEN

Frauencafé Hexenkessel e.V., Kölner Straße 216. Tel: 7 8 24 79.

Frauen-Kommunikation e.V., Luisenstraße 7. Tel: 3 8 38 61.

Frauenhaus Düsseldorf, Frauen helfen Frauen e.V. (Women's Aid Society), P.O. Box 180 138. Tel: 7 10 34 88.

Frauenbücherzimmer, Becherstraße 2. Tel: 4 6 44 05.

Treffpunkt für Frauen in Not, Notruf für vergewaltigte Frauen e.V. (Meeting Place for Women in Need, emergency number for raped women), Ackerstr. 144. Tel: 02311/68 68 54.

ADDRESSES FOR CHILDREN

JUB - Jugendberatungsstelle (Youth Counselling Office), Wallstraße 3. Tel: 80 40 6, open daily except Thursday, 2.00 to 11.00 p.m.

Jugendamt (Youth Welfare Office, open round-the-clock). Tel: 8 99 24 00.

Drug Counselling Office, Bolkerstr. 14. Tel: 13 16 17.

Kinder-Aids-Hilfe (Children Aids Assistance). Tel: 3 2 67 02.

ADDRESSES FOR HANDICAPPED

ASB-Behindertenfahrdienst (ASB Chauffeur Services for the Handicapped). Tel: 3 9 15 05.

Koordination der Behindertenhilfe (Co-ordination of Aid for the Handicapped), Heinrich-Heine-Allee 53. Tel: 899 64 68, 899 64 75.

The majority of the public facilities, museums, theatres as well as many shops are accessible to persons on a wheel-chair.

ART/PHOTO CREDITS

Photographs by

Page 210	**Britta Lauer**
3, 232	**Dupedia**
14/15, 16/17, 18/19, 25, 53, 55, 59, 64, 104, 146, 147, 167, 229	**Erhad Pansegrau**
62/63, 86, 205	**F Medau**
24	**Germanisches National Museum**
9, 56, 120/121, 126, 137, 142, 228	**Hans Höfer**
181	**Henkel Archives**
94/95, 96, 98, 99, 107, 143	**Horst Müller**
138/139	**Ingo Jezierski**
212/213	**J. Sackermann**
47	**Konrad R. Müller**
32/33, 37, 38, 39	**Landesbildstelle Rheinland**
105, 108	**Pohling**
207	**Politisches Schatzkästlein**
216	**Press and Information Office of Soligen City**
20, 26, 29, 31, 36, 39, 40, 42, 46, 48/ 49, 50/51, 52, 54, 57, 60/61, 65, 67, 71, 72, 81, 84/85, 86/87, 90L, 90R, 91, 92, 93, 97, 100/101, 102, 106, 112/ 113, 114/115, 122/123, 127, 129, 130, 134, 144, 148, 149, 151, 155, 159, 160, 161, 168, 169, 171, 175, 176/177, 180, 183, 184, 191, 192, 194, 196, 197, 198, 202/203, 206, 208L, 208R, 220, 224/225, 226, 231	**R. Kiedrowski**
74/75, 116/117, 133, 153, 158	**Stephan Weiner**
78, 79, 103, 132, 163, 200, 201	**Thomas Mayer**
73	**Uwe Loesch**
76R, 80, 190	**V. Barl**
209	**Volker Döhne**
34, 35, 58, 66, 68/69, 89, 125, 128, 131, 145, 150, 152, 156, 157, 165, 166, 172, 174, 188, 214, 219	**Wolfgang Fritz**
70, 136, 173, 182	**W. Schmerfeld**
Maps	**Berndtson & Berndtson**
Illustrations	**Klaus Geisler**
Visual Consulting	**V. Barl**

INDEX

A
C
D
E
F
G
H
I
J
b
c
d
e
f
g
h
i
j
k
l